Academic Capitalism in the A

Academic Capitalism in the Age of Globalization

Edited by
BRENDAN CANTWELL
and ILKKA KAUPPINEN

Foreword by Sheila Slaughter

Johns Hopkins University Press
Baltimore

© 2014 Johns Hopkins University Press
All rights reserved. Published 2014
Printed in the United States of America on acid-free paper
2 4 6 8 9 7 5 3 1

Johns Hopkins University Press
2715 North Charles Street
Baltimore, Maryland 21218-4363
www.press.jhu.edu

Library of Congress Cataloging-in-Publication Data

Academic capitalism in the age of globalization / Brendan Cantwell and
Ilkka Kauppinen, editors; foreword by Sheila Slaughter.
pages cm
Includes bibliographical references and index.
ISBN 978-1-4214-1537-6 (hardcover : alk. paper)—ISBN 978-1-4214-1538-3
(pbk. : alk. paper)—ISBN 978-1-4214-1539-0 (electronic)—ISBN 1-4214-1537-2
(hardcover : alk. paper)—ISBN 1-4214-1538-0 (pbk. : alk. paper)—ISBN
1-4214-1539-9 (electronic) 1. Education, Higher—Economic aspects. 2. Business
and education. 3. Capitalism and education. 4. Knowledge economy.
I. Cantwell, Brendan, 1980– II. Kauppinen, Ilkka.
LC67.6.A26 2014
338.43378—dc23   2014004989

A catalog record for this book is available from the British Library.

Special discounts are available for bulk purchases of this book.
For more information, please contact Special Sales at 410-516-6936 or
specialsales@press.jhu.edu.

Johns Hopkins University Press uses environmentally friendly book materials,
including recycled text paper that is composed of at least 30 percent post-
consumer waste, whenever possible.

CONTENTS

Academic Capitalism: Politics, Policies and the Entrepreneurial University (1997) was written as an attempt to describe the politics and policies shaping the beginnings of a period of intense marketization for universities in four English-speaking countries. *Academic Capitalism: Markets, State, and Higher Education* (2004) was an effort to theorize this phenomenon more fully, concentrating on the United States, where we believed dissection of the belly of the beast would offer the richest understanding of its etiology.* We understood the academic swivel toward the market as being framed by opportunities created by the rise of the neoliberal state, the knowledge economy, globalization, and the growth of transnational capitalism. We tried to work out mechanisms that connected academics to the market possibilities opening up and focused on organizational processes—new circuits of knowledge, interstitial organizational emergence, intermediating organizations, expanded managerial capacity—and also narratives, discourses, social technologies, resources, rewards, and incentives that moved actors within the university from the public good knowledge/learning regime to the academic capitalist knowledge/learning regime. We always understood, however, that colleges and universities were not corporations, that whatever markets in which these organizations participated were heavily state subsidized, whether by the federal government (through federal student

---

*Although I have been asked to write the foreword to this volume, I do not regard myself as the sole or even coauthor of the several volumes on academic capitalism. Rather, I see exploration of the academic capitalist knowledge/learning regime as a joint project, enabled by the many people who worked together on it: first and foremost, Larry Leslie and Gary Rhoades, also Cynthia Archerd, Sondra Barringer, Teresa Campbell, Jen Croissant, Rachel Hendrickson, Margaret Holleman, David R. Johnson, Samantha King, Christine Maitland, Matt Mars, Charles Mathies, Amy Metcalfe, Jennifer Olson, Brian Pusser, Kelly Ochs Rossinger, Barbara Sporn, Barrett J. Taylor, Scott Thomas, Leasa Weimer, Liang Zhang, and of course the editors of this volume, Brendan Cantwell and Ilkka Kauppinen, among many others.

financial aid or research dollars) or the several states (through block grants or tuition assistance), and that market-like behaviors were often irrational strategies for the higher learning, were there any serious concerns for the "bottom line." We knew that corporations and foundations were interested in universities as sites of knowledge production and human capital creation but understood that a number of academics, professional staff, and senior managers also participated by internally embedding competition and a profit orientation that centered on developing universities' capacity to market products created by faculty and to develop commercializable products outside of but connected to conventional academic structures. We tried to look beyond research and technology transfer to market and market-like practices such as online education and those that touched student life (branding, sales of university paraphernalia, privatization of dormitories, food services, special education services, etc.), all of which created a hidden curriculum of consumer capitalism. Although we focused primarily on research universities, we intuited that all sectors of higher education were confronting, considering, and resisting the academic capitalist knowledge/learning regime.

Overall, we are delighted with the reception the theory of academic capitalism has had. The first book came out in 1997, based on work we had done in the 1980s and in Australia in 1991, so, give or take a few years, one way or the other, a quarter of a century ago. Behaviors we associated with academic capitalism morphed beyond our wildest (post-)Marxist imaginings. Who prior to the nineties would have foreseen auctioning off departments to corporate bidders, as was the Department of Plant and Microbial Biology at University of California, Berkeley, to Novartis in 1998?[†] We regarded the theory—as is the case with all theory—as provisional and as something to explore, modify, expand, and interweave with other theories, such as globalization or strategic action fields. Or reject. This volume is a wonderful example of (re)theorizing the academic capitalist knowledge/learning regime.

Of course, we were disappointed with the previous books' reception in some regards. Perhaps the biggest surprise and disappointment for me was that a number of readers missed the critique and took our work as a how-to manual. We also wished that theorists and scholars would go beyond what we saw as a

[†]Lawrence Busch et al., "External Review of the Collaborative Research Agreement between Novartis Agricultural Discovery Institute, Inc., and the Regents of the University of California," Institute for Food and Agricultural Standards, East Lansing, MI, 2004. http://cs3.msu.edu/d/pubs/Berkeley_Final_Report_071204.pdf.

rather narrow focus on a limited array of revenue generation—tuition, research grants and contracts, technology transfer—and also examine how marketization has become deeply imbricated in so many aspects of the academy. Sometimes we are impatient with critiques of our work that see it as another example of American exceptionalism, or as something that should manifest itself uniformly across the globe. In our 1997 book we were careful to deal with the different politics and policies of the four English-speaking countries we studied, illustrating how they came to somewhat similar policies. We thought that what we saw as underlying processes—neoliberalism and globalization, the centrality of knowledge and an educated workforce, the massification of higher education—would create possibilities for expansion of academic capitalist knowledge/learning regimes across the planet, but expected them to play out differently in countries other than English-speaking nations. We hoped then and still hope now that scholars will explore and theorize these developments.

Areas we consider to have been somewhat neglected by scholars, especially in the field of higher education, are expanded managerial capacity, the corresponding diminishment of professorial power, and the dramatic drop in the number of tenure track faculty as a part of the work force. Areas that we believe need to be incorporated into theorizing about academic capitalism are segmentation within universities among fields (i.e., STEM and the humanities), increased stratification among universities, and the part played by universities as state or 501(c)(3)/nongovernmental organizations in facilitating and expanding privatization opportunities, many of which flourish because of continued state subsidies. As we have said elsewhere, colleges and universities may be the model neoliberal organization. We need to research the ways in which actors within them reshape organizational structures, networks, and fields to enable various organizational segments of managers, faculty, and academic professionals to deploy competitive strategies and tactics to create, in the recent theorizing of Brendan Cantwell and Ilkka Kauppinen, constellations of activities and resources across corporations, foundations, state agencies, and transnational networks that may defy our current understandings of the boundaries of organizations. Actors within colleges and universities may be able to engage in such activities because they derive advantages from *not* being corporations— such as state and federal subsidies, exemption from taxation, exemption on the part of public universities from prosecution for liability and various forms of malpractice, not being held to corporate accounting standards, or risks they take with state and donor funds. This unique position may make (some) actors within universities key players in the (re)organization and capitalization of a wide variety of new organizational forms, perhaps reshaping organizations in ways that change our world, as did trust formation at the end of the twentieth century.

Also missing from the corpus of work surrounding academic capitalism are rich studies of resistance: how do we roll it back, re-create universities by building new conceptions of the higher learning to which to which a middle class and intellectuals of all stripes will eagerly respond? Our purpose in theorizing academic capitalism was to enable academics who want another future to understand what is happening and work for alternatives. Like all academics, in our heart of hearts, we believe that knowledge is power, and understanding what is happening will enable us to change it.

Sheila Slaughter

ACKNOWLEDGMENTS

The idea for this book was conceived when both of us editors were postdocs at the Institute of Higher Education at the University of Georgia in 2011. During that time we worked under the advisement of Sheila Slaughter, whom we thank for helping to provide the intellectually fertile environment that spawned this project. Brian Pusser also gave both good advice and kind support in the early stages of this project. We are grateful to Greg Britton from Johns Hopkins University Press for his support throughout the process. Also thanks to the sociology unit at the University of Jyväskylä, Finland, for providing financial help for editorial work as well as to Riikka Aro for proofreading our initial book plan. Finally, we thank Claire Gonyo, whose research and editorial assistance has been indispensable.

PART ONE

ACADEMIC CAPITALISM REVISITED

CHAPTER ONE

Academic Capitalism in Theory and Research

BRENDAN CANTWELL AND ILKKA KAUPPINEN

During the nineteenth and twentieth centuries, universities were organizations central to modern state-building processes. For example, Clark Kerr (2001) described the "multiversity" as an institution central to the pluralist national welfare state. Over the course of the late twentieth and early twenty-first centuries, broad social transformations have drawn many universities into market activities, often on a global scale. This does not mean that universities are fully unmoored from their national political and cultural contexts, but we should take seriously efforts to understand the complex ways in which universities are integrated into local, national, and global political economies (Marginson and Rhoades 2002). Nearly all aspects of higher education (e.g., student recruitment and learning, governance, organizational administration and strategy, public policy, and the academic profession) are embedded in the political economy with links to the market, nonprofit and nongovernmental organizations, and the state.

The theory of academic capitalism (Slaughter and Rhoades 2004) has proved to be one fruitful perspective from which to study how higher education is integrated with the political economy. Academic capitalism offers systematic interdisciplinary theorization that demonstrates the ways in which higher education relates to states, markets, and globalization. But we believe there is a need to revisit the theory of academic capitalism. Rather than elaborate a new or revised theory, in this volume we bring together scholars from different national settings who are working on a number of important topics and who operate from various theoretical and normative positions to help draw out the contributions and limitations of academic capitalism as a framework for understanding the contemporary social, political, and economic conditions of higher education. As such, this book is intended to contribute to a growing collection of work, including Rhoads and Torres's (2006) *The University, State, and Market*; King,

Marginson, and Naidoo's (2011) *Handbook on Globalization and Higher Education*; Pusser, Kempner, Marginson, and Ordorika's (2012) *Universities and the Public Sphere*, and others too numerous to name here. Like these books, the present volume largely takes a critical perspective to understand the condition of higher education in an increasingly interconnected world. Unlike the works listed above, however, the concept of academic capitalism anchors our book.

Each chapter draws on the model of academic capitalism as developed in books by Slaughter and Leslie (1997) and Slaughter and Rhoades (2004). Introduced in 1997, academic capitalism is part of a revolution in higher education scholarship that places universities and higher education policy within a wider set of social and economic arrangements. The focus of the theory expanded with publication of *Academic Capitalism and the New Economy* (Slaughter and Rhoades 2004). Earlier Slaughter and Leslie (1997) predominantly analyzed technology transfer and marketization of the academic research enterprise, but Slaughter and Rhoades (2004) more broadly addressed "the intensified commercialization of instruction, educational materials, and software/courseware, in relation to changes in copyright policies nationally and at the institutional level" (10). Yet, in expanding its scope, Slaughter and Rhodes limited their analysis of academic capitalism to the United States and kept a substantive focus on revenue generation through the exploitation of intellectual property (IP).

Revenue generation and IP within the context of US higher education remain central to the study of higher education. But researchers have deployed academic capitalism theory to understand an array of topics, including undergraduate student entrepreneurship (Mars, Slaughter, and Rhoades 2008), doctoral student socialization (Mendoza 2007), the treatment of migrant academic workers (Cantwell and Lee 2010), faculty perceptions of organizational change (Gonzales, Martinez, and Ordu 2013), as well as the cultural meaning of money within the academy (Szelényi 2013). Other scholars have documented the expansion of academic capitalism outside of the United States (Kauppinen and Kaidesoja 2013; Metcalfe 2010; Slaughter and Cantwell 2012; Tang 2012), and the development of a transnational academic capitalism (Kauppinen 2012).

Like with any theory, as the influence and breadth of academic capitalism studies expand, there is a danger that the concept could become overly descriptive and lose some of its analytical and empirical currency. For this reason, we argue for taking stock of academic capitalism in order to reassess its theoretical and empirical uses. *Academic Capitalism in the Age of Globalization* takes important empirical and theoretical steps to achieve this goal.

This volume has two main objectives. The first is to revisit academic capitalism nearly two decades after the publication of Slaughter and Leslie's (1997) book. In doing so, the contributors build upon the theory of academic capitalism, extending and refining it, and at times challenging its application. The second objective is to explore the relationship between academic capitalism and the globalization of higher education. Since academic capitalism was first introduced, a substantial body of literature on higher education and globalization has developed. This literature has been influential in making sense of contemporary higher education. Yet there are few systematic efforts to revisit academic capitalism within the context of globalization. Such an approach offers important insights for understanding contemporary higher education internationally and transnationally. These two objectives provide the organizing framework of the book. Part I, Academic Capitalism Revisited, revisits the theory of academic capitalism, while Part II, Academic Capitalism and Globalization, gives special attention to globalization.

Understanding Academic Capitalism

In defining academic capitalism, we point to two elements of what Slaughter and Rhodes (2004) call the academic capitalist knowledge/learning regime. The first element is structural and constitutes a neoliberal policy and governance regime that restructures higher education systems and organizations through regulation, funding streams, and linking organizations that tie the academy to the state and the market. The second is behavioral and constitutes a variety of market and market-like actions taken by policymakers, administrators, faculty, and students. Research into academic capitalism has attended to both the structural and behavioral elements of the phenomenon.

Academic capitalism is of course not the only possible approach for exploring the political, economic, and social conditions of higher education. Why, then, does this volume take up the subject? Several interrelated reasons underpin our focus. The theory of academic capitalism has provided two path-breaking contributions: (1) a conceptual framework for making sense of a shift in higher education policy from social welfare regimes to private welfare and competition regimes; and (2) methodological tools useful for tracing the formation and reformation of linkages between higher education organizations (and individuals therein), nonprofit organizations, corporations, and the state. Academic capitalism provides a vehicle for exploring the theoretical dimensions of higher education studies within the context of knowledge-driven economies because of its broad use as a concept and theory that addresses both structure and behavior and because it has intellectual linkages to many other concepts and theories that are useful in making sense of knowledge-driven economies.

Sheila Slaughter's work, of which academic capitalism is the most prominent, is among the first to deploy critical social theory in order to understand the place of higher education in processes of social change (Pusser 2008). Academic capitalism makes explicit connections between higher education studies, organizational sociology, political economy, and globalization studies by drawing from classical Marxian and Weberian thought along with Foucauldian concepts of government and regime, as well as the work of contemporary social theorists of globalization, including David Held and Manuel Castells. It is this root in social theory that makes academic capitalism so useful and fruitful in assessing the social, political, and economic conditions of higher education. Its social theory origins have also guaranteed that academic capitalism has generated considerable interest not only among higher education scholars but also in other academic fields, including sociology, science and technology studies, and geography. Academic capitalism is one of the few concepts that link higher education studies with research policy and other areas of scholarship that are interested in globalization, and especially the globalization of knowledge production (Metcalfe 2007).

Academic capitalism is furthermore treated both as an object of study and a theory, making it particularly suited as the centerpiece of a volume taking up the problem of how globalization has transformed higher education. As an object of study, academic capitalism refers to the origins, extent, and consequences of "market and market-like behavior" in higher education (Slaughter and Leslie 1997), and as a theory, academic capitalism has been used as a frame to predict and explain shifting organizational patterns and modes of production within universities as well as the changing relationships between universities, states, and markets (Slaughter and Rhoades 2004), permitting work that takes transnational networks or structures as the unit of analysis to be presented side by side with work that takes individual or collective actors as the unit of analysis. The contributions to this volume reflect this shift.

The theory of academic capitalism has also generated controversies and critical debate. Some scholars have questioned the theoretical status of academic capitalism, for example, arguing that it is a descriptive account rather than an explanatory theory (Välimaa and Hoffman 2008). Others are even more critical and claim that academic capitalism rests on anecdotes, amounting to little more than a gripe over waning Mertonian norms in higher education (Geiger and Sá 2008). Given these critiques, it is useful to engage academic capitalism at different scales (local, national, and global) in order to reassess its conceptual utility and fruitfulness. Because academic capitalism engages several theoretical traditions and addresses both structural and behavioral levels of analysis, the theory offers an ideal place to begin to explicate connections between higher education and social theory related to globalization.

Academic Capitalism Revisited

Part I reexamines the theory of academic capitalism. In chapter 2, Sheila Slaughter evaluates the explanatory power of academic capitalism within the context of globalization. In doing so, she revises academic capitalism theory by comparing it with other contemporary theories on institutional fields and policy networks. Highlighting the case of board interlocks between elite US universities, Slaughter argues that her updated version of academic capitalism is best suited for explaining how higher education is complexly networked with other important global actors.

In chapter 3, Jussi Välimaa situates academic capitalism within broad historical context. Välimaa traces the historical development of higher education from its medieval European roots to the contemporarily globally networked university. He analyzes the periods of "university revolutions" since the Gutenberg revolution (1460s–1560s) in order to critically evaluate the explanatory power of the theory of academic capitalism. Välimaa argues that academic capitalism is not a universal theory because there are differences between nation-states in how universities respond to pressures to adopt market and market-like behaviors. Välimaa also emphasizes that the real value of this theory, in his view, lies in how it has focused attention on changes taking place inside universities.

Judith Walker, in chapter 4, also focuses on academic capitalism and time. Rather than address historic periods that demarcate governance paradigms, she critically theorizes time as a dimension of academic capitalism that affects individuals. Walker argues that academic capitalism imposes a new time regime on academic subjects, including students, faculty, and staff. In doing so, she opens new avenues for theorizing academic capitalism as a temporal, as well as structural and behavioral, process.

Chapter 5, by Jacob H. Rooksby and Brian Pusser, updates one of the central concerns of academic capitalism, namely, technology transfer and IP. Rooksby and Pusser further our understanding of how academic capitalism and technology may expose universities to increased financial risk rather than serve as a revenue panacea. Exploitation of intellectual property has long been considered a hallmark of academic capitalism, but Rooksby and Pusser show that filing a patent application is only the beginning. Profiting from intellectual property requires defending against patient infringement, and universities are at a distinct disadvantage against corporations that spend millions of dollars in patent litigation.

Chapters 6 and 7 address academic labor. In chapter 6, Keijo Räsänen draws into sharp focus the condition of academic subjects. Working out of the traditions of moral philosophy and practical sociology, he explores how individual academics can find meaning in their day-to-day work even as policies that promote academic capitalism proliferate. Räsänen reminds us that resisting academic capitalism does not always involve large-scale conflict and political maneuvering but may be a more subtle part of everyday academic practice.

Finally, in chapter 7, Gary Rhoades considers labor in updating the theory of academic capitalism. Rhoades explains that power relations embedded in academic work had always been central to the theory of academic capitalism, but notes that this aspect of the theory is often overlooked. Using contemporary examples, he provides a vivid account of how labor restructuring not only affects individual academics but also transforms the social relations that underlie the provision of higher education. Rhoades's contribution demonstrates the complex interconnections between individual conditions and transnational processes that constitute academic capitalism.

REFERENCES

Cantwell, Brendan, and Jenny J. Lee. 2010. "Unseen Workers in the Academic Factory: Perceptions of Neoracism among International Postdocs in the United States and the United Kingdom." *Harvard Educational Review* 80, no. 4: 490–517.

Geiger, Roger, and Creso M. Sá. 2008. *Tapping the Riches of Science: Universities and the Promise of Economic Growth*. Cambridge, MA: Harvard University Press.

Gonzales, Leslie D., E. Martinez, and C. Ordu. 2013. "Exploring Faculty Experiences in a Striving University through the Lens of Academic Capitalism." *Studies in Higher Education* doi:10.1080/03075079.2013.777401.

Kauppinen, Ilkka. 2012. "Towards Transnational Academic Capitalism." *Higher Education* 64, no. 4: 543–56.

Kauppinen, Ilkka, and Tuukka Kaidesoja. 2013. "A Shift towards Academic Capitalism in Finland." *Higher Education Policy* doi:10.1057/hep.2013.11.

Kerr, Clark. 2001. *The Uses of the University*. 4th ed. Cambridge, MA: Harvard University Press.

King, Roger, Simon Marginson, and Rajani Naidoo, eds. 2011. *Handbook on Globalization and Higher Education*. London: Edward Elgar.

Marginson, Simon, and Gary Rhoades. 2002. "Beyond National States, Markets, and Systems of Higher Education: A Glonacal Agency Heuristic." *Higher Education* 43, no. 3: 281–309.

Mars, Matthew M., Sheila Slaughter, and Gary Rhoades. 2008. "The State-Sponsored Student Entrepreneur." *Journal of Higher Education* 79, no. 6: 638–70.

Mendoza, Pilar. 2007. "Academic Capitalism and Doctoral Student Socialization: A Case Study." *Journal of Higher Education* 78, no. 1: 71–96.

Metcalfe, Amy S. 2007. "Research Policy Studies: Between Science and Higher Education." *Higher Education Perspectives* 3, no. 2: 11–19.

———. 2010. "Revisiting Academic Capitalism in Canada: No Longer the Exception." *Journal of Higher Education* 81, no. 4: 489–514.

Pusser, Brian. 2008. "The State, the Market and the Institutional Estate: Revisiting Contemporary Authority Relations in Higher Education." In *Higher Education Handbook of Theory and Research*, vol. 23, edited by John C. Smart, 105–39. Netherlands: Springer. doi:10.1007/978-1-4020-6959-8_4.

Pusser, Brian, Ken Kempner, Simon Marginson, and Imanol Ordorika, eds. 2012. *Universities and the Public Sphere: Knowledge Creation and State Building in the Era of Globalization*. New York: Routledge.

Rhoads, Robert A., and Carlos A. Torres, eds. 2006. *The University, State, and Market: The Political Economy of Globalization in the Americas*. Stanford, CA: Stanford University Press.

Slaughter, Sheila, and Brendan Cantwell. 2012. "Transatlantic Moves to the Market: The United States and the European Union." *Higher Education* 63, no. 5: 583–606.

Slaughter, Sheila, and Larry L. Leslie. 1997. *Academic Capitalism: Politics, Policies, and the Entrepreneurial University*. Baltimore: Johns Hopkins University Press.

Slaughter, Sheila, and Gary Rhoades. 2004. *Academic Capitalism and the New Economy*. Baltimore: John Hopkins University Press.

Szelényi, Katalin. 2013. "The Meaning of Money in the Socialization of Science and Engineering Doctoral Students: Nurturing the Next Generation of Academic Capitalists?" *Journal of Higher Education* 84, no. 2: 266–94.

Tang, Hei-hang Hayes. 2012. "Universities Empowered or Endangered? Academic Capitalism and Higher Education in Macao." Paper presented at the annual meeting of the Association for Asian Studies, Toronto, Ontario.

Välimaa, Jussi, and David Hoffman. 2008. "Knowledge Society Discourse and Higher Education." *Higher Education* 56, no. 3: 265–85. doi:10.1007/s10734-008-9123-7.

CHAPTER TWO

Retheorizing Academic Capitalism

Actors, Mechanisms, Fields, and Networks

SHEILA SLAUGHTER

A number of theorists focus on connections between entrepreneurial universities and markets, generally drawing on functionalist, institutionalist, or neo-institutionalist perspectives that concentrate primarily on higher education as a system or set of institutions within a given country (Bok 2003; Clark 1998; Fallis 2007; Gumport and Pusser 1995; Morphew and Eckel 2009). These theorists see "third stream" funding as important to creating entrepreneurial universities and ties with commercial entities, but they do not usually dwell on the details of connections between academe and industry or philanthropy, let alone the relations between these organizational fields. In contrast, theorists studying research policy focus intensely on the connections between academic science and industry, usually from an economic or business perspective that assumes such connections should be intensified to better stimulate discovery, technology development, economic growth, and job creation (Bercovitz and Feldman 2007; Colyvas 2007; D'Este and Patel 2007; Etzkowitz, Weber, and Healey 1998; Gibbons et al. 1994; Lam 2007; Shinn and Lamy 2006; Stuart, Ozdemir, and Ding 2007). Science policy theorists are not usually concerned with higher education as a whole; rather, they focus heavily on STEM (science, technology, engineering, and mathematics) fields, omitting the majority of actors, organized and otherwise, within any given research university.

Building on my 1997 work with Larry Leslie (Slaughter and Leslie 1997), Gary Rhoades and I (Slaughter and Rhoades 2004) developed a theory of academic capitalism that focused on mechanisms through which multiple segments of higher education moved toward quasi-markets and markets; this work was recently extended (Slaughter and Cantwell 2012). We drew on what can be loosely called a critical tradition and viewed universities' shift toward the market from a political economy perspective in which organizations were embedded.[1] In addition to understanding individual institutions and the field, we also wanted to know how institutions other than higher education shaped and were shaped by higher learning.

Other theorists are also concerned with these issues, seeking to look beyond the organization, or even the field, to understand broad dynamics of change. In this chapter, I look at several of these theorists—including Neil Fligstein and Doug McAdam (2012), authors of *A Theory of Fields*, and Stephen J. Ball (2012), author of *Global Education Inc.: New Policy Networks and the Neo-Liberal Imaginary*—and compare their work to the theory of academic capitalism. I begin by introducing the major elements of the several theories, understanding that the confines of a book chapter limit a rich, deep exploration of these well-developed, complex, and highly nuanced explanations of the dimensions of organizations', fields', and networks' patterns of change or stability. Next, I attempt to illustrate the strengths and weaknesses of the theorists' explanations for change by considering how each would explain a particular problem: what part do trustees of research universities play in linking universities to markets and quasi-markets?

Genuflecting to positionality, I understand that as a theorist I have an interest in extolling the power of my theory. Moreover, I am able to select the problem that potentially illustrates the explanatory power of the several theories— all of which could lead to the ascendance of academic capitalism as the theory of choice. I hope to be able to rise above my vested interests, striving for a Mertonian disinterest, and to learn from this exercise. Should this chapter turn out to be no more than a paean to academic capitalism, however, I expect to be called to account by readers.

Elements of the Theories

Historically, higher education theorists have tried to explain change in higher education by concentrating on the organization, field, system, or postsecondary policy arena at the state or federal level. Little attention has been paid to how other groups, fields, or organizations of actors external to higher education affect the higher learning. As the pace of change in higher education accelerates, however, a broader understanding of change seems more relevant to comprehending our future. Each of the theories examined in this chapter are characterized by a focus on change that goes beyond the incremental or by an understanding of organizations that does not see their culture as unified or organized by broadly supported logics or scripts, taken-for-granted understandings, or relatively unified actors within the organization, network, or field. The theories also see groups or fields or organizations of actors external to the organization/field in question as able to influence the focal actors, networks, and fields.

A Theory of Academic Capitalism

Slaughter and Rhoades (2004) attempt to tease out the ways in which new institutional and organizational structures that link state agencies, corporations, and universities develop to take advantage of the openings provided by the neoliberal state to move toward the market. Segments of all sectors—state agencies, nonprofits and nongovernmental organizations (NGOs), corporations, and universities—are involved. Universities are not simply acted upon by outside forces. Segments of the university, including faculty, administrators, and students, embrace market activity and its associated competition, while other segments are resistant (or neglected).

Elements of the Theory

Philanthropic policy organizations often intermediate among public, nonprofit, and private sectors to initiate policy that facilitates the entrepreneurial activity of universities. For the most part, these policies reconfigure laws, opportunities, and organizations so they are more amenable to markets. Although diverse, the participants in intermediating organizations represent a rather limited segment of society. Participants are generally business elites, middle- to high-ranking government officials, or professionals with advanced degrees. They tend to see advantage from rearranging the traditional, distinct sectors of state, nonprofits, and for-profits to create new opportunities configured in a neoliberal frame.

Intermediating networks promote new circuits of knowledge that link state agencies, corporations, and universities in entrepreneurial research and educational endeavors. New circuits of knowledge incorporate business and industry, patenting, licensing, start-ups, and other entrepreneurial activities, such as university funding of research parks and incubators as well as curricula and student market activity; for example, e-learning and recruitment of full-fees-paying overseas students, academic tourism.

New funding streams emerge to support entrepreneurial science and education. The narratives and discourses that surround entrepreneurial science often present new funding streams as tightly coupled to markets. New circuits of knowledge are often funded by redirecting and expanding government funding, however. For example, the case is often made that federal student financial aid, which underwrites undergraduate student tuition across all fields, is redirected to support research and development (R&D) in STEM fields (Ehrenberg, Rizzo, and Jakubson 2007; Newfield 2008; Taylor, Cantwell, and Slaughter

2013), which in turn yields overheads that are redirected to broaden and expand STEM fields. Such redirection and expansion occurs regardless of whether STEM fields yield marketable discoveries that lead to technology transfer.

Actors within the university, sensitive to the opportunities attached to new resources, create interstitial organizations that emerge to facilitate new entrepreneurial knowledge constellations. Interstitial organizations emerge from the interstices of existing organizations within the university (Mann 1986). Obvious interstitial organizations are those that deal with research commercialization or technology transfer, or with marketing to and recruitment of full-fees-paying students from overseas. These interstitial organizations act like switching devices, channeling energy, effort, and revenues to the new circuits of knowledge. They create new careers and a host of new rewards.

Universities concurrently build extended managerial capacity that enables them to function as economic actors. At the same time that interstitial organizations emerge from the interstices of traditional organizations such as departments, centers, and institutes and are eventually institutionalized, the managerial structures of universities change to enable universities to conform with and participate in shaping relations with agencies within the nation-state and among neoliberal states. Universities expand managerial capacity to monitor, incent, and discipline the increasingly differentiated faculty as well as the increasing numbers of nonacademic professionals that make up the growing tertiary education work force.

All the players develop, elaborate, and articulate the narratives, discourses, and social technologies that justify and normalize these changes. For example, human capital and competitiveness narratives and discourses are often initiated in intermediating organizations that span public, private, and nonprofit organizations, and reconfigure those sectors in ways that promote individuals, competition, and markets or quasi-markets in spaces designed to foster the success of knowledge economy corporations.

There is no particular order in which these phenomena occur. They can take place sequentially, simultaneously, independently, and always recursively. They explain how universities become marketized not only in science and engineering fields, but also across a variety of fields.

A Theory of Fields

Fligstein and McAdam (2012), both sociologists, propose a general theory of social change and stability at the mesolevel. They see strategic action fields as the "basic structural building block of modern political/organizational life in the economy, civil society and the state" (3). Individual and collective actors within the fields interact on the basis of shared, although not consensual, "understandings about the field, relationships to others in the field (including who has power and why), and the rules governing legitimate action in the field" (9). These shared understandings are not the same as organizational or institutional logics, nor taken-for-granted realities that imply consensus leading seamlessly to reproduction. Instead, the authors see fields as being conflict ridden, with constant jockeying for position and opportunity. Despite deep contention among actors within fields, fields are nonetheless often able to achieve stability, reproducing themselves over time.

Within each field are incumbents and challengers. Incumbents are actors who hold power in the field and whose conceptions of the field hold sway. Challengers have a critique of the field and their position in it. They usually conform to the dominant conception of the field but await moments when they can challenge its logic and structure. Most fields have internal governance units, such as trade associations, that aid in reproduction and usually bear the incumbents' imprint, making it more difficult for challengers to push for change.

Social skill is the ability of individual and collective actors to understand people and environments, enabling them to develop a compelling plan of action and to mobilize others to support them. Incumbents draw on these skills to reproduce fields when challenged, and challengers deploy them when fields become unstable to foment change. In other words, fields have social or institutional entrepreneurs.

Fields are not isolated but embedded in complex webs of other fields, nested like Russian dolls. Fields are proximate or distant for the strategic action field under study, or dependent, interdependent, or independent. There are state and nonstate fields: the state fields often hold the trump cards because "state actors alone have the formal authority to intervene in, set rules for, and generally pronounce on the legitimacy and viability of most nonstate fields" (Fligstein and McAdam 2012, 19).

Interdependent fields are "a source of routine, rolling turbulence in modern society" (Fligstein and McAdam 2012, 19). Contention within any given field is routine, although stability usually prevails. Change is most likely to occur as a result of exogenous shock, leading to an episode of contention, which challengers seize to mobilize for change. Incumbents are often able to restore order despite challenges because they hold material, cultural, and political advantages. Regardless of whether challengers or incumbents prevail, a new institutional settlement emerges from episodes of contention that encompasses field rules and cultural norms.

Networks, Neoliberalism, and Policy Mobilities

Although Ball (2012) does not offer a specific theory, he presents a rich explanation of the abrogation of state authority and marketization of education, drawing on neo-Marxian and Foucauldian understandings of neoliberalism to comprehend how these changes occur. From the Marxian tradition, he draws on "the 'economisation' of social life and the 'creation' of new opportunities for profit," and from Foucault he takes the "analytics of governmentality . . . particularly the governing of populations through the production of 'willing,' 'self-governing,' entrepreneurial selves" (3). He sees neoliberalism not as an economic doctrine or concrete political project but "as a complex, often incoherent, unstable and even contradictory set of practices that are organized around a certain imaginary of the 'market' as a basis for the universalization of market-based social relations, with the corresponding penetration in almost every single aspect of our lives of the discourse and/or practice of commodification, capital-accumulation and profit-making" (Shamir 2008, as quoted by Ball 2012, 3).

He theorizes and analyzes policy networks, which he sees as reducing the privileged authoritative position of the state, replacing it—to a degree—with "self-organising, inter-organizational networks characterized by interdependence, resource-exchange, rules of the game, and significant autonomy from the state" (Rhodes 1997, 15, as quoted by Ball 2012, 7), blurring the boundaries between state and society and privatizing policy making. Although far from coherent and stable, these networks are a new form of governance. They proliferate nationally and globally, introducing new voices to policy conversations, offering new sites and conduits for policy to enter discourse with regard to educational fields, and creating a new type of policy space somewhere between "multilateral agencies, national government, NGOs, think-tanks and advocacy groups, consultants, social entrepreneurs and international businesses in and beyond the traditional sites and circulations of policy-making" (Ball 2012, 10). These networks create a shadow hierarchy that mixes bureaucracy, markets, and networks, stimulating policy mobility across the shadow hierarchy that the networks simultaneously legitimate.

Ball (2012) sees policy entrepreneurship as a way of understanding the role of agency in policy making and policy mobility. Following Kingdon (1995), he regards policy entrepreneurs as able to take advantage of constructing and opening policy windows. But Ball critiques Kingdon for focusing primarily on actors within the state sector, and expands the concept of policy entrepreneurship by emphasizing money, the role of philanthropic policy organizations, and discourse. He sees policy networks as essential to policy entrepreneurship because policy is constructed discursively, flooding networks and forums, and because successful policy is often "fully funded" by philanthropic endeavors, including think tanks, that recursively support actors within the networks and create new opportunities for them. He sees philanthropic activity and NGOs as providing the essential financial underpinning for policy entrepreneurs operating in policy networks.

Ball (2012) studies educational policy flows by looking primarily at K–12 education, and occasionally at postsecondary education, examining trends with regard to parental choice and privatization of schooling as well as reform of education systems along managerial and entrepreneurial lines. He does this by following the educational policy networks in which business expresses an interest at the national, global, and local levels, arguing that we are shifting from government (state/bureaucracy) to networks, and from delivery of education to contracting. In Peck and Tickell's (2002) terms, the state is rolled back and the opportunity for contracting and private sector profit making is rolled out.

The Problem

I want to consider a problem through each theoretical lens: what part do trustees of private institutions that are part of the Association of American Universities (AAU) play in linking universities to markets and quasi-markets? This problem is appropriate for the theorists discussed here because it is relevant to elements each seeks to explain. Academic capitalism sees trustees as an intermediating network, moving academic science in entrepreneurial directions (Mathies and Slaughter 2013; Slaughter, Thomas, Johnson, and Barringer 2014). From the theory of fields' perspective, trustees pose a puzzle. They are generally business leaders who often head large firms and sit on the boards of directors of other firms and who were chosen to be trustees of research universities because they hold these positions. As trustees, however, they hold legal, fiduciary, and moral responsibility for nonprofit entities technically classified as charities. Trusteeship opens new ways to consider fields that encompass higher education, other nonprofits, and corporations. The policy network approach is useful for the consideration of trustees of private universities because they are tightly networked (see below) and are undoubtedly connected to other networks that are able to shape discourse and to fund policy entrepreneurs who are able to shape state and federal policy to roll back public support for higher education, creating opportunities for private business.

Context of the Problem

Trustees of private AAU universities may be different than most other university trustees. The AAU is the oldest (est. 1900) and arguably most elite association of research universities in North America. It develops national policy positions on issues related to academic research and graduate and professional education and provides a forum for discussing a broad range of other institutional issues. It is a "principals only" organization: only the presidents of these universities are at the table for meetings; substitutes are not acceptable. AAU membership is highly sought after, granted by invitation only. There are sixty AAU institutions in the United States. They consistently score among the highest on all indicators of research, including grant and contract funds, citations in research and patent literature, patents, revenue generated by licensing, start-up companies, and quality ratings by peers in specialized fields as well as national and international rankings.

Historically and presently, the trustees of institutions in the AAU are drawn from the boards of directors of large corporations and are often tightly networked (Beck 1947; Pusser, Slaughter, and Thomas 2006; Veblen 1918). But there is a stark difference in the connectivity of public and private universities (see fig. 2.1 and Slaughter et al. 2014). Trustees at private universities extensively link their universities to corporate directorships in terms of the number of corporations to which they are directly and indirectly tied, whereas public university trustee interlocks are far less dense.

Despite the dense network of private university trustees, little is known about the trustee selection process. About 70% of the trustees in private AAU samples are alumni. Given that these universities routinely graduate men and women who disproportionately head powerful institutions ranging from corporations to government, sitting trustees have an ample alumni base from which to select distinguished new trustees (Domhoff and Dye 1987; Dye 1989, 1994, 2002). But there are no data that suggest why particular corporate leaders are selected. Nor do we know why the 30% who are not alumni are chosen, although we do know that they have 1.5 times as many corporate ties as alumni, suggesting that board members may be chosen for strategic reasons, including the research interests of the science corporations that many of them represent. Many of the trustees sat on one or more boards of directors of corporations, creating a dense network.

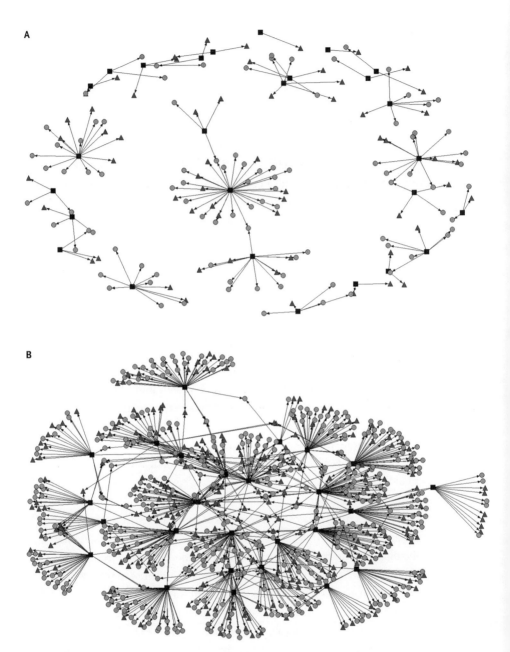

Figure 2.1. The 2005 AAU organizational network by institutional type. (*A*) Public subnetwork. (*B*) Private subnetwork. Key: black squares = universities; gray triangles = patenting firms; light gray circles = nonpatenting firms.

Applying the Various Theories to the Trustee Problem

Although the problem has been specified as understanding whether trustees link research universities to markets and quasi-markets, and how this occurs, the various theorists would likely frame specific research questions somewhat differently. I thus analyze the theories in terms of how the theorists would likely cast the research questions, the assumptions they may bring to the problem, and their explanatory approach (mechanisms, networks, fields, actors, methods). Finally, I consider the strengths and weaknesses of the several theoretical approaches.

Theory of Academic Capitalism

There are a number of broad research questions about trustees that academic capitalism poses: What was the function of trustees in the public good knowledge/learning regime? Did that role change over time? And was the change a move toward the market or the academic capitalist knowledge/learning regime? The assumption underlying these questions is that the rise of neoliberalism created many openings for entrepreneurial educational and scientific endeavor. The rise of neoliberalism is not explored in depth but serves as a taken-for-granted backdrop.

Under the public good regime, trustees were understood to be a buffer between universities and state as well as the economy. Under the academic capitalist knowledge/learning regime, trustees instead would be expected to promote entrepreneurial science and shift universities toward research that met corporate needs: universities become corporate laboratories that focus on broad questions with entrepreneurial promise, replacing the industrial laboratories that historically performed such functions. Although researchers closely study the mechanisms that move universities toward markets, they leave relatively unexamined the mechanisms by which various groups within and external to universities may resist the entrepreneurial university and attempt to maintain the public good knowledge/learning regime.

The trustees are conceptualized as actors who accomplish these changes, but they are not presented as social or organizational entrepreneurs, as would Fligstein and McAdam (2012), nor are they analyzed as policy entrepreneurs, as would Ball (2012), linked to multiple networks beyond the university, many dominated by business leaders, that are aimed at changing policies. Rather, trustees who are heads of or on the boards of directors of science corporations are seen as acting together to realize narrow interests related to the broad fields of science with which their corporations are concerned. Interests (rational ones at that) are what shape these actors' choices. Manifestations of the interests of the trustees are their patenting and research investment activities.

Over time, the patenting behavior of corporations represented by private research university trustees becomes more similar to the universities of which they are stewards. In a study of similarity between trustees' corporations' patent classes and university patent classes that relied on structural equivalence analysis, we found that the percentage of total ties to trustees' patenting corporations within a university's profile grew from 5.61% in 1997 to 19.01% in 2001 and 26.06% in 2005 (Slaughter et al. 2014). Another study (Mathies and Slaughter 2013) suggests that AAU private research universities' corporate science fields and research fields converged between 1997 and 2005.

We read the convergence of trustees' science corporations' areas of research and universities' broad research fields as suggesting that private research university trustees act as an intermediating network that likely serves as an executive science network that is important in shaping national research agendas and securing research funding in fields where shared corporate science and university research meet. Trustees are unlikely to impose their will on universities' research agendas, however; the arrow points both ways. University senior management likely seeks out trustees who represent science corporations in areas where universities are strong and want to expand.

New circuits of knowledge emerge. As indicated above, patenting classes are shared between trustees and universities and the research areas of trustees' science corporations and universities' broad fields of research converge. Pilot research indicates that science corporations represented by trustees may provide a range of activities for faculty who work in shared research areas, including consulting, contract research, testing and field trials, training, and special conferences devoted to the research areas that are sometimes attended by both university faculty and corporate scientists.

The new circuits of knowledge call for expanded managerial capacity. Technology transfer offices grew in number and staff along with entrepreneurial science, for example, as did legal counsel devoted to patent defense, grants management personnel, and information technology offices that provided infrastructure. Trustees had to approve these expansions, as well as sanction commercial strategies such as patent litigation for university patent families.

New funding streams that privileged STEM fields thought likely to produce entrepreneurial science emerged. Particularly sought after were fundamental fields with the entrepreneurial possibility to create entire new commercial technologies. Examples are computer science, biotechnology, and, more recently, nanotechnology and the brain-mapping project. Although we have not studied the part trustees may have played in shaping federal science policy funding priorities through mission agencies, nor conceptualized the mechanisms by which they may exercise policy influence, we suspect trustees may be active in these policy circuits; see the section on Ball (2012) below.

Theory of Fields

A theory of fields addresses the question of "how stability and change are achieved by social actors in circumscribed social arenas," which they conceive of as strategic action fields (Fligstein and McAdam 2012, 3). As the authors acknowledge, defining a field is often somewhat problematic. Any organization such as a university can be a field, for example, yet universities as a group may also be a field, or perhaps only research universities, or possibly AAU universities. And universities (depending on the case) may be simultaneously components of many fields (e.g., the field of higher education in some specific nation-state or region), and the field of economy in that same nation-state or region or even the global field of economy. Fields can also be constructed as the need arises, bringing together new constellations of actors as situations change.

Trying to understand the part AAU private university trustees play in linking universities to markets and quasi-markets illustrates the difficulty of delineating a field. Does the field consist of AAU institutions, which would include trustees as a segment of the universities? Yet trustees are likely selected because of their business connections, whether as heads of firms or as members of firms' boards of directors. Are the firms then the field? A case could be made that the firms and the universities are the field, although that conception would likely break down given that the "rules of the game" are quite different for business and universities. Perhaps trustees (who, as fig. 2.1 indicate, are closely linked to one another) are themselves a strategic action field. Trustees often sit on more than one board, and a number of them may interact regularly. The trustees could also be conceived of as a network, however, raising the perplexing question of the difference between networks and fields.

Perhaps trustees' strategic action field may best be conceptualized as one shared by trustees of universities and other nonprofit organizations that are moving away from an understanding of their role as stewards of universities understood as charitable—i.e., 501(3)(c)s—or state organizations and toward a more corporate or market conception. In other words, trustees may look to other trustees, especially those in charge of nonprofit organizations that provide and increasingly charge for products and services, such as health care and insurance, or museums.

To comprehend patterns of change and stability, a theory of fields ask us to understand the settlement (rules of the game) that created stability for trustees in the past, to identify the incumbents and challengers, as well as the episodes of contention that lead to change and the contours of the new settlement. As with the definition of strategic action fields, the time frame of change is sometimes difficult to specify and is often sweeping. Given that the authors see (contested) stability as the norm, and exogenous shocks as often the precipitators (although not the drivers) of change, broad scope and deep historical knowledge on the part of the analyst are assumed.

With regard to trustees, we propose a time frame from roughly the 1970s until the present. Prior to the 1970s, trustees were guided by the "prudent man" principle, established in 1830 by the Massachusetts Supreme Court in *Harvard College v. Amory* (Humphreys et al. 2010). Trustees were regarded as stewards who have an obligation to manage and protect property or money, acting for the benefit of the institution rather than out of self-interest, calling for conservative investment strategies likely to lead to sure returns. Some states even had statutes that listed the type investments allowable under the prudent man principle. Trustees of nonprofits were understood to be morally responsible for preserving the integrity of their organizations.

In the early 1970s, the settlement that saw nonprofits as charities intent on providing support to worthy recipients, such as students in higher education or patients in health care, began to change. The incumbents in the nonprofit strategic action field were presumably trustees who adhered to the norms and logics that favored prudent man stewardship, while the challengers were probably trustees who wanted to maximize endowments or entrepreneurial research. A small group of financiers, lawyers, academics, and endowment trustees began to push for reforms that would allow trustees to engage in more risk taking with endowments. In 1972, the Ford Foundation–funded Barker Report promoted a shift of "investment objectives from securing income to maximizing long term total return" (Humphreys et al. 2010, 18). Shortly thereafter, the Uniform Management of Institutional Funds Act was enacted, codifying this more (neo)liberal approach to investments. The National Association of College and University Business Officers came out of these endeavors, perhaps serving as internal governance unit for the university segment of the nonprofit sector.

While this shift could be considered as part of the contention and jockeying for position that occurs routinely within fields, there is evidence of change that was more than incremental, that the settlement indeed changed. As Weisbrod (1988) says, nonprofits may have become disguised for-profits, or, in James's (1998) words, many nonprofits may have become "false non-profits." In the 1990s, the Yale endowment model of investing became dominant among private research universities. This model moved beyond the changes of the 1970s and 1980s, which had preferred "transparent, publicly traded equities, bonds and money market instruments to largely illiquid 'alternative investments' such as hedge funds, venture capital and other private equity, commodities, private real estate and other 'real assets'" (Humphreys et al. 2010, 12). Nonprofits were able to profit from market volatility, velocity, and scale because they were subsidized by tax exemption, simultaneously reducing and encouraging risk. Endowments ballooned. In his study of six New England private universities, three of which were in the AAU, Humphreys et al. (2010) noted a "striking" number of trustees who worked with investment firms managing endowments for the schools for which they served as stewards.

During the time that trustees of finance, insurance, and real estate (FIRE) firms may have framed opportunities in terms of the Yale model, however, there is no obvious evidence of exogenous shocks followed by episodes of contention that spilled out into the private research university field. Rather, the neoliberal state's blurring and opening of previously fixed boundaries between public, private, and nonprofit entities created opportunities. Although the economic collapse of 2008 could be considered as an exogenous shock, given the amount of endowment funds lost, the behavior of trustees with regard to aggressive stewardship that links universities to markets does not seem to have changed.

Nor were there reports of contention within boards. But we cannot know for certain because trustees of private AAU institutions tend to be powerful men (and some women) who are not required by law to make public their deliberations as members of public university boards of trustees and rarely do. But the challengers seem to have convinced the incumbents that their strategy for endowment investment and exchanges between science corporations and research universities was the right one without much fuss or fanfare.

Perhaps if we considered the corporations and universities represented by trustees as a field, rather than nonprofits as a whole, then we could come to a different understanding of change and stability. Yet expanding the field to that degree would come close to encompassing the economy and polity as a totality— or at least the oligopolistic and neoliberal segment of it—which diminishes the explanatory power of fields. A theory of fields may work well to explain fields where social movements intersect and alter stable organizations, but it seems to do less well in explaining changes within elite networks that nonetheless may be consequential for broad segments of society.

Networks, Neoliberalism, and Policy Mobilities

Were Ball (2012) to look at university trustees, he would look for policy networks that express business interests and education. He would expect these networks to work at rolling back the state and rolling out opportunities for business. If trustees are such a network, he would expect them to generate policy that reduce the privileged, authoritative position of the state and ultimately create a shadow hierarchy of philanthropic and business organizations that work with the state but also privatize governance. To some degree, philanthropic organizations are the key because they provide deep funding for policy entrepreneurs who are credentialed experts outside of academe and government and yet are able to work as change agents within it, creating more opportunities for business to profit from education.

As Ball (2102) suggests, trustees may have been committed to rolling back the state in that they sought opportunities to mesh or insert their science corporations' research agendas with their universities, and their businesses likely benefit from patents, licenses, and discoveries made through research sponsored by corporations. Research universities are also engaged in a number of other types of exchanges with their trustees' corporations. If we use corporations represented on Northwestern University's board of trustees as an example, we find that Abbott Laboratories, Baxter, Boeing, Kraft, and Motorola are each engaged in research partnerships with more than one institute at the university. At Caltech, we observed two centers: the Center for Neuromorphic Systems Engineering and the Materials Research Science and Engineering Center, both funded by the National Science Foundation and each with two trustees' corporations—Intel and General Motors—as industrial affiliates (four other trustee corporations were also tied to these institutes, but not as industrial affiliates; see Slaughter and Taylor 2012). Such collaborations highlight exactly why this field may be understood as an executive science network, as they suggest ways members of corporate boards of directors and chief executives of major scientific corporations both oversee and participate in strategic science initiatives involving commerce, the federal government, and premier research universities.

In so doing, private universities—which perhaps can be considered as philanthropic entities, and certainly as 501(c)(3) organizations (the legal designation for nonprofit organizations in the United States)—may have participated in transmuting public funds historically geared for public missions to profits for trustees' corporations. AAU private universities' senior management and trustees may constitute an executive science network intent on setting what amounts to industrial policy through their research strategies and investments, but success depends heavily on federal R&D, which still foots approximately 60% of the bill for academic science. The trustee network may work with the shadow hierarchy of philanthropy and business to privatize government authority, yet, rather than rolling back the state, the network likely lobbies for increasing government spending to more fully subsidize commercial endeavor. In contrast to Ball, the state is not rolled back; rather, it subsidizes academic research that corporations then appropriate.

We did not look at the other networks in which trustees may participate, but trustees and senior managers may play a part in shaping national research policy that promotes technology discovery, economic innovation, and (perhaps) job creation. We know that trustees are joiners and participate in many philanthropic and policy networks beyond university boards (see below) and anecdotally that they are in policy groups, such as the Business-Higher Education Forum, that promote integration of universities with the knowledge economy (Slaughter 1990).

We focused rather narrowly on AAU trustees as a network of science corporations, and looked at how the relationships between firms' science interests and trustees' universities' broad fields of science were manifested by patents and research funding. But we know that the largest subnetwork among trustees is FIRE, not science corporations. Trustees who represent FIRE firms may be engaged in different networks than trustees who represent science corporations. And they may have different policy strategies, aims, and goals.

If we randomly choose several current nonscience trustees of the Massachusetts Institute of Technology and look them up in the online *Encyclopedia of American Biography*, we find that many are rich, businessmen, Republican or Libertarian, and heavy participants in variety of policy networks. For example, Board Chair John S. Reed was CEO of Citibank as well as the New York Stock Exchange, sits on multiple boards of directors, and is a trustee of Stanford's Center for Advanced Study in the Behavioral Sciences, a member of the Council on Foreign Relations, and a member of the board of directors of MDCR.

Some of the trustees, such as Samuel Wright Bodman III, a life member of MIT's board and former US secretary of energy as well as secretary of commerce, bring together government, business, and research. Bodman was head of Cabot, a chemical corporation, Fidelity Management and Research Corporation, served on the board of American Research and Development Corporation, and is credited as the father of venture capitalism (Hsu and Kenney 2005).

These examples indicate that trustees participate in multiple policy networks, many of which may be amenable to a shift from a prudent man understanding of trusteeship to one that prefers a broader conception of risk and looks to markets as an arena to exercise this understanding. That said, the AAU trustees' network participation is so extensive that comprehending the meaning of their network activity may be difficult. Indeed, the more that technology and education have increased, the more tightly people are networked, which raises multiple questions: How can network participation be measured? Does membership in multiple networks hinder or increase participation? Are there hierarchies among and within networks, and how might hierarchy be mapped? If networks promote policies, how can we know whether these policies are enacted? If enactment is taken to be legislation, then how is it implemented, if at all? And what about the shadow hierarchy? Is it a network or a bundle of networks? How exactly does it intersect the state? Ball (2012) does not dwell on any of these questions, instead focusing on illustrative policy entrepreneurs and relatively obvious philanthropic money trails.

Conclusion

The several theories have a number of similarities. All want to explain change of some magnitude, whether conceptualized as a shift away from a public good academic knowledge/learning regime to an academic capitalist knowledge/learning regime, or a shift from a settlement characterized by one set of "rules of the game" to another quite different set, or a shift from a liberal to a neoliberal political economy that reshapes education. All see organizations as turbulent sites where actors jockey for position and opportunity to promote or preserve and defend their strategies. All see study of single organizations as insufficient to understand change within the organization or even the field. Actors may share an understanding of their organization and its relationships to other similar organizations, but there is no taken-for-granted understanding that unites them. Groups of actors want to push or pull the organization or network in one direction or another, to challenge or change the organizational logic, to move in different directions.

That said, there are many areas of difference. A theory of fields argues that life is lived in mesolevel fields, but the theory seeks to offer a general theory of change and stability, applicable to all fields, which sounds like a macrolevel the-

ory and which may be its undoing. When a theory of fields brings social movement theory (change) together with various institutionalisms (stability), it necessarily focuses on broad changes as well as multiple fields, making specification
of unit(s) of analysis—fields by any other name—an art rather than a (social)
science. Fligstein and McAdam (2012) also might put analysis of change in fields
in clearer perspective if they attended more closely to their deep understanding
that the deck is stacked in favor of the incumbents, whom they acknowledge are
well positioned and fortified to withstand pressures for change.

Episodes of contention, when challengers and incumbents clash, are analytically problematic. When episodes of "true" contention are presented as
spanning decades, then it seems that understanding settlements depends on
hindsight and has little to offer actors involved in struggle. What looks like a
settlement that favors the challengers may be just one round in a protracted
episode of contention that is slowly and routinely picked apart by former incumbents (the abortion rights movement in the United States is one such
example). Fligstein and McAdam (2012) offer the Russian doll metaphor to
describe the structure of fields. Yet their depiction of fields is not nested—it is
more like networks. And are not exogenous shocks, which we understand as
frequently precipitating episodes of contention, an overly economistic conception that prevents us from looking at how organizations and fields deal with
shocks, which despite their differences may be routine, or at least should be
expected?

Ball's (2012) approach, focused on networks, raises the question of the relation of the analytical strength of networks as compared to fields. The standard
critiques of networks are that they are a method of tracing relations among
actors, but they can say little about what the relations mean and how they work,
other than drawing inferences from closeness and separation (Burt 1992;
Granovetter 1973). In many ways, Ball's work illustrates this critique. The networks he follows—such as the strand in the Clinton Global Initiative tracing a
network promoting policy that pushes for-profit, low-cost, private school initiatives from the United States to Hyderabad, India, where the schools are insti-
tuted, back to the United States, where the purported successes in India are
used to justify similar initiatives at home—are difficult to follow with any precision. Ball tries to counter this lack of precision by introducing the concept of
policy entrepreneurs to illustrate the workings of the network he has studied.
But, in the end, we are not quite sure about the importance and strategies of
policy entrepreneurs apart from knowing they are active and may profit from
their initiatives as they roll back the state and roll out openings for business in

education. It is not clear how policy entrepreneurs articulate the "complex set of political and economic processes involving advocacy, by policy entrepreneurs . . . and transnational advocacy groups . . . business interests (new profit opportunities), 'new' philanthropy" (Ball 2012, 87), which are at the heart of the new global paradigm, nor is the process through which change occurs.

Academic capitalism, not a theory of fields, may be the theory that looks at the mesolevel organizational fields of higher education. But the fields are backgrounded, assumed rather than foregrounded. Instead, the theory relies on the concept of mechanisms—including new circuits of knowledge, interstitial organizations, intermediating organizations, expanded managerial capacity, new funding circuits, discourse, and social technologies rather than contenders within fields, nested or otherwise—to explain change. Despite the arbitrary elements of field boundaries, academic capitalism could nonetheless profit from drawing on the concept of fields to better understand the rules of the game that govern the AAU research university playing field and the part trustees play within it. Boundaries and boundary crossing would be of particular interest in understanding the move from prudent man conceptions of stewardship to stewardship best served by risk taking in markets that benefit universities and trustees' related corporations. Among the questions that might be asked are: When do trustees govern? When do they delegate? Or do they work so closely with senior management that there are few boundaries? If so, are the boundaries between nonprofit and for-profit worlds represented by the trustees? How do the (proximate? distant?) fields of nonprofits (all? some?) shape what occurs with regard to stewardship in research universities?

Academic capitalism has actors, but the motivations of those who seek to bring universities closer to the market are seen as narrow, representing interests that are ironically not too different than rational choice theory, being either self-interests or those of economic men. Closer consideration of actors' motivations would allow a greater understanding of how the shift from the public good knowledge/learning regime to the academic capitalist knowledge/learning regime occurs. This would include analyzing the social skills of organizational entrepreneurs, which Fligstein and McAdam (2012) see as important to inducing cooperation, setting agendas, convincing others that goals are achievable, brokering agreements, and linking actors across fields to better understand how they try to accomplish change or defend the status quo.

Ball's (2012) work on policy mobility centers on analysis of networks. While we claim that the AAU trustees are a network, we have not systematically analyzed patterns of interaction within that network. Fligstein and McAdam (2012) make the case that there is no network-based theory of fields. A network-based theory of fields may be problematic, but networks perhaps could be used by academic capitalism to connect fields and understand the way change moves through fields, whether proximate or distant, dependent or interdependent. In other words, it would be possible to trace flows of people, ideas, money, and mechanisms between fields. Given current methods of network analysis, computer power, and multiple new software programs, it is probably possible to understand the degree to which trustees participate in policy networks, how active they are, and what they seek to accomplish. Their participation would have to be established systematically through procedures such as those we developed to capture trustees' positions as members of boards of corporate directors, but for multiple networks that may be less fully documented. Policy language could probably be traced through networks via programming languages such as R. The density of overlapping network activity may present the biggest challenge to understanding the meaning of networks because imputing causality would likely be problematic. Were we able to accomplish this, we may end up with a clearer understanding of how change occurs in mesolevel fields such as research universities that are networked to actors and organizations in the larger political economy.

NOTE

1. Throughout I use "we" rather than "I" because academic capitalism has never been an individual project. My coauthors have contributed as heavily as I to the development of academic capitalism as a theory as well as to analyzing various topics, such as trustees, from our theoretical perspective.

REFERENCES

Ball, Stephen J. 2012. *Global Education Inc.: New Policy Networks and the Neo-Liberal Imaginary.* New York: Routledge.

Beck, Hubert P. 1947. *Men Who Control Our Universities: The Economic and Social Composition of Governing Boards of Thirty Leading American Universities.* New York: King's Crown Press.

Bercovitz, Janet E. L., and Maryann P. Feldman. 2007. "Fishing Upstream: Firm Innovation Strategy and University Research Alliances." *Research Policy* 36, no. 7: 930–48. doi:10.1016/j.respol.2007.03.002.

Bok, Derek. 2003. *Universities on the Marketplace: The Commercialization of Higher Education*. Princeton, NJ: Princeton University Press.

Burt, Ronald S. 1992. *Structural Holes: The Social Structure of Competition*. Cambridge, MA: Harvard University Press.

Clark, Burton R. 1998. *Creating Entrepreneurial Universities: Organizational Pathways of Transformation*. Issues in Higher Education. New York: Emerald Group.

Colyvas, Jeannette A. 2007. "From Divergent Meanings to Common Practices: The Early Institutionalization of Technology Transfer in the Life Sciences at Stanford University." *Research Policy* 36, no. 4: 456–57. doi:10.1016/j.respol.2007.02.019.

D'Este, Pablo, and Pari Patel. 2007. "University-Industry Linkages in the UK: What Are the Factors Underlying the Variety of Interactions with Industry?" *Research Policy* 36, no. 9: 1259–313. doi:10.1016/j.respol.2007.05.002.

Domhoff, William G., and Thomas R. Dye, eds. 1987. *Power Elites and Organizations*. Newbury Park, CA: SAGE.

Dye, Thomas R. 1989. *Who's Running America? The Bush Era*. 5th ed. Englewood Cliffs, NJ: Prentice Hall.

———. 1994. *Who's Running America? The Clinton Years*. 6th ed. Englewood Cliffs, NJ: Prentice Hall.

———. 2002. *Who's Running America? The Bush Restoration*. 7th ed. Englewood Cliffs, NJ: Prentice Hall.

Ehrenberg, R. G., M. J. Rizzo, and G. H. Jakubson. 2007. "Who Bears the Growing Cost of Science at Universities?" In *Science and the University*, ed. P. Stephan and R. G. Ehrenberg, 19–35. Madison: University of Wisconsin Press.

Etzkowitz, Henry, Andrew Webster, and Peter Healey, eds. 1998. *Capitalizing Knowledge: New Interactions of Industry and Academe*. Albany: State University of New York Press.

Fallis, George. 2007. *Multiversities, Ideas, and Democracy*. Toronto: University of Toronto Press.

Fligstein, Neil, and Doug McAdam. 2012. *A Theory of Fields*. New York: Oxford University Press.

Gibbons, Michael, Camille Limoges, Helga Nowotny, Simon Schwartzman, Peter Scott, and Martin Trow. 1994. *The New Production of Knowledge: The Dynamics of Science and Research in Contemporary Societies*. Thousand Oaks, CA: SAGE.

Granovetter, Mark S. 1973. "The Strength of Weak Ties." *American Journal of Sociology* 78, no. 6: 1360–80.

Gumport, Patricia J., and Brian Pusser. 1995. "A Case of Bureaucratic Accretion: Context and Consequences." *Journal of Higher Education* 66, no. 5: 493–520.

Hsu, D. H., and M. Kenney. 2005. "Organizing Venture Capital: The Rise and Demise of the American Research Development Corporation, 1946–1973." *Industrial and Corporate Change* 14, no. 4: 579–616.

Humphreys, Joshua, Christi Electris, Yewande Fapohunda, Justin Filosa, James Goldstein, and Katie Grace. 2010. *Educational Endowments and the Financial Crisis: Social Costs and Systemic Risks in the Shadow Banking System. A Case Study of Six New England Schools*. Boston: Center for Social Philanthropy and Tellus Institute.

James, Estelle. 1998. "Commercialism among Nonprofits: Objectives, Opportunities, and Constraints." In *To Profit or Not to Profit: The Commercial Transformation of the*

Non-Profit Sector, edited by Burton A. Weisbrod, 271–86. Cambridge: Cambridge University Press.

Kingdon, John W. 1995. *Agendas, Alternatives, and Public Policies.* 2nd ed. New York: Harper-Collins College.

Lam, Alice. 2007. "Knowledge Networks and Careers: Academic Scientists in Industry-University Lines." *Journal of Management Studies* 44, no. 6: 993–1016. doi:10.1111/j.1467-6486.2007.00696.x.

Mann, Michael. 1986. *The Sources of Social Power*, vol. 1. Cambridge: Cambridge University Press.

Mathies, Charles, and Sheila Slaughter. 2013. "University Trustees as Channels between Academe and Industry: Toward an Understanding of the Executive Science Network." *Research Policy* 42, no. 6–7: 1286–300. doi:10.1016/j.respol.2013.03.003.

Morphew, Christopher C., and Peter D. Eckel, eds. 2009. *Privatizing the Public University: Perspectives from the Across the Academy.* Baltimore: Johns Hopkins University Press.

Newfield, C. 2008. *Unmaking the Public University.* Cambridge, MA: Harvard University Press.

Peck, Jamie, and Adam Tickell. 2002. "Neoliberalizing Space." *Antipode* 34, no. 3: 380–404. doi:10.1111/1467-8330.00247.

Pusser, Brian, Sheila Slaughter, and Scott L. Thomas. 2006. "Playing the Board Game: An Empirical Analysis of University Trustee and Corporate Board Interlocks." *Journal of Higher Education* 77, no. 5: 747–75.

Rhodes, Rod A. W. 1997. *Understanding Governance: Policy Networks, Governance, Reflexivity and Accountability.* Buckingham: Open University Press.

Shamir, Ronen. 2008. "The Age of Responsibilization: On Market-Embedded Morality." *Economy and Society* 37, no. 1: 1–19. doi:10.1080/03085140701760833.

Shinn, Terry, and Erwan Lamy. 2006. "Paths of Commercial Knowledge: Forms and Consequences of University-Enterprise Synergy in Scientist-Sponsored Firms." *Research Policy* 35, no. 10: 1465–76. doi:10.1016/j.respol.2006.09.024.

Slaughter, Sheila. 1990. *The Higher Learning and High Technology: The Dynamics of Higher Education Policy Formation.* Albany: State University of New York Press.

Slaughter, Sheila, and Brendan Cantwell. 2012. "Transatlantic Moves to the Market: Academic Capitalism in the United States and European Union." *Higher Education* 63, no. 5: 583–603. doi:10.1007/s10734-011-9460-9.

Slaughter, Shelia, and Larry L. Leslie. 1997. *Academic Capitalism: Politics, Policies, and the Entrepreneurial University.* Baltimore: Johns Hopkins University Press.

Slaughter, Sheila, and Gary Rhoades. 2004. *Academic Capitalism and the New Economy: Markets, State, and Higher Education.* Baltimore: Johns Hopkins University Press.

Slaughter, Sheila, and Barrett Jay Taylor. 2012. "The Executive Science Network: University Trustees and the Organization of University Industry Exchanges." NSF Grant Proposal 1262522, Science of Science Policy. Washington, DC: National Science Foundation.

Slaughter, Sheila, Scott L. Thomas, David R. Johnson, and Sondra N. Barringer. 2014. "Institutional Conflict of Interest: The Role of Interlocking Directorates in the Scientific Relationships between Universities and the Corporate Sector." *Journal of Higher Education* 85, no. 1: 1–35.

Stuart, Toby E., Salih Zeki Ozdemir, and Waverly W. Ding. 2007. "Vertical Alliance Network: The Case of University-Biotechnology-Pharmaceutical Alliance Chains." *Research Policy* 36, no. 4: 477–98. doi:10.1016/j.respol.2007.02.016.

Taylor, Barret J., Brendan Cantwell, and Sheila Slaughter. 2013. "Quasi-markets in US Higher Education: Humanities Emphasis and Institutional Revenues." *Journal of Higher Education* 84, no. 5: 675–707.

Veblen, Thorstein. 1918. *The Higher Learning in America: A Memorandum on the Conduct of Universities by Business Men*. New York: B. W. Huebsch.

Weisbrod, Burton Allen. 1988. *The Nonprofit Economy*. Cambridge, MA: Harvard University Press.

CHAPTER THREE

University Revolutions and Academic Capitalism

A Historical Perspective

JUSSI VÄLIMAA

Changing means of organizing the relationship between higher education institutions (HEIs) and surrounding societies characterize the history of universities. Academic capitalism as a midrange social theory aims to offer, perhaps, only one of the possible explanations of the recent changes in these relationships. In order to see better what aspects of change the theory of academic capitalism explains, one should analyze from a historical perspective the different roles played by universities and knowledge production in societies. It is especially useful to analyze the periods of radical changes, or university "revolutions," because they help illuminate how universities have responded—or refused to respond—to changes in their societal environments. The concept of "university revolution" refers to the periods of time when historical continuities of universities and/or knowledge production have been challenged by new ideas or technologies or policies (Nybom 2007).

When analyzing revolutions in higher education, one should bear in mind that higher education institutions are, and have always been, connected with their societies through a number of different ways, and universities have always been rather complex social entities as organizations serving many different functions in and for their societies (Clark 1983; de Ridder-Symoens 1992, 1996; Rüegg 2003a, 2003b, 2004a, 2004b). For this reason, one should pay attention to the alterations in the content of academic work, structures of organizations, and relationships with society in order to see which of them have changed and which have not as well as the consequences of these different foci and rhythms of changes. Higher education and knowledge production should be taken into consideration because technological innovation in knowledge production— such as in printing or the Internet—influences the content, foci, and ways of working in academia and may challenge universities' traditional academic and administrative practices and functions. Similarly, policies and politics may change internal power relations in universities and influence the content of academic work.[1]

Following the reasoning of Nybom (2007), we should pay attention to the following dimensions when analyzing rapid changes in HEIs and knowledge production:[2]

- Changes in the institutional and/or organizational aspects of universities. Such changes help show how the relationship between societies and HEIs has been organized. This relationship also helps explain the internal organization of universities and other HEIs.
- Changes in the pedagogical practices and/or the organization and content of curricula. These changes—or lack thereof—help us understand what is changing in the content of teaching and learning.
- Changes in the professional identities and practices. Taking into account changes in the ideals and practices of academic and professional work helps us understand how formal structures and actual academic work are related. Tensions within these relationships help to explain the need for or outcomes of changes.
- Changes in the social relationships and mental climate of academics. It is helpful to pay attention to potential changes in the purposes and goals of universities and academic work and how these have been defined.
- Finally, changes in the relationship with the prince (or state or other similar representative of political power) are normally defined as the most important aspect of higher education changes and reforms. It is also a popular topic in European higher education research (see Saarinen and Välimaa 2012). But the analyses of the changes in the politics and policies of the prince should be analyzed only in relation with the abovementioned dimensions to examine their importance for the organization, power relations, and academic work of higher education institutions.

Taking support from Nybom (2007), these five dimensions help to examine six periods of major changes in the history of European universities called in this study: (1) the Gutenberg revolution (1460s–1560s); (2) the scientific revolution (1600–1750); (3) the Humboldt revolution (1810s–1860s); (4) the modern research university revolution (1860s–1920s); (5) the mass higher education revolution (1960s–1970s); and (6) the knowledge society revolution (1990–).

Using these dimensions, it is easier to examine how changes in universities may touch either all their functions or focus only on certain aspects while leaving others intact. When thinking about the nature of changes in higher education, we should remember that changes may originate either from inside (like organic growth) or outside of higher education institutions (like a political reform). The nature of changes may also be a continuous development or a sudden change (Saarinen and Välimaa 2012). In this study I focus on radical changes in higher education and knowledge production.

The first main research question I ask in this chapter is how universities have changed during these university revolutions. I base my discussion on existing research literature, and it opens historical perspectives to the development of universities. The second main aim is to reflect on how academic capitalism can be used to explain current changes in higher education. I begin with the reflection of historical foundations of European universities because changes are difficult to understand without knowing the starting points of universities. Following this discussion is an analysis of six different revolutions. In the conclusion, I reflect on academic capitalism as an intellectual device to explain the changes taking place in contemporary higher education.

The Cornerstones of Universities

In order to understand changes in universities, one must first understand how and why they were established. Historically speaking, tensions between societies and universities emerged even before the first universities were established. One of the ironies of history is the fact that the first European universities—such as Bologna and Paris—were never officially established. Instead, they emerged and developed together with developing medieval European societies. Universities offered a solution to vocational needs of medieval societies, which needed qualified lawyers, clerical officials, and citizens who were able to read, write, and defend their arguments in expanding social life and commerce. Even their name—*universitas*—referred originally to several types of corporate bodies such as craft guilds and municipal councils (in the eleventh through thirteenth centuries) that were typical in medieval societies. It was only during the fourteenth century that *universitas* as a concept began to mean universities (Cobban 1988).

It is fair to say that universities are an indigenous European social innovation. Crucial for the future success of universities was their corporative character: European universities were from the beginning "privileged corporate associations of masters and students with their statutes, seals, administrative machinery and degree procedures," as Cobban (1988) puts it. Typical of traditional universities was the fact that they were multidisciplinary institutions (with traditional disciplines of theology, law, medicine, and arts) helping to promote the idea that students need a broad education before leaving the university. A medieval innovation was the relationship between teaching and degrees, which in turn justified and structured curricula. Typical forms of teaching were lectures and disputations that introduced medieval students to a tradition of knowledge accumulated and commented on by recognized authorities. Owing to a lack of printed books, the verbal and literal argumentation skills of students were practiced in exercises and repetitive work at masters' homes or in colleges, thus supporting the concept that learning was based on memorizing (Schwinges 1992).

These may seem to be small innovations, but they were crucially important because they shaped both the content of academic work (teaching and learning and scholarship) and the administrative structures of universities. From the beginning, universities were able to defend their institutional autonomy with the help of their corporate structures against the political pressures represented by bishops, princes, and city councils.

The intellectual cornerstones of the European universities, however, were beliefs and convictions that supported the development of future academic practices. According to Cobban (1988, 11–14), these cornerstones were as follows:

- "The belief in the dignity of man, who, even in his fallen state, was capable of impressive mental and spiritual growth." In other words, medieval academics valued education and believed that students could be educated.
- "The belief in an ordered universe open to rational understanding." In a modern context, this means that man can and should conduct research in order to better understand the world. That is, medieval academics valued research and scholarship. This is an important principle (and conviction), even though the methods, foci of studies, and academic approaches of research have changed over the course of centuries.
- "The belief in the prospect of man's mastery of his environment through his intellect and his mounting knowledge and experience." In a modern context, this means that research can be useful. It was important for the future development of universities that medieval academics respected the

utility of research, even though the meaning and understanding of "man's mastery of his environment" has been defined and understood differently during the history of universities.

In addition to these intellectual cornerstones, two practical matters strongly supported the development of universities and their intellectual curiosity driven–functioning. Namely, as Cobban (1988) emphasized, supported by Christian humanisms, there developed

- a culture that encouraged questioning and analytical approaches to both classical and contemporary material, meaning that the critical thinking of academics was encouraged.

Walter Rüegg has, in turn, emphasized that medieval universities also supported

- publicity of research and open debates (Rüegg 2003a, 32–34).

These beliefs and values, which have been tested by historical processes over centuries, continue to stay alive in the intellectual heartland of universities for all (European) universities. They continue to be vital even in modern universities because they emphasize the value of critical thinking and the importance of research, teaching, and learning. It is equally important that higher education institutions have institutional autonomy and social structures to defend it.

What is said above may seem to be naïve and simplistic thinking that aims to glorify past and present universities, but this is not the purpose of this chapter. We need to understand the value basis of European universities to better understand why and how they have changed during their history. Universities have expanded outside Europe from the nineteenth century onward. The cornerstones of European universities have been and are being tested in other cultural contexts, leading to new cultural interpretations and social roles of higher education institutions.

The Gutenberg Revolution, 1460s–1560s

The first information technology revolution that really challenged many of the practices of European universities was the printing of books, invented by Johannes Gutenberg in the 1450s. According to Nybom (2007), this innovation rapidly changed the social role of knowledge dissemination and had both professional and curricular implications. It changed the role of the university professor, who was challenged to change from a transmitter of a canonical tradition to a critical interpreter of knowledge and who was even expected to produce new, original knowledge. Humanism as a change movement also crept into universities by demanding active life (*vita activa*) and the interpretation of original sources as a goal for critical studies of academics (Rüegg 2003b). However, as Nybom (2007) pointed out this radical information and communication technology (ICT) reform had practically no impact on existing modes of teaching or educational thinking in universities. Medieval social practices—like academic guilds and colleges—continued, and dynastic and confessionally bounded universities began to ossify (Rüegg 2003b).

What is crucial with this revolutionary period is the notion that information technology has always had an influence on the production and distribution of knowledge. It has also influenced the way universities—and their knowledge production—relate to their surrounding societies. Important for the future of universities, however, was that this first ICT revolution did not influence universities, which reformed neither their organizational structures nor medieval pedagogical practices.

The Scientific Revolution, 1600–1750

According to Nybom (2007), a second critical period for European universities was the expansion of empirical sciences, which began to develop outside universities in semi-independent science academies established in practically every European country. The first ones were L'Académie Française (in 1635) and the Royal Society (in 1660). There have been academic debates on the role universities played in the scientific revolution because they trained the majority of members of first scientific academies, as Porter (2003) has shown. But there seems to be common agreement that universities, with the exceptions of Padua and Leiden, were not active contributors to the development of this scientific revolution (Porter 2003). According to Rüegg (2003b), one of the reasons for this development was the fact that humanism, which started as university reform movement in the fifteenth century, degenerated into activity that turned from the contemporary world toward antiquity, and "university research became more and more an alien theatre in which world was presented" (Rüegg 2003b, 41). Traditional (ecclesiastical and dynastic) universities had begun to decline into parochial teaching-oriented institutions serving mainly the needs of the Church and the prince. Nepotism was a strong social phenomenon, especially in German universities, but it was known elsewhere as well (Charle 2004; Nybom 2007).

Outside universities, this revolutionary period introduced a new intellectual mentality of "a modern scientist" as a new professional and European ideal. This ideal helped to transform a traditional natural philosopher into an objective and impartial scientist who was beginning to take a new kind of authority and who was able to provide cognitive standards for any kind of enquiry. This was one of the starting points for the modern standing of science, as Gaukroger (2006) put it. The scientific revolution also strongly supported the internationalization of empirical scientific research, which began to be understood as a common international enterprise. Traditional theological and humanist scholars had more dogmatic approaches.

The scientific revolution in knowledge production left universities mainly intact regarding their organization, pedagogy, and academic work. Socially, one of the consequences of this development was the fact that universities began to decline into parochial institutions that recruited local or national students and academics. No new universities in England were established after the Middle Ages, for example, even though Scottish universities were radical exceptions to sleepy Oxbridge and European universities also incorporating empirical sciences as early as the eighteenth century (Hammerstein 1996; Perkins 1984). But Scottish universities in the nineteenth century did not provide a model for new European universities, which began to follow the German university model. The need for rapid reforms became apparent during the French Revolution and Napoleonic Wars in Europe at the turn of the nineteenth century.

The Humboldt Revolution, 1810s–1860s

According to a number of scholars (see Charle 2004; Nybom 2007; Wittrock 1993), the period of the Napoleonic Wars was the most critical period in the history of European universities, which were regarded—with good reason—as out-of-date institutions corrupted by nepotism and not serving the needs of their societies. One of the indicators of the crisis is the fact that the number of European universities decreased from 143 (in 1798) to eighty-three (in 1815). The decline was especially remarkable in France, where twenty-four universities were discontinued or transformed into professional schools, and in Germany, where eighteen of thirty-four universities disappeared. In Spain, only ten out of twenty-five universities had some academic life left (Rüegg 2004a). It took more than one hundred years for Europe to recover from this crisis, using the number of universities as a measure. From an institutional point of view, this crisis meant a total external, internal, intellectual, and institutional decline of the

French and German university systems, whereas traditional universities managed to survived in the British Isles and in the southern and northern parts of Europe (Charle 2004).

There were two solutions to this crisis among continental European universities. The first was implemented by Napoleon, who established and strengthened the system of *grandes écoles* in France. These highest-status higher education institutions trained the elite of and for the emerging French republic and nation-state. Universities became teaching-only institutions, consequently influencing both intellectual productivity and academic careers, which could be advanced only in Paris. In universities outside Paris, research was forbidden, leading to what has been called "an intellectual desert" (Charle 2004). But other European nation-states did not follow this system of higher education even though it did have an influence on Russian higher education, for example, which has typified a combination of French and German university ideals (Rüegg 2004a).

The salvation of and for the European universities came from Berlin, where the defeat of the Prussian army created a suitable social and identity crisis that supported the search for new directions for Prussian society (Charle 2004; Rüegg 2004a). Wilhelm von Humboldt managed to convince the rulers of Prussia that new state building should be based on the idea of *Bildung* in the spirit of German neo-humanists and German idealism. In politics, this meant that the aim of the new nation-state should be a cultural state (*Kulturstaat*), which can be reached with the help of education and research (*wissenschaft*). This political situation thus helped realize the need for university reform by connecting this reform to the reformulation of goals for the Prussian state. The reform of the university of Berlin was thus not only about reforming the university but also reforming the status and position of education in society. What is often forgotten is that Humboldt also reformed German education, thus creating a new system by connecting secondary-level education (*Gymnasium*) to the university system through *abitur*, which allowed access to university (Nybom 2007).

As for universities, this reform had significant consequences with regard to their organization, pedagogy, academic work, and academic careers. One of the leading ideas of the reform was to secure the autonomy of universities in relation to the state. Basically, the state gave the money but did not interfere with the internal matters in university. The only exception was the nomination of professors by the Prussian king in order to fight against the traditional vice of nepotism. As for research and teaching, *lernfreiheit* (freedom to study) and *lehrfreiheit* (freedom to teach) helped to secure academic freedom for students and academics. As for pedagogy, research seminars were introduced to all disciplines to strengthen the relationship between teaching and research. The unity of teaching and research was crucially important as a goal, because it was thought that knowledge is an indivisible entity. The main goals of the university were science and scholarship (*wissenschaft*), or the pursuit of truth. The unity of teaching and learning (*forschung und lehre*) was a strong ideal, which also influenced the nature of the academic work. One of the consequences was that the faculty of philosophy replaced theology as the most important faculty in university. It was thought that philosophy was the most crucial discipline to secure the indivisibility of knowledge. The *Privatdozent* system—whereby scholars had permission to teach in a university without salary from the university—strongly supported academic careers and mobility in German universities because talented young doctors were trying to create their reputations and careers in a competitive academic environment. As a consequence of planned reforms and the emerging social dynamics in Prussian society and higher education, new German universities became dynamic places for the pursuit of truth and academic careers (Charle 2004; Nybom 2004; Rüegg 2004b).

This is not to say that all German universities—which were called Humboldtian universities only in the twentieth century, when an unfinished memo by Humboldt was "found"—followed this model (Humboldt 1896–99). However, this ideal was important as a goal because it helped to revitalize and reform German universities indifferent to how well they managed to implement it. It also gave a successful model to be imitated by academics and politicians in other countries. As Nybom (2007) points out, however, one of the historical ironies is that this ideal of knowledge as indivisible entity and even the unity of teaching and research started to disappear when the rest of the world began to admire the German university system during the end of the nineteenth century. The vital and dynamic German research universities, which were admired by American, British, French, and Japanese colleagues, were no longer following Humboldtian ideals (Nybom 2007; Perkins 1984).

The Modern Research University Revolution, 1860s–1920s

The development of the research university is, according to Nybom (2207), the fifth university revolution. It is a revolution because it changed the function of universities, the funding of research, the production of scientific knowledge, academic careers, and academic communities. One of the most difficult principles to maintain in the new research universities was the unity of knowledge, because sciences and humanities began to be divided by more specific curricula and interests of knowledge. In this context it is quite natural that German philosophers like Wilhelm Dilthey started the tradition of differentiating between disciplines explaining "nature" (sciences) and disciplines understanding "culture" (*geistwissenschaft,* or humanism). The expansion of sciences forced universities to create new and more specified curricula, while science was becoming more like an "intellectual industry" practiced by highly qualified professionals. There emerged also a new type of universities, namely, technical universities. The strengthening of research universities also led to the professionalization of academic careers. This process was supported by disciplinary communities, which grew stronger with emerging international and national conferences, and the expanding number of academic journals, which brought elevated status to academic professions and disciplinary fields. Academic degrees and careers became more closely intertwined, and state bureaucracy expanded (Nybom 2007). As Wittrock (1993) has stated, universities made a good deal with the emerging nation-states, benefiting both parties.

Problems integrating research with teaching emerged, which in turn contributed to the establishment of research institutes. Scientific laboratories and clinics appeared as new sites for academic research and teaching, while seminars continued in all disciplines to be social spaces for seeking truth by both students and academics.

To make a long story short, the changes in knowledge production, pedagogical practices, and academic careers were related to the institutional aspects of the German universities. Institutional autonomy supported the development of academic careers and academic work. University professors, who became independent mandarins of their chairs, managed faculties, which consisted of many related disciplines. This way, the chair system supported not only academic freedom and academic careers by providing academic career perspectives for a group of *Privatdozent,* but it also created a hierarchical social relationship inside faculties. Mentally, the combination of research and teaching freedoms gave an impetus for combined research and teaching activities that emerging scientific communities supported.

The Mass Higher Education Revolution, 1960s–1970s

Similar to the Humboldt revolution of the early nineteenth century, the expansion of mass higher education is strongly related to political goals, as Western societies built welfare states after the Second World War in an effort to enhance the international competitive capacities of nation-states with the help of education and research. With this expansion, however, the role played by higher education institutions in society changed remarkably. Martin Trow (1974) was first to conceptualize this transformation by highlighting how the social role of higher education changes when the number of students exceeds a certain proportion in the age cohort. It has been estimated that when more than 15% of a certain age cohort enters higher education, we can no longer speak about an elite system of higher education, but rather a mass system of higher education producing a qualified workforce for the labor markets.

With the expansion of higher education the social dynamics of teaching, learning, administration, and management in universities also changed. There were introduced a number of new pedagogical approaches (e.g., focus on different learning styles, student-centered learning, problem solving, development of expertise) and different pedagogical isms that suggested solutions to the problems related to and caused by expanding numbers of different kinds of students in HEIs. The expansion also introduced new professional groups into higher education institutions (i.e., managed professionals; see Rhoades 1998), thus making academics more dependent on technical and administrative staff. But the most radical changes to universities during the 1960s focused on reforming the old administrative and management structures and processes to open university senates to academics other than university professors (Bourdieu 1988; Cerych and Sabatier 1986; Välimaa 2005). Mass education is one of the factors that promote assessment, evaluation, and audit systems of higher education, opening the "black box" of HEIs. "Accountability," "quality," and "making more with less" are common slogans repeated by a number of ministries of higher education influenced by higher education policy objectives defined by the Organisation for Economic Co-operation and Development and International Monetary Fund (Kallo 2009). Such slogans and policy goals are related to the increasing costs that come with the rapid expansion of higher education. This is the case with both private and public HEIs because the funding of students and research depends heavily on public funding sources all over the globe. The costs of higher education are, in turn, a political issue practically everywhere. The global funding crisis of traditional welfare states has also hit HEIs, which have been a strong part of publicly funded social services. During the mass higher education revolution, changes have taken place in pedagogical, professional, political, and organizational aspects of and in higher education.

Knowledge Society Revolution, 1990–

The last revolutionary period of higher education began in the 1990s with the rapid expansion of three different social and technological developments related, first, to the expansion of Internet and later wireless information technology (Castells, Fernandez-Ardevol, Qiu, and Sey 2006) and, second, to the expansion of network as a form of social life, communication, and industrial production (Castells 2009). The third and fundamental alteration is the expanding role of knowledge in every sphere of society (Stehr 1994). These three simultaneous, overlapping, and mutually enforcing processes have led to societal situation that can be called a networked knowledge society (Välimaa 2012). Without going deeper into this complex sociological theory, it is perhaps sufficient to say that higher education and knowledge production are facing fundamental challenges because of the changes in ICT, networked social forms of knowledge production, and dissemination and also because of multiple needs to produce reliable and up-to-date knowledge for citizens, societies, nongovernmental organizations (NGOs), industry, and business. All these global societal trends are also challenging the traditions of academics, HEIs, and the position of HEIs in societies. According to Altbach, Reisberg, and Rumbley (2010), "one can, without risk of exaggeration, speak of academic 'revolution'—a series of transformations that have affected most aspects of postsecondary education worldwide" as quoted in Kwiek 2012, 17).

The trend of supporting economies with the help of research had its beginning in the research university revolution, when the funding of research was seen as a fundamental competitive factor for industry, business, and national economies at large (Nybom 2007). What is crucial with the current revolution is the speed of changes and the increase of knowledge produced and consumed in every sphere of society. In a globalized world, the social function of knowledge production has been taken into the core of political agendas practically everywhere. This is the case even though there is clear evidence that the task of transferring knowledge from "knowledge factories" (universities) to industry is a complex task (Kwiek 2012).

In order to see what these changes in societies and economies may pose for higher education, we must examine the most important changes by comparing the emerging networked knowledge society with traditional society on the basis of controlled and hierarchical social relationships and clearly defined borders between, inside, and outside of an organization.

There are many changes in the production, dissemination, and storage of knowledge that are related to the traditional basic functions taken care of by higher education institutions. First, it is more than evident that the locus of knowledge is changing from only local and national institutions toward global networks. Second, the nature of knowledge is changing because in a traditional hierarchical society the knowledge producers or public authorities controlled knowledge, whereas in networked knowledge societies the ideal is to have open access to freely distributed knowledge. The mode of knowledge production is also changing. In a traditional society, academics employed by universities and research institutes primarily produced new knowledge, whereas in a networked knowledge society, cooperation with many partners located both in academic and business environments in global settings produces new knowledge. This is a broader phenomenon than just Mode 2 production of knowledge, which emphasizes the context of application as being essential for the knowledge production, or a triple helix kind of research, which focuses on cooperation between the state, universities, and industry (Etzkowitz and Leydesdorff 2000; Gibbons et al. 1994). The mode of knowledge production is based on networks where all members can benefit, instead of aiming for patent-protected and closed information (Benkler 2006). The production of knowledge, which used to be the responsibility of more or less heroic academics, or public intellectuals, is increasingly becoming a cooperative business, which is based on peer production of knowledge (Benkler 2006). In addition, the storage of knowledge, which used to be the responsibility of (national) archives and libraries only physically accessible to users is transitioning into Internet- and open access–based virtual archives and electronic databases often accessible to global users—at least to those who have access to Internet. Access to knowledge, which used to be controlled strictly by public authorities, is being replaced by the idea of free and open access to documents by all users. Finally, student-centered approaches are challenging teaching or knowledge transmission through traditional teacher-centered pedagogical practices. This change is made possible by different technological innovations (such as clouds and electronic learning environments) enabling new forms of Internet-based distribution of courses and curricula (like massive open online courses, or MOOCs). Social media can also be simultaneously used for the delivery of ideas and even teaching materials. For a number of reasons, this new ICT-based technology has the potential of changing academic teaching and learning environments because learning no longer requires a physical presence of students in the same classroom, or even in the same country. Teaching and learning face 24/7 learning processes that can take place everywhere and any time. All these changes challenge academic teachers to change their attitudes and also their pedagogical perspectives and skills.

Constructive theories of learning support the ideals where teachers become more like couches to learners than distributors of authoritative knowledge, whereas neoliberal attitudes help to define students as consumers who should be served as clients. All these changes take place in a globalized and networked knowledge society. They also have the potential to challenge the traditional status of university studies and traditional practices of teaching and learning and management in universities. For all these reasons, it is justified to define these changes as an academic revolution.

In addition to these transformations in the nature of academic work and the relationship between HEIs and their societies, one should not forget the changes in the policy environments of HEIs. A number of countries have simultaneously faced budget cuts in higher education with shifts of funding from "soft" disciplines (humanities, social sciences, education) toward "hard" ones, and especially the applied sciences (ICT, technology; see Kwiek 2012). A recent phenomenon is the rise of world-class university status as a policy goal in most developed and developing countries, supported by the growing importance of HEI rankings. This goal is often based on the idealized image of an American research university (Välimaa 2012).

Is Academic Capitalism an Analysis of a New University Revolution?

Before analyzing how academic capitalism manages to explain recent changes in higher education, I must first give my interpretation of this theory. Academic capitalism as a midrange social theory aims to explain how the dynamics of neoliberal economies are embedded in higher education institutions. Slaughter and Leslie (1997) use academic capitalism as a concept to study institutional and professional market or market-like efforts to secure external moneys. They describe how academic staffs have become state-subsidized entrepreneurs who exploit their academic capital in increasingly competitive situations. Market-like behaviors refer "to institutional and faculty competition for moneys" (e.g., patenting, spinoff companies, university-industry partnerships), whereas market behavior refers to "for-profit activity on the part of institutions" and "more mundane endeavors, such as the sale of products and services from educational endeavors" (11). They also state that "a quiet revolution has already taken place" (11).

Slaughter and Rhoades (2004) further developed this theoretical reasoning by focusing on the United States, which is ruled by neoliberal politics. They show how boundaries between higher education, the market, and government are blurring when for-profit behaviors are adopted by and embedded in HEIs.

Slaughter and Cantwell (2012) in turn argue that the academic capitalism regime also exists in European higher education, even though the developmental path differs from the US one. In US higher education, the driving force has been the exploitation of regulatory openings and policy shifts that favor competitiveness among NGOs and universities, whereas in Europe the driving force is the state-supported new public management (NPM) agenda, which has led to a number of higher education reforms in the spirit of neoliberal policies (see also Weimer 2013).

The research question this chapter seeks to answer is this: how well does academic capitalism as concept and as a theoretical perspective manage to explain this academic and "quiet revolution" taking place in higher education? I try to answer to this question by using the defined dimensions and questions derived from them:

- How have institutional and organizational aspects of HEIs changed?
- How have pedagogical practices and curricula changed?
- How have professional identities and practices changed?
- How have the social relationships and mental climate of academics changed?
- How has the relationship with the state changed?

How Have Institutional and Organizational Aspects Changed?

On the basis of empirical evidence, the era explained by of academic capitalism has not witnessed new types of HEIs. But shifts in the balance of power related to and caused by market forces and state policies have occurred inside HEIs. According to Slaughter and Leslie (1997), those units, which receive their own funding independently from their mother institution, gain more power inside HEIs, leading to differentiation among units, with units closer to markets benefiting from the situation. State policies, especially NPM in Europe, have given more power to central institutional administration and management (Ferlie, Musselin, and Andresani 2008). However, the consequences at the basic academic unit level are more blurred because market trends and NPM policies may also act against each other. As Slaughter and Leslie (1997) put it, "power is becoming both more and less centralized" (230–31). This seems to be the case in continental Europe in addition to Anglo-American higher education. As a theoretical explanation, academic capitalism helps to show that universities are not monolithic entities, but organizations characterized by conflicting interests between disciplines and academics and their managers.

48   Jussi Välimaa

How Have Pedagogical Practices and Curricula Changed?

Academic capitalism does not take into consideration the issue of higher education pedagogics. This is an understandable shortcoming of this theory, which is focused on knowledge production. However, the lack of teaching and learning perspective is problematic because it pays no attention to one of the most important relationships between universities and society: the flow of students with their ideas and human capital to the labor market. As discussed above, ICT represents a remarkable challenge for higher education institutions. MOOCs are just one example of possible future trends in this regard.

How Have Professional Identities and Practices Changed?

The theory of academic capitalism pays extensive attention to changes in the understanding and definitions of work done by academics (or faculty) and administrative staff. The authors discuss in detail the ways academic identities and working profiles are influenced both by competition with colleagues and by closer cooperation with business and industrial enterprises (representing markets). This increasing cooperation has the potential of changing academic identities as well. The authors also suggest, with a reference to Clark Kerr, that there is a "paradigm shift in academic life whereby faculty members have become committed less to the academic community and more to economic factors" (Slaughter and Leslie 1997, 226). Even though they do not give exact answers to the question, Slaughter and Leslie discuss elegantly and profoundly the pressures created by market and market-like forces in a globalized higher education environment. This discussion is most seminal because it opens new perspectives on emerging tensions and potential problems in the autonomy of academics and academic profession.

How Have the Social Relationships and Mental Climate of Academics Changed?

The social relationships and mental climate of academics are closely related to professional identities and practices. Market and market-like behaviors influence the self-understanding of academics as teachers and researchers in two ways. First, research is the most efficient way to get more money individually as well as for the unit and the institution. As a consequence, HEIs, basic academic units, and individuals consider research to be a more important activity than teaching. In addition, research has been and continues to be the most secure path to a university career. Second, most HEIs and academics—at least in the

Western world—feel the pressure of making more with less. One might assume that academics feel more pressure in their work than before. Surprisingly, however this does not seem to be case based on empirical Changing Academic Profession and EuroAc studies (Teichler and Hähle 2013). One possible explanation is that working conditions in HEIs have deteriorated less than those in outside labor markets. As for academic capitalism, these empirical findings are intriguing because they indicate that academics may have managed to survive quite well the pressures created by markets and market-like behaviors.

How Has the Relationship with the State Changed?

The books *Academic Capitalism* and *Academic Capitalism and the New Economy* analyze the changing relationship between HEIs and society. They show empirically and discuss theoretically how neoliberal policies have changed—or have the potential to change—the social role of HEIs and the nature of academic work as well as power structures inside HEIs and between disciplines. In other words, they help explain why applied "hard disciplines (science and technology) are gaining more public and private funding and why "soft disciplines (education, humanities, and social sciences) are on the losing side of the funding game.

According to the basic assumptions of academic capitalism as a theory, HEIs are willing to adopt to market behaviors and to make money in competitive settings as much as they can, often at the cost of academic freedom and institutional autonomy. Yet these are hardly universal explanations of HEI behavior, as Leasa Weimer (2013) explains. On the basis of empirical evidence, she shows that Finnish universities do not follow the logic of academic capitalism because Finnish HEIs are not willing to make money at any cost by charging tuition fees from international students coming from outside the European Union (EU). Weimer also shows that there are contradictory opinions about the purposes of higher education. Incumbents see that higher education benefits Finnish society as whole, whereas challengers maintain that tuition fees are the best way to respond to international pressures in the global economy. Incumbents define higher education as a public good and resist strongly the basic assumptions of academic capitalism, which would lead to the rule of market forces and defining students as consumers. Challengers, in turn, see higher education more as private good that can be bought and sold in the international marketplace, as the theory assumes (Weimer 2013). At the moment, however, there is no decision in Finland to charge international students tuition fees. National and EU students pay no tuition in any case.

Weimer's dissertation helps to develop an argument that if the theory of academic capitalism does not explain the behavior of HEIs and academics in one country, then the theory is not a universal one, but rather a particular one that explains social dynamics in some societies. It has been proven empirically that academic capitalism explains the social dynamics related to higher education in Anglo-American world, but its explanatory power outside this cultural context is more than uncertain. In addition to Finland, a similar social dynamic may be found in other Nordic countries and countries where higher education has a strong nation-building function, such as in Mexico and other Latin American countries (Ordorika and Pusser 2007).

Conclusion

This chapter intends to show that the history of universities is not an evident success story. Universities have often had conflicts and challenges in their relationships with their societies. There have been periods when universities have lost their societal legitimacy and credibility and even their importance as teaching institutions. Radical and rapid transformations in societies and economic environments have forced universities to change or adapt.

When explaining contemporary changes in higher education, academics figure in at least three arenas. One of them is the policy arena, where politicians and policymakers tend to use different academic theories as performative ideologies, as Michael Peters (2007) put it. In this arena, Machiavellian ideologies of policy-making rule and academic research only serve political purposes. The second arena is that of the academic career. In this arena, academics fight for the best explanation of historical or contemporary phenomena—whether in the humanities or social sciences. In this arena, reputation is the currency. Books and articles and reports can translate into power and positions. The third arena is that of academic contemplation, where academics struggle for the best explanation or best theory of a phenomenon indifferent of the reputation it may help to gain or lose. They search for the truth. Normally, and in the speeches of rectors and reputational academics, this is the arena in which most academics claim to play because it is most closely and firmly rooted in the core values of (European) universities. All these arenas derive from different theoretical families of explanations, which I will not explore in detail because here the aim is to reflect on the arenas in which academic capitalism has been used.

Based on citation indexes, academic capitalism has a strong presence in the arena of academic careers because it has a strong reputation in the field of higher education. This edited volume is in itself an evidence of that reputation. Based on academic awards, academic capitalism has become an ambitious search for the truth. It has been recognized as a true example of excellent research in the arena of academic contemplation. But academic capitalism has a much weaker presence in the arena of policy making. This matter of fact is quite natural because, as a theory, academic capitalism criticizes neoliberal political practices, which have been the most influential policy perspectives (e.g., NPM) in global higher education policy-making agendas in recent decades.

The real value of the theory of academic capitalism lies in the fact that it has focused on the process of change taking place inside academia. This is more important than focusing only on political ideologies aiming to change management structures in HEIs or their relationship with the prince, which is what critics of NPM often do. Even though these relationships are important, they are not the most important social phenomena to be studied in higher education. As academic capitalism shows, we should be sensitive to gradual changes, "quiet revolutions" that are taking place below the policy screens of higher education. In a similar vein, the relationship between management and academic work is important, but even more important are the dynamics of fundamental changes affecting the nature of academic work. For these reasons, we should analyze the transformations of different aspects, dimensions, and academic functions of universities in order to understand how and where the changes take place at the basic operational level of HEIs and knowledge production, as well as how and where these transformations challenge HEIs and academics to change or not change.

NOTES

1. "Academic work" is used as a neutral term, which includes the work academics and students do in higher education institutions: teaching, learning, research, administration, and management.

2. "Higher education institutions" and "universities" are used interchangeably here because there were only universities before the seventeenth century, whereas the modern term higher education institution became popular during the 1960s and 1970s with the expansion of higher education and new tertiary-level institutions.

REFERENCES

Altbach, Philip G., Liz Reisberg, and Laura E. Rumbley. 2010. *Trends in Global Higher Education: Tracking an Academic Revolution.* Paris: UNESCO.

Benkler, Yochai. 2006. *The Wealth of Networks: How Social Production Transforms Markets and Freedom.* New Haven, CT: Yale University Press.

Bourdieu, Pierre. 1988. *Homo Academicus.* Translated by Peter Collier. Stanford, CA: Stanford University Press.

Castells, Manuel. 2009. *Communication Power.* Oxford: Oxford University Press.

Castells, Manuel, Mireia Fernandez-Ardevol, Jack Linchuan Qiu, and Araba Sey. 2006. *Mobile Communication and Society: Global Perspective.* Cambridge, MA: MIT Press.

Cerych, Ladislav, and Paul A. Sabatier. 1986. *Great Expectations and Mixed Performance: The Implementation of Higher Education Reforms in Europe.* Stoke-on-Trent, UK: Trentham Books.

Charle, Christopher. 2004. "Patterns." In *A History of the University in Europe,* vol. 3, edited by Walter Rüegg, 33–81. Cambridge: Cambridge University Press.

Clark, Burton R. 1983. *The Higher Education System: Academic Organization in Cross-National Perspective.* Berkeley: University of California Press.

Cobban, Alan B. 1988. *The Medieval English Universities: Oxford and Cambridge to c. 1500.* Aldershot, UK: Scolar Press.

de Ridder-Symoens, Hilde, ed. 1992. *A History of the University in Europe.* Vol. 1, *Universities in the Middle Ages.* Cambridge: Cambridge University Press.

————. 1996. *A History of the University in Europe.* Vol. 2, *Universities in Early Modern Europe (1500–1800).* Cambridge: Cambridge University Press.

Etzkowitz, Henry, and Loet Leydesdorff. 2000. "The Dynamics of Innovation: From National Systems and 'Mode 2' to a Triple Helix of University-Industry-Government Relations." *Research Policy* 29, no. 2: 109–23. doi:10.1016/S0048-7333(99)00055-4.

Ferlie, Ewan, Christine Musselin, and Gianluca Andresani. 2008. "The Steering of Higher Education Systems: A Public Management Perspective." *Higher Education* 56, no. 3: 325–48. doi:10.1007/s10734-008-9125-5.

Gaukroger, Stephen. 2006. *The Emergence of a Scientific Culture: Science and the Shaping of Modernity, 1210–1685.* Oxford: Oxford University Press.

Gibbons, Michael, Camille Limoges, Helga Nowotny, Simon Schwartzman, Peter Scott, and Martin Trow. 1994. *The New Production of Knowledge: The Dynamics of Science and Research in Contemporary Societies.* London: SAGE.

Hammerstein, Notker. 1996. "Relations with Authority." In *A History of the University in Europe,* vol. 2, *Universities in Early Modern Europe (1500–1800),* edited by Hilde de Ridder-Symoens, 114–54. Cambridge: Cambridge University Press.

Humboldt, W. 1896–99. "Denkschrift and Antrag auf Einrichtung der Universität Berlin Juli 1808." In *Wilhelm von Humboldt als Staatsman I-II,* edited by B. Gebhardt. Stuttgart.

Kallo, Johanna. 2009. *OECD Education Policy: A Comparative and Historical Study Focusing on the Thematic Reviews of Tertiary Education.* Research in Educational Sciences 45. Jyväskylä: Finnish Educational Research Association.

Kwiek, Marek, ed. 2012. *Knowledge Production in European Universities: State, Markets, and Academic Entrepreneurialism.* Frankfurt: Peter Lang.

Nybom, Thorsten. 2007. "A Rule-Governed Community of Scholars: The Humboldt Vision in the History of the European University." In *University Dynamics and European Integration,* vol. 19, *Higher Education Dynamics,* edited by Peter A. M. Maassen and Johan P. Olsen, 55–80. Dordrecht: Springer.

Ordorika, Imanol, and Brian Pusser. 2007. "La Maxima Casa de Estudios: Universidad Nacional Autonóma de México as a State-Building University." In *World Class World-*

wide: Transforming Research Universities in Asia and Latin America, edited by Philip G. Altbach and Jorge Balán, 189–215. Baltimore: Johns Hopkins University Press.

Perkins, Harold. 1984. "The Historical Perspective." In *Perspectives on Higher Education: Eight Disciplinary and Comparative Views*, edited by Burton R. Clark, 17–55. Berkeley: University of California Press.

Peters, Michael A. 2007. *Knowledge Economy, Development and the Future of Higher Education*. Vol. 10, *Educational Futures, Rethinking Theory and Practice*. Rotterdam: Sense.

Porter, Roy. 2003. "The Scientific Revolution and Universities." In *A History of the University in Europe*, vol. 2, *Universities in the Early Modern Europe*, edited by H. de Ridder-Symoens, 531–62. Cambridge: Cambridge University Press.

Rhoades, Gary. 1998. *Managed Professionals: Unionized Faculty and Restructuring Academic Labor*. Albany: State University of Press.

Rüegg, Walter. 2003a. "Themes." In *A History of the University in Europe*, vol. 1, *Universities in the Middle Ages*, edited by H. de Ridder-Symoens, 3–34. Cambridge: Cambridge University Press.

———. 2003b. "Epilogue: The Rise of Humanism." In *A History of the University in Europe*, vol. 1, *Universities in the Middle Ages*, edited by H. de Ridder-Symoens, 442–68. Cambridge: Cambridge University Press.

———, ed. 2004a. *A History of the University in Europe*. Vol. 3, *Universities in the Nineteenth and Early Twentieth Centuries (1800–1945)*. Cambridge: Cambridge University Press.

———. 2004b. *A History of the University in Europe*. Vol. 4, *Universities Since 1945*. Cambridge: Cambridge University Press.

Saarinen, Taina, and Jussi Välimaa. 2012. "Change as an Intellectual Device and as an Object of Research." In *Managing Reform in Universities: The Dynamics of Culture, Identity and Organizational Change*, edited by Bjørn Stensaker, Jussi Välimaa, and Claudia Sarrico, 41–60. New York: Palgrave Macmillan.

Schwinges, Rainer Christoph. 1992. "Admission." In *A History of the University in Europe*, vol. 1, *Universities in the Middle Ages*, edited by Hilde de Ridder-Symoens, 171–94. Cambridge: Cambridge University Press.

Slaughter, S., and B. Cantwell. 2012. Transatlantic Moves to the Market: The United States and the European Union. *Higher Education* 63, no. 5: 583–606.

Slaughter, Shelia, and Larry L. Leslie. 1997. *Academic Capitalism: Politics, Policies, and the Entrepreneurial University*. Baltimore: Johns Hopkins University Press.

Slaughter, Sheila, and Gary Rhoades. 2004. *Academic Capitalism and the New Economy: Markets, State, and Higher Education*. Baltimore: Johns Hopkins University Press.

Stehr, Nico. 1994. *Knowledge Societies*. London: SAGE.

Teichler, Ulrich, and Ester Ava Hähle, eds. 2013. *The Work Situation of the Academic Profession in Europe: Findings of a Survey in Twelve Countries*. The Changing Academy—The Changing Academic Profession in International Comparative Perspective 8. New York: Springer.

Trow, Martin. 1974. "Problems in the Transition from Elite to Mass Higher Education." In *General Report on the Conference on Future Structures of Post-Secondary Education*, 55–101. Paris: OECD.

Välimaa, Jussi. 2005. "Social Dynamics of Higher Education Reforms: The Case of Finland." In *Reform and Change in Higher Education: Analysing Policy Implementation*, edited by Åse Gornitzka, Maurice Kogan, and Alberto Amaral, 245–68. Dordrecht: Springer.

―――. 2012. "The Corporatization of National Universities in Finland." In *Universities and the Public Sphere: Knowledge Creation and State Building in the Era of Globalization*, edited by Brian Pusser, Ken Kempner, Simon Marginson, and Imanol Ordorika, 101–20. New York: Routledge.

Weimer, Leasa. 2013. "Tuition Fees for International Students in Finland: A Case Study Analysis of Collective Action and Social Change." PhD diss., University of Georgia.

Wittrock, Björn. 1993. "The Modern University: Its Three Transformations." In *The European and American University Since 1800*, edited by Sheldon Rothblatt and Björn Wittrock, 303–62. Cambridge: Cambridge University Press.

CHAPTER FOUR

Exploring the Academic Capitalist Time Regime

JUDITH WALKER

> Rather than pass time, we must invite it in.
>
> —*Walter Benjamin*

Each of us in the academy chooses how we spend our time. As an example, I opted to invest X number of hours in writing this chapter in exchange for an imagined amount of capital to use within the "prestige economy" of academia (Blackmore and Kandiko 2011). I can later withdraw on this deposit to apply for jobs, to receive merit pay, or to foster research collaborations; this use of my time has value (albeit limited). Inherent is the belief that I have a certain amount of time that I can contribute to a certain task—be it teaching a class, sitting through a committee meeting, or writing this paper. The time is mine to give, just as the dollar in my wallet is mine to pay for what I please. We understand the concept of time as resource, capital, or investment. Each of us knows, to some extent, that this reification and commodification of time is an illusion. But the idea of time as tangible, definable, and exchangeable has been ingrained into our collective consciousness since the advent of capitalism (Marx 1967; Weber 1958). Furthermore, the changes in capitalism and the associated technological inventions of our globalized postmodern era bring forth different conceptualizations and operationalizations of time. Think about some ideas recently incorporated into popular discourse, such as "real time," "networked time," "just-in-time production," and "synchronous" or "asynchronous" conversations. This altered use of (and thinking about) time permeates our individual and collective psyches; it also pervades our higher education institutions, our teaching, and our learning.

This book is about academic capitalism within an era of globalization, or the ways in which universities have become more entrepreneurial, more connected with business, more competitive, and better linked to more marketable subject areas as higher education and the labor market have become increasingly globalized (e.g., Bok 2003; Brown and Lauder 2012; Marginson and Considine 2000;

Mendoza 2012; Slaughter and Rhoades 2004). Slaughter and Leslie's (1997) insights into what they called academic capitalism are as relevant today as they were seventeen years ago. Our academies, if anything, are becoming more academically capitalist—in different countries and in many ways (e.g., Mars and Rhoades 2012; Metcalfe 2010; Choi 2010; Slaughter and Cantwell 2012). While these empirical and theoretical analyses are important to better understanding the academic capitalist knowledge/learning regime (Slaughter and Rhoades 2004), we need to look more explicitly at what I call the academic capitalist time regime (ACTR). We need to "invite time in" if we are to have a firmer grasp of what academic capitalism means for us as teachers, researchers, students, and administrators.

This chapter is my attempt at further theorization of time in academic capitalism under globalization, a topic I first explored in 2009 (Walker 2009). ACTR is the result of a reconfigured relationship among academia, capitalism, and time, reflecting primarily both modernity and postmodernity. In developing this theory, I examine the relationships between (1) time and capitalism, (2) time and academia, and (3) academia and capitalism. From this, I highlight some of ACTR's paradoxes and then bring in the added dimensions of *kairos* and *chronos* to help us further understand how time now functions within higher education. To further concretize this theory, I illustrate how ACTR operates globally in the case of massive open online courses (MOOCs). The chapter ends with a more in-depth discussion of the perils of ACTR as well as its current and potential influence on the way we think and act in academia.

Time Relationships of the Academic Capitalist Time Regime

Timescapes typify both capitalism and academia (Adam 2004). In this section, I divide society's relationship with time into three main eras—(1) premodern, (2) modern, and (3) postmodern—focusing principally on modernity and postmodernity.[1]

Time and Capitalism

Capitalism radically shifted how people use and think about time (Fenves 2010; Marx 1967). In premodernity/precapitalism, time was marked by events and was generally thought about as cyclical, and change was gradual (Castells 2000; Lash and Urry 1994). Knowledge was considered somewhat fixed as wisdom passed from generation to generation (Hongladarom 2002). With the Industrial Revolution, time began to be divorced from space and nature, and instead became a precise unit of measurement, necessary to meet the needs of an industrializing economy (Giddens 1991). The new division of labor required the division of time into quantifiable units for planning, scheduling, and routine production of goods (Marx 1967). This new time sense was essential to ensure speed, discipline, order, precision, and efficiency (Thompson 1992).

We cannot think about capitalism without thinking about time (Marx 1967; Weber 1958). The time ethos of industrial/modern capitalism is by most accounts oppressive, and time disciplining is commonplace in its hierarchical structure. In Marx's and Engels's (1978) descriptions of the alienating world of the worker of industrial capitalism, we see workers slaving away on the factory floor, directed to produce meaningless products only to be separated from the fruits of their labor. The irony of creating that which you cannot afford to possess! An inefficient use of time became a moral failing as we moved from "passing" to "spending" time (Thompson 1992). "Time is money," Weber (1958, 48) proclaimed, and thrift is the name of the game. As Weber observed, punctuality and working long hours are moral virtues within a capitalist society. The Protestant ethic is one of time in which we sacrifice in the here and now to validate our worth; our Calvinist predestination can be demonstrated by how we use time. Working hard in the factory or business office and delaying our gratification is a sign of our deservingness of later reward.

Time Moves from Modern/National to Postmodern/ Global Capitalism

Under industrial capitalism and modern time, the focus was on production of goods within a mainly national context. There was a clear delineation of roles (Engels 1978; Smith 1826), as well as a clear demarcation of time for most workers, with the introduction of the working week (e.g., nine to five, Monday through Friday) and the nonworking weekend.

In global capitalism, starting in the later part of the twentieth century, we move, in part, from goods and manufacturing-based economies to service and knowledge-based ones (particularly in the West), and from a material to a more immaterial economy. Thanks to technological inventions and changes in capitalism, there is a shift in the roles of workers and we see the rise of a creator class (Castells 2000), the knowledge worker (Drucker 1993), and the symbolic analyst (Reich 1991). Our relationship with space begins to change. We witness the rise of the global citizen (e.g., Friedman 2005) for whom where she works is of little importance. Porous borders and supply-side economics have meant the economy has become more intensely competitive (Castells 2000). Even higher education cannot save us from this competition (Brown and Lauder 2012).

Intrinsically connected to changes in space are further commodification and compression of time (Harvey 2010). Thanks to e-markets, transportation systems, and information and communication technologies (ICTs) more generally, the global transmission of ideas is almost instantaneous and goods are much more efficiently transported across the globe, manufactured "just in time" to meet the demand of the consumer (Castells 2000). With the exponential growth in—and dissemination of—information, the shelf life of products and knowledge is often short. Employment has also become more short term to maximize profit and to ensure flexibility (Harvey 2010). Although postmodern time has led to greater efficiency, time has become the ultimate resource we just do not have enough of (Stix 2006).

Capitalism under postmodernity (Lyotard 1984) has prompted a change in time ethic, with speed and efficiency being further pronounced as values (Stein 2001). In addition, the postmodern, globalized knowledge worker continues to use time to her advantage as she seamlessly adapts, innovates, reinvents, and seizes new opportunities within the shortest time possible (Friedman 2005; Reich 1991). Professional and service workers alike may appear to have more time flexibility within their jobs and less external time disciplining, but because of falling real wages and rising costs, they may have less absolute time.

Time and Academia

From pre- to postmodernity, time has shifted within academia. The Platonic Academy was arguably predicated on a long-term timescape. Students entered the academy to explore subjects such as philosophy, mathematics, and law, as well as what it means to be a good person, to be happy, to live in a functioning society (Plato 2007). The Socratic method of questioning can be understood as a journey of exploration, with winding paths and dead ends; these conversations take time and are often circular. Mastery of material took time, too. Within this premodern academy, deadlines, schedules, and official curricula were absent. Ideas were historically grounded and tended not to have the relatively short lifespan they do today.

Modern universities created academic disciplines, provided structure to study, and demanded greater personal discipline (Delanty 2003; Gould 2003). They started to become both more time permanent and time bound. Thanks to the printing press, ideas were more accessible to a wider audience, more permanent, immortalized. At the same time, institutions began to grant degrees, and programs became scheduled and time bound. With the massification of higher education in the twentieth century, timed lectures became the primary mode of instruction.

Academia, like capitalism, has shifted under globalization, having entered an era of mobility, flexibility, and immateriality (Delanty 2003). With increased emphasis on individualized, self-paced learning, degrees have become less bound by time in certain cases. Over the past decades, we have also witnessed greater internationalization with an influx of students to Western universities, primarily from India, China, and Middle Eastern nations, who often can have different conceptions of time. Likewise, well-known universities of developed nations are opening international branch campuses for students in other countries. But one of the most transformative changes in the relationship between time and academia could be the massive growth of the virtual student, enrolled at a university within a city or country into which she may never set foot. We have entered an era of virtual education where 30% of all college students now learn online—up from less than 10% in 2002 (*Economist* 2012a). Students are there, but not there, as they engage in virtual, asynchronous, and synchronous forms of learning.

In addition, there is increasing evidence of time compression for academics (Grove 2012), as academic knowledge workers are "sleepless in academia" (Acker and Armenti 2004) with "no time to think" (Menzies and Newson 2007). Yet faculty reflect different time perspectives, and even premodern conceptions of time still exist; not all academics are bound by the proverbial clock (Ylijoki and Mäntylä 2003).

A Closer Look at the Academic Capitalist Time Regime

Academic capitalism explores the ways in which higher education is becoming more capitalist owing to neoliberal globalization, for both exogenous and endogenous reasons (Slaughter and Rhoades 2004). In seeking to meet the demands of the knowledge economy, improve their national and international rankings, and attract more students, star faculty, and money, universities across the world have become more enterprising (Marginson and Considine 2000; Slaughter and Cantwell 2012). Time is the missing ingredient in understanding academic capitalism and its relationship with globalization. The academic capitalist time regime brings together primarily modern and postmodern amalgamations of time, academia, and capitalism.

Paradoxes

The ACTR is paradoxical on a number of levels. Below I illuminate five different paradoxes.

First, despite demands for greater speed and efficiency (e.g., Wildavsky 2012), there is much evidence of inefficiency and stagnation in the academy. In their attempts to integrate into the global knowledge economy, universities focus on cost efficiency, productivity, and performance (Walker 2009). Publishing more in less time is a message that has only increased in intensity since academic capitalism was first identified. Students, as consumers, now demand more responsiveness. Do more with less—money and time—is the mantra of the twenty-first-century academy. However, those of us working in universities know the rate of change can be almost glacial. If the university is a business, it is a bad business, as scholars have mused (e.g., Bok 2003; Manicas 2007). Universities are partly stuck in a highly hierarchical and industrial model of capitalism with bloated and inefficient bureaucracies. The *Wall Street Journal* (2012) recently noted that between 2001 and 2011, the number of university administration personnel hired across the United States to manage people, programs, or policies increased 50% faster than the number of instructors. Instead of a nimble, dynamic twenty-first-century corporation, in this alternative discourse, the university is an institution unfriendly to innovation, efficiency, and cost effectiveness.

Second, while ACTR means working longer hours, we seem to spend less time on each task. This "speeding-up" has a negative effective on quality. As noted above, academics are working longer hours in the postmodern capitalist era (Castells 2000; Grove 2012; Menzies and Newson 2007). Academia is a "long hours culture" (Rutherford, quoted in Ylijoki and Mäntylä 2003), where to be taken seriously one must show that she is (constantly) working. At the same time, there is the sense that no one really has time for anything (Cabin 2010). According to Cabin, academics rarely write in-depth reviews or closely read anything anymore; at best, he claims, material receives superficial treatment. Academia has experienced an acceleration of clock time (Adam 2004), but less time spent on a task—whether it be researching, writing, or teaching—means a sacrifice of quality.

Third, time personalization grows alongside time standardization and limitation. A major trend in the "academic capitalist knowledge/learning regime" (Slaughter and Rhoades 2004) is personalized, differentiated, and self-paced instruction.[2] In this new timescape, students can take as long or as little as they need to learn material. Competency-based education—fast becoming the norm in health professions education—is about mastery of competencies, not finishing a four-year program. Our degrees are still very much time based, however. Medical (MD) and dental programs (DMD or DDS), for example, generally take four years. Perhaps a few students at some institutions may repeat a year; however, because fees are often exorbitantly high—sometimes upward of $50,000 per year in tuition alone (e.g., at Harvard School of Dental Medicine)—students rarely repeat or drop out (e.g., American Dental Association 2012). In addition, we see greater time standardization in degree programs with the implementation of the Bologna process in Europe, for example, where undergraduate programs are standardized to three or four years to help with international mobility, causing some to worry about the undermining of institutional (and national) autonomy (e.g., Pechar and Pellert 2004).

Fourth, while time in the academy is becoming more short term and linear, longer-term views of time continue. We are now in an era of what Enders (2000) called the "casualisation of higher education," with the proliferation of short-term contracts and projects. For example, researchers are likely to be locked into time-limited projects funded by industry or government. At the same time, not everyone is a slave to the clock (Ylijoki and Mäntylä 2003). Scientists still refuse to give time-bound answers to how long a discovery might take, continuing to work on the big problems. Even the limited-term researcher does not conceive of time as merely linear and short term. For example, the contract researcher-participants in Hockey's (2002) study were structured by two kinds of time. First, they saw time as linear and linked to value in consideration of the duration of their contracts as well as their actual research projects. Second, they viewed time as cyclical; for example, as marked by calls for proposals, or starting new projects or contracts that represented a return to the beginning of a cycle.

Finally, ACTR means freedom within a context of being more controlled. Accountability demands, surveillance, and techniques of managerialism have intensified and exert greater control over academic work (e.g., Menzies and Newson 2007). Ylijoki and Mäntylä (2003) note that the more academics invest in their work, the greater hold that work has over them. There is freedom, at least often officially, to produce as much or as little as you can or want, however, and the standards of academic success are still often implied rather than explicitly communicated. Usually, control is internal. The failure to produce "enough capital" as an academic working within the prestige economy (Blackmore and Kandiko 2011) is often experienced personally in comparing oneself to others. There are, of course, also external ramifications of not producing enough in the amount of time—lack of merit pay, promotion, or tenure. The disciplining of one's time is both heteronomous and autonomous. And there is constantly an internal and external battle over time; for example, whether to spend it on service, research, or teaching. Hockey (2002) showed that sessional researchers can "steal" time from their jobs to use toward helping them secure an occupational future; for example, they reclaim work time and redirect it toward academic publishing, which can bring them greater capital in a highly competitive academic labor market. Yet as competition increases, capital from publishing or receiving grants decreases. There is always someone who will work longer hours and produce even more "products" to justify their position in the pecking order of the academy.

Kairos and Chronos

Time as the substance of our academic lives, as the material through which we work, is elusive, illusionary, and indefinable. But it is useful to explore different conceptions (metaphors) of time in being able to better understand the ACTR. *Kairos* and *chronos* come from ancient Greek and elicit two divergent ideas of time. *Kairos* refers to the moment. When we live in *kairos*, we live presently. *Kairos* is ahistorical; it is about the now. It can be positive (e.g., *carpe diem*, the "power of now," Csikszentmihalyi's [1975] "flow"). It can also be understood in a similar way as Walter Benjamin's *Messianic Time*, as now-time, standing outside history, bringing together intense feelings of immediacy and eternity, and characterized by ruptures (Fenves 2010). In the way I use the term, *kairos* also refers to the idea that we do not think beyond today, our desires, ourselves. *Chronos*, however, describes the continuity or progression of time—as moving toward progress. It also could encompass Benjamin's notion of homogenous or empty time—which he believed characterized (modern) capitalism—representing a monotonous ennui of continuity; it is more of the same rather than a march toward progress (Fenves 2010). For the purposes of this chapter, we can understand *kairos* as the short, instant view and *chronos* the longer view of time.

Our academies are becoming both less and more *kairos* based. Growing pressures, expanding work hours, and multitasking impede the ability to pay attention, to be present to one another. Checking our smartphones or tablets during a conversation or a lecture means we cannot be also in the moment. Rushing to publish, to become relevant or influential as academics, means we cannot fully reflect or be present in our minds and in our thinking. The credit-based society is *kairos*; making hedonistic decisions based purely on the here and now is *kairos*. As twenty-first-century students and faculty, we can live in what Adams and Groves have called a "present-future" (cited in Clegg 2010). In a *kairos* state, we are present oriented and time optimists (or perhaps time illiterate!), only thinking about our work now, not grounding what we are doing in the past nor thinking much about the future. The present-future-oriented individual sees the future as the new frontier, something wide open to be colonized (Clegg 2010; Giddens 1991). In capitalist postmodernity, we receive the message that the future is ours for the taking; we can continually reinvent ourselves. In her research into contract staff in Finland, Ylijoki (2010) discovered three future orientations, two of which could be considered mainly *kairos* oriented or present-future: (1) instant living, whereby faculty would concentrate solely on the present, and (2) multiple futures, where faculty were working and living in the present but with one foot placed in the future as they explored their future options.

In contrast, *chronos* is the notion of continuity, of time passing. In academia, our knowledge and information still build on past information; medical advances come on the backs of the advances before them. We build on each other's work. The continuity of present into the future has become more intensified through technology. We can log our thinking and activities on Facebook or Twitter, where data never truly get deleted. We blog or publish online as we struggle against our own obsolescence as researchers, teachers, and students. Universities encourage us to look forward, to develop a "temporal orientation toward the future" (Brooks and Everett 2008, 355), where we engage in continuous self-improvement, self-surveillance, and self-promotion. This is the self-regulated self who works now for future rewards. This is also the third type of time orientation that Ylijoki (2010) uncovered in her study of Finnish sessional academics: scheduled future, which described those respondents who had highly detailed and structured plans for an alternative future—working now but turned toward the future in their goals of attaining a different career outcome.

MOOCs and the Online Teaching/Learning Regime

While distance education has been with us for over a century and online education since the 1990s, MOOCs are a relatively new phenomenon. MOOCs are massive (ranging from hundreds to hundreds of thousands of students) open (no prior credit, no entry requirements, no fees) online courses (i.e., stand-alone courses that are not part of a broader program). The first MOOC was started in 2008 by two University of Manitoba professors (Daniel 2012). Since that time, MOOCs have exploded, and they are today considered by some to be a threat to traditional higher education (e.g., Manjikian 2013). There are currently three main players (Udacity, edX, and Coursera) in the MOOC world (*Economist* 2012a, 2012b). We are entering an era of the "moocification" of higher education as MOOCs change the university landscape across the globe.

MOOCs provide an ideal case study to explore ACTR within globalization. MOOCs reflect the paradoxes of ACTR explored above. At first blush, they appear to be decidedly uncapitalist. MOOCs buck the trend of rising costs of higher education (*Economist* 2012b). Although fees within traditional universities are increasing across the world, MOOCs are almost entirely free. They also represent a bulwark against the craze of credentialism: most MOOCs offer little in the form of credit (but this is beginning to change). They have no bloated technocracy (as we see within the growing administration costs of universities), and instructors are not necessarily paid anything additional for teaching a MOOC; faculty and students are both there for the love of teaching and learning. In addition, none of the educational technology companies (as of yet) make a profit (*Economist* 2012b).

At the same time, MOOCs embody the ethic of post-Fordist, neoliberal, academic capitalism. First, the three MOOC providers above grew out of universities as spin-off companies or organizations. Second, they are based on a partnership model (public-private or public nonprofit). For example, universities partner with Udacity, Coursera, or edX to provide MOOCs on their platform; Udacity has links to Google (see *Economist* 2012a, 2012b). Furthermore, the educational technology company decides whether to accept a university partnership or to bid for providing a course, in essence assuming the process of academic quality control and taking away some of the power from universities. Third, Udacity, Coursera, and edX were created by entrepreneurs-cum-university professors as entrepreneurial "companies." While edX is university funded, both Udacity and Coursera are funded through venture capital, like most start-ups of the early twenty-first century (*Economist* 2012b). Fourth, up until recently, most courses have been concentrated in science, technology, engineering, and mathematics; at the time of writing, Udacity only offered courses in engineering, computer science, statistics, and physics, with one course in "how to build a start-up" (see www.udacity.com). Fifth, while still mostly "free," MOOC providers are starting to charge students for accreditation and identification as they partner with testing, facial recognition, and other companies to be able to ensure student identity and to grant certification as the desire for credentials grows (*Economist* 2012b; Koller and Ng 2013). Since January 2013, Coursera has offered a "signature track" on some of its courses, where students pay $50 to $100 to get an authentic certificate (Koller and Ng 2013). In addition, Coursera charges companies for referrals to its best students, as there is a sense that talent spotting will become a model for revenue production (*Economist* 2012b).

For our interests in this chapter, MOOCs also shift our relationship with time in accordance with what we have previously read. They are built for the virtual student who can access the Internet from anywhere in the globe. For the most part, MOOCs are based on a compilation of short (approximately eight- to ten-minute) prerecorded lectures. They adapt traditional university lectures to fit within this new time frame. In addition, MOOCs tend to run for less time than a regular university semester. Horn and Christensen (2013) presage that "the need for customization will drive us toward just-in-time mini-courses." MOOCs also can operate in *kairos*—with instantaneous, synchronous interactions enabled through chat rooms or Google hangouts. The permanence of the lectures and written asynchronous interactions that remain also reflect the continuity of knowledge. And a *chronos* sense of time is seen in the underlying lifelong learning paradigm that lies at the heart of MOOCs: learning is for all and continues until we die.

MOOCs represent personalized "unbundling of education" (*Economist* 2012b). We can take as much of a course as we like, engage in as little or as much of the topic as we want. This is the ultimate in flexibility, and the ultimate in the neoliberal value of choice. At the same time, the courses generally still last a fixed amount of time and their (massive) nature does not allow for the same level of personalization. Taking a MOOC requires time discipline. To keep up with the material, one must complete the weekly quizzes and assignments. With freedom comes extreme need for self-control when it comes to time. Only 10% of people who start a MOOC finish (*Economist* 2012b), and while it is not always the case that the student intends to finish the course (Koller and Ng 2013), she will need intense time management to complete it on top of her daily demands. The self-regulated MOOC student is future oriented as she invests her precious "spare" time in learning, thus delaying gratification. She often does not even receive a certificate for her efforts, not knowing when and for what she can withdraw her MOOC capital.

MOOCs shift the balance of time from instructor to student. Because most MOOC instructors are also faculty members, MOOCs can take away from face-to-face time between instructors and their students in their physical home institutions. At the same time, control moves to the consumer (student), who can decide what they will do and when. MOOCs also can destabilize power in enabling more peer learning than in a traditional lecture-based course (Koller and Ng 2013). A more capable student in India could speedily reply and support a struggling student in Canada; peers can grade each other's work (*Economist* 2012b). Study groups have arisen all over the globe as students meet in person to work on course content outside of class (Koller and Ng 2013).

While MOOCs are globally accessible, there is concern that they reinforce the unbalanced power dynamic of globalization (Liyanagunawardena, Williams, and Adams 2013; Regalado 2012). For the most part, they bring Western university courses, ways of teaching and learning, and underlying hegemonic cultural assumptions and practices to the developing world. It appears that they also currently disproportionately attract the already-educated student living in a developed country (Koller and Ng 2013), perhaps owing to differences in resource access (including time). Someone who works three jobs on limited-term contracts just to get by may not have the luxury of taking a MOOC. Similarly, someone who can only access the Internet at certain times of day may also be less likely to take a MOOC. Furthermore, differences in time perception persist between Western countries and others. MOOCs are still time bound with tight deadlines for exams and assignments; while deadlines may be more considered "approximations" in countries in Latin America or Africa, the leniency does not exist in a Western-style MOOC. Time zone variations may additionally make it difficult for students to participate in the synchronous chats or other aspects of the courses. The cross-border flow of ideas, including a particularly modernist time ethic (Weber 1958), still appears unidirectional, but this situation may change as more non-Western universities deliver MOOCs in different languages adapted to different cultures (Koller and Ng 2013).

MOOCs bring together globalization, capitalism, time, and academia in a reconfigured, modern, and postmodern ethos. We see a shift in power/control over time, from instructor to student, from university to MOOC provider (e.g., Coursera). The modernist conceptualization of time remains. The sage is still on the stage—or, more aptly, the queen is on the screen—in transmitting official knowledge to students in a condensed but recognizable lecture format. The hierarchy is still there. As the courses become increasingly credit based, they will act as they have done in the marketplace for decades: as a signal to employers of competence (Spence 1973).

Discussion

The ACTR intensifies both capitalism and time within the context of higher education. It reconfigures relationships, decenters power, and renders our notions of past, present, and future as problematic, posing challenges to who we are as individuals and as a society.

Shifts in Time/Power Relations

The academic capitalist time regime means a shift in who gets to make time demands. Administrators demand that faculty members better account for their time—especially in places such as the United Kingdom (Brown and Carasso 2013) and Australia (e.g., Marginson and Considine 2000). In a consumer-based education model, student is king, deciding when and on what he should spend his time. Teaching primarily in an online context (though not MOOCs), I am sometimes struck by students' resentment at my assignments that require them to read articles or write papers longer than ten pages, or at participation criteria that ask them to engage in ongoing small and large group discussions—in essence, asking them to spend more "time" on their education. A priceless comment I received from a student in a recent teaching evaluation says it all: "I spent too much time participating in this class that it took away from my learning."

There is—and likely will continue to be—a shift in ownership of the products of our synchronous and asynchronous conversations, whether they be on wikis, Google hangouts or docs, Blackboard, or within MOOCs. The recent outcry in the United States over the National Security Agency's PRISM program (Greenwald and MacAskill 2013)—which allows government access to the content of citizens' Internet search history, chats, and file transfers—highlights the salience of this question. The more we use ICTs in our teaching and research, the more we give up ownership of what we do with our time. This situation arises in part because, while the shelf life of knowledge is reducing, the permanence of information is increasing. Our ideas are recorded in cyberspace for all time; words, claims, mistakes can no longer be erased with the passage of time. ACTR in part means the immortalization of ideas, of information.

Furthermore, work time and personal time become more enmeshed thanks to new technologies such as smartphones, and, perhaps soon, Google Glass (www.google.com/glass/start/). As we enter more fully into a "cyborg era," there are clear implications for those who control our time. Multitasking—going back and forth between technology, application, and task—is already commonplace. And, from the research done so far, it seems to be making us stupid (Medina 2009). We have not (yet) evolved to go back and forth in time.

The Morality of the Academic Capitalist Time Regime

The ethos of ACTR accentuates the Protestant ethic. We are further asked to morally justify our use of time; we are asked to make additional sacrifices, to be more self-regulated and future oriented (Clegg 2010). We put in our time now (e.g., writing publications) to withdraw on our deposits later (e.g., for tenure). At the same time, the capital we draw on is worth less and less. The flip side of this prestige economy is a shame-based one, where we feel bad about ourselves for procrastinating, for not "using" time well. And sometimes, no matter how much time we "spend," it is never enough. We study longer for undergraduate and graduate degrees only to meet under- or unemployment upon graduation (Brown and Lauder 2012). We receive tenure only to become unhappier and to spend more time publishing and performing service commitments (Wilson 2012). It is as though we are willing to forgo the pleasures of this world in the belief that our efforts will be rewarded in the afterlife. In the ACTR, however, the after(tenure) life can feel more like hell than heaven.

In ACTR, speed is even more of a virtue. To save money—and in the pursuit of the virtue of efficiency—there is an effort to condense teaching, in what Hartman and Darab (2012) have called "speed pedagogy." In a telling example, Wildavsky and Litan (2012) praise Carnegie Mellon University for pioneering technology-based teaching techniques with "adaptive" instruction that has allowed students to take an accelerated version of a fifteen-week course within an eight-week schedule with (apparently) no detriment to learning. Students seem to enroll expecting speed pedagogy, and expecting to invest minimal time for maximum output (Rose 2012). But learning and research require reflection, engagement, collaboration, trial and error, processing, and practice, all of which take time. Perhaps, as Hartman and Darab (2012) alternatively suggest, it is time for "slow scholarship."

Insights from the field of psychology chime additional warning bells of the moral costs to working within an ACTR. We are thinking more about money within the context of academia: university presidents pressed for financial support seek out funding; students spend time applying for financial aid; faculty members spend more time applying for grants. Thinking about money or profit makes us more selfish, more independent, more individualistic, less collaborative, and less trusting (Kahneman 2013). In addition, the further divorced from cash, which is the reality of our new cashless society, the less ethical we are. People are much more likely to steal food and drink from a shared refrigerator than they are to take an actual $1 bill (Ariely 2008). The antics of Bernie Madoff and the financial playboys on Wall Street make more sense when viewed from this perspective on real humans responding to neoliberal capitalism. Likewise, when we are hurried or low on time, we tend to be more self-focused and less likely to help a stranger in need, even if lending a hand is absolutely integral to our values (Darley and Batson 1973). In sum, it appears that ACTR is bad for the quality of what we are doing, bad for our self-esteem, and bad for higher education.

Conclusion

In this chapter, I have attempted to provide a description of ACTR as being a particular configuration of premodern, modern, and postmodern capitalism; of the academy and approaches to teaching and learning; and of time itself within an era of globalization. I took *kairos* and *chronos* as conceptual, metaphorical frames to help explain how time operates within this new academic capitalistic knowledge/learning regime. Finally, I examined MOOCs as reflecting this new ACTR ethos on a global level. This further theorization of time within academic capitalism draws on initial insights put forth in my 2009 article (Walker 2009). ACTR requires additional theorization and empirical research; for example, to examine how ACTR is gendered, classed, racialized, spatially organized, or differentially affects someone depending on the academic capital they possess.

Readers might have noticed the somewhat negative tone of this chapter. In concluding my thoughts, I feel I must clarify. Although we should be cautious in our brave new world, it is important to acknowledge the opportunities we enjoy in this globalized academic capitalist time regime. I like MOOCs. I like connecting with people faster than ever. I like the fact my students in Congo, Qatar, and Vancouver can all communicate and learn from one another regardless of time zone. I like that, through Skype, I can engage easily with a research collaborator in London, Spain, or New Zealand in real time. Never before have we had so much "free" time that we can put toward exploring new ideas or to creating new knowledge. We can wax nostalgic, like *New York Times* journalist David Brooks (2013a, 2013b), who wishes to return to a bygone era where we were less individualistic and more community oriented, rooted more squarely in the place we live, before a time when we had internalized the values of postmodernity, capitalism, and global time. We cannot go back to earlier times, for example, when I as a woman would not have been given the time to write this chapter. We have to live within what is, recognizing the opportunities and perils of the present day.

Premodern conceptions of time teach us to be patient, to accept that everything has its time, and that everything takes time. The time has come to explore seriously the academic capitalist time regime. Thinking more purposefully and deliberately about how and why we use our time is important. We need to have our eyes wide open as we move about our days and working lives as faculty members, administrators, instructors, or students. With awareness, we can become more mindful of how we use our time—and respond more thoughtfully to the ways in which it uses us.

NOTES

1. The three main time epochs I explore (premodern, modern, and postmodern) cannot be entirely chronologically delineated; however, there have been conceptual shifts over certain periods of time that are useful for our analysis.

2. Another research project maps the citation incidences of the terms "differentiated instruction," "differentiated learning," "personalized instruction," and "self-paced learning" over time. These terms have exploded in the literature since 2000.

REFERENCES

Acker, Sandra, and Carmen Armenti. 2004. "Sleepless in Academia." *Gender and Education* 16, no. 1: 3–24. doi:10.1080/0954025032000170309.

Adam, Barbara. 2004. *Time*. Cambridge: Polity Press.

American Dental Association. 2012. *2010–2011 Survey of Dental Education: Academic Programs, Enrollment, and Graduates*. Volume 1. Chicago: American Dental Association. www.ada.org/sections/professionalResources/pdfs/survey_ed_vol1.pdf.

Ariely, Dan. 2008. *Predictably Irrational: The Hidden Forces That Shape Our Decisions.* New York: HarperCollins.

Blackmore, Paul, and Camille B. Kandiko. 2011. "Motivation in Academic Life: A Prestige Economy." *Research in Post-Compulsory Education* 16, no. 4: 399–411. doi:10.1080/13596748.2011.626971.

Bok, Derek. 2003. *Universities in the Marketplace: The Commercialization of Higher Education.* Princeton, NJ: Princeton University Press.

Brooks, David. 2013a. "What Our Words Tell Us." *New York Times*, May 20. www.nytimes.com/2013/05/21/opinion/brooks-what-our-words-tell-us.html?ref=davidbrooks.

———. 2013b. "Religion and Inequality." *New York Times*, June 13. www.nytimes.com/2013/06/14/opinion/brooks-religion-and-inequality.html?ref=davidbrooks.

Brooks, Rachel, and Glyn Everett. 2008. "The Prevalence of 'Life Planning': Evidence from UK Graduates." *British Journal of Sociology of Education* 29, no. 3: 325–37. doi:10.1080/01425690801966410.

Brown, Phillip, and Hugh Lauder. 2012. "The Great Transformation in the Global Labour Market." *Soundings* 51: 41–53. doi:10.3898/136266212802019489.

Brown, Roger, and Helen Carasso. 2013. *Everything for Sale? The Marketisation of UK Higher Education.* London: Routledge / Society for Research into Higher Education.

Cabin, Robert J. 2010. "Skim This Article (or Just Skip It)." *Chronicle of Higher Education*, March 7. http://chronicle.com/article/Skim-This-Article-or-Just/64462/.

Castells, Manuel. 2000. *The Rise of the Network Society*. 2nd ed. Malden, MA: Blackwell.

Choi, Po King. 2010. "'Weep for Chinese University': A Case Study of English Hegemony and Academic Capitalism in Higher Education in Hong Kong." *Journal of Education Policy* 25, no. 2: 233–52. doi:10.1080/02680930903443886.

Clegg, Sue. 2010. "Time Future: The Dominant Discourse of Higher Education." *Time and Society* 19, no. 3: 345–64. doi:10.1177/0961463X10381528.

Csikszentmihalyi, Mihaly. 1975. *Beyond Boredom and Anxiety: Experiencing Flow in Work and Play.* San Francisco: Jossey-Bass.

Daniel, John. 2012. "Making Sense of MOOCs: Musings in a Maze of Myth, Paradox and Possibility." *Journal of Interactive Media in Education* http://jime.open.ac.uk/article/2012-18/pdf.

Darley, John, and C. Daniel Batson. 1973. "From Jerusalem to Jericho: A Study of Situational and Dispositional Variables in Helping Behavior." *Journal of Personality and Social Psychology* 27, no. 1: 100–108.

Delanty, Gerald. "The University and Modernity: A History of the Present." In *The Virtual University? Knowledge, Management, and Markets*, edited by Kevin Robins and Frank Webster, 31–48. Oxford: Oxford University Press.

Drucker, Peter F. 1993. *Post Capitalist Society*. New York: HarperBusiness.

Economist. 2012a. "Higher Education: Not What It Used to Be." *Economist*, December 1. www.economist.com/news/united-states/21567373-american-universities-represent -declining-value-money-their-students-not-what-it.

———. 2012b. "Free Education: Learning New Lessons." *Economist*, December 22. www .economist.com/news/international/21568738-online-courses-are-transforming -higher-education-creating-new-opportunities-best.

Enders, Jürgen. 2000. "Between State Control and Academic Capitalism: A Comparative Perspective on Academic Staff in Europe." In *Academic Staff in Europe: Changing Contexts and Conditions*, edited by Jürgen Enders, 1–24. Westport, CT: Greenwood Press.

Engels, Frederich. 1978. "On the Division of Labour in Production." In *The Marx-Engels Reader*, edited by Robert C. Tucker, 718–27. London: W. W. Norton.

Fenves, Peter. 2010. *The Messianic Reduction: Walter Benjamin and the Shape of Time*. Stanford, CA: Stanford University Press.

Friedman, Thomas L. 2005. *The World Is Flat: A Brief History of the 21st Century*. New York: Farrar, Strauss & Giroux.

Giddens, Anthony. 1991. *Modernity and Self-Identity: Self and Society in the Late Modern Age*. Cambridge: Polity Press.

Gould, Eric. 2003. *The University in a Corporate Culture*. New Haven, CT: Yale University Press.

Greenwald, Glenn, and Ewen MacAskill. 2013. "NSA Prism Program Taps in to User Data of Apple, Google and Others." *Guardian*, June 7. www.guardian.co.uk/world /2013/jun/06/us-tech-giants-nsa-data.

Grove, Jack. 2012. "Stressed Academics Are Ready to Blow in Pressure-Cooker Culture." *Times Higher Education*, October 4. www.timeshighereducation.co.uk/421388.article.

Hartman, Yvonne, and Sandy Darab. 2012. "A Call for Slow Scholarship: A Case Study on the Intensification of Academic Life and Its Implications for Pedagogy." *Review of Education, Pedagogy, and Cultural Studies* 34, no. 1–2: 49–60. doi:10.1080/10714413.2 012.643740.

Harvey, David. 2010. *The Enigma of Capital and the Crisis of Capitalism*. Oxford: Oxford University Press.

Hockey, John. 2002. "Occupational Time: The Case of UK Social Science Contract Researchers." *Research Papers in Education* 17, no. 3: 323–42. doi:10.1080/02671520210158082.

Hongladarom, Soraj. 2002. "The Web of Time and the Dilemma of Globalization." *Information Society* 18: 241–49.

Horn, Michael, and Clayton Christensen. 2013. "Beyond the Hype: Where Are MOOCs Going?" *Wired*, February 20. www.wired.com/opinion/2013/02/beyond-the-mooc-buzz -where-are-they-going-really/.

Kahneman, Daniel. 2013. *Thinking, Fast and Slow*. New York: Farrar, Strauss & Giroux.

Koller, Daphne, and Andrew Ng. 2013. "The Online Learning Revolution: Learning without Limits." Centre for Teaching and Learning Technology Institute, University of British Columbia video, 1:54:32, May 31. http://mediasitemob1.mediagroup.ubc.ca /Mediasite/Play/62ddb199ab024a73b72cb4c63e1e88481d.

Lash, Scott, and John Urry. 1994. *Economies of Signs and Space.* London: SAGE.

Liyanagunawardena, Tharindu, Shirley Williams, and Andrew Adams. 2013. "The Impact and Reach of MOOCs: A Developing Countries' Perspective." *eLearning Papers* 33: 1–8.

Lyotard, Jean Francois. 1984. *The Postmodern Condition: A Report on Knowledge.* Minneapolis: University of Minnesota Press.

Manicas, Peter T. 2007. "Globalization and Higher Education." In *The Blackwell Companion to Globalization,* edited by George Ritzer, 461–77. Malden, MA: Blackwell.

Manjikian, Mary. 2013. "Why We Fear MOOCs." *Chronicle of Higher Education,* June 14. http://chronicle.com/blogs/conversation/2013/06/14/why-we-fear-moocs/.

Marginson, Simon, and Mark Considine. 2000. *The Enterprise University: Power, Governance and Reinvention in Australia.* Cambridge: Cambridge University Press.

Mars, Matthew M., and Gary Rhoades. 2012. "Socially-Oriented Student Entrepreneurship: A Study of Student Change Agency in the Academic Capitalism Context." *Journal of Higher Education* 83, no. 3: 435–59. doi:10.1353/jhe.2012.0015.

Marx, Karl. 1967. *Capital: A Critique of Political Economy.* Vol. 1. New York: International.

Medina, John. 2009. *Brain Rules: 12 Principles for Surviving and Thriving at Work, Home, and School.* Seattle: Pear Press.

Mendoza, Pilar. 2012. "The Role of Context in Academic Capitalism: The Industry Friendly Department Case." *Journal of Higher Education* 83, no. 1: 26–48. doi:10.1353/ jhe.2012.0002.

Menzies, Heather, and Janice Newson. 2007. "No Time to Think: Academics' Life in the Globally Wired University." *Time and Society* 16, no. 1: 83–98. doi:10.1177/09 61463X07074103.

Metcalfe, Amy Scott. 2010. "Revisiting Academic Capitalism in Canada: No Longer the Exception." *Journal of Higher Education* 81, no. 4: 489–514. doi:10.1353/jhe.0.0098.

Pechar, Hands, and Ada Pellert. 2004. "Austrian Universities under Pressure from Bologna." *European Journal of Education* 39, no. 3: 317–30. doi:10.1111/j.1465-3435.2004.00186.x.

Plato. 2007. *The Republic.* London: Penguin Books.

Regalado, Antonio. 2012. "Online Courses Put Pressure on Universities in Poorer Nations." *MIT Technology Review,* November 12. www.technologyreview.com/news /506336/online-courses-put-pressure-on-universities-in-poorer-nations/.

Reich, R. 1991. *The Work of Nations: Preparing Ourselves for 21st Century Capitalism.* New York: First Vintage.

Rose, Jeanne M. 2012. "Writing Time: Critical Approaches to Teaching Literature, Language, Composition, and Culture." *Pedagogy* 12, no. 1: 45–67. doi:10.1215/15314200-1416522.

Slaughter, Sheila, and Brendan Cantwell. 2012. "Transatlantic Moves to the Market: Academic Capitalism in the United States and European Union." *Higher Education* 63, no. 5: 583–603. doi:10.1007/s10734-011-9460-9.

Slaughter, Shelia, and Larry L. Leslie. 1997. *Academic Capitalism: Politics, Policies, and the Entrepreneurial University.* Baltimore: Johns Hopkins University Press.

Slaughter, Sheila, and Gary Rhoades. 2004. *Academic Capitalism and the New Economy: Markets, State, and Higher Education.* Baltimore: Johns Hopkins University Press.

Smith, Adam. 1826. *An Inquiry into the Nature and Causes of the Wealth of Nations*. London: J. F. Dove.

Spence, Michael. 1973. "Job Market Signaling." *Quarterly Journal of Economics* 87, no. 3: 355–74. doi:10.2307/1882010.

Stein, Janice Gross. 2001. *The Cult of Efficiency*. Toronto: House of Anansi Press.

Stix, Gary. 2006. "Introduction: Real time." *Scientific American*, June 2–5.

Thompson, Edward P. 1992. *Customs in Common: Studies in Traditional Popular Culture*. New York: New Press.

Walker, Judith. 2009. "Time as the Fourth Dimension in the Globalisation of Higher Education." *Journal of Higher Education* 80, no. 5: 483–509. doi:10.1353/jhe.0.0061.

Wall Street Journal. 2012. "Dean's List: Hiring Spree Fattens College Bureaucracy—and Tuition." *Wall Street Journal*, December 28. http://online.wsj.com/news/articles/SB10 001424127887323316804578161490716042814.

Weber, Max. 1958. *The Protestant Ethic and the Spirit of Capitalism*. New York: C. Scribner.

Wildavsky, Ben. 2012. "An Entrepreneurial Approach to Reforming Higher Education." *Chronicle of Higher Education*, June 7. http://chronicle.com/blogs/worldwise/an -entrepreneurial-approach-to-reforming-higher-education/29781.

Wildavsky, Ben, and Robert E. Litan. 2012. "It's Time to Go Back to School on Higher Education Reform." *Huffington Post*, May 7. www.huffingtonpost.com/ben-wildavsky /higher-education-reform_b_1651914.html.

Wilson, Robin. 2012. "Why Are Associate Professors So Unhappy?" *Chronicle of Higher Education*, June 3. http://chronicle.com/article/Why-Are-Associate-Professors/132071/.

Ylijoki, Oili-Helena. 2010. "Future Orientations in Episodic Labour: Short-Term Academics as a Case in Point." *Time and Society* 19, no. 3: 365–86. doi:10.1177/0961463X10356220.

Ylijoki, Oili-Helena, and Hans Mäntylä. 2003. "Conflicting Time Perspectives in Academic Work." *Time and Society* 12, no. 1: 55–78. doi:10.1177/0961463X03012001364.

CHAPTER FIVE

Learning to Litigate

University Patents in the Knowledge Economy

JACOB H. ROOKSBY AND BRIAN PUSSER

Over the nearly two decades since the publication of *Academic Capitalism: Politics, Policies, and the Entrepreneurial University* (Slaughter and Leslie 1997), the model of academic capitalism has become one of the more widely cited conceptual frameworks in the global literature on higher education. Works in the academic capitalist canon have relied on the two basic understandings of the theory of academic capitalism and the new economy, as articulated by Slaughter and Leslie (1997), Slaughter and Rhoades (2004), and Rhoades and Slaughter (2006). Rhoades and Slaughter (2006) summarize these two conceptual strands as "the increasing engagement of higher education institutions and participants in the market-like and market behaviors in creating and taking to the marketplace (1) research and education products and services that commodify higher education's basic work and (2) nonacademic products and services that feature higher education as a nonacademic consumption item (dimensions of the new economy)" (104).

In this chapter we turn attention to the first of two conceptual arenas articulated in the conceptual model of academic capitalism, with specific attention on the patenting of university research. We hope to refine the scholarly understanding of the commercialization of academic research through focusing on universities' approaches to extracting revenue from their patents by asserting infringement claims against outside parties. University patents provide a useful lens for understanding the future of academic capitalism in global higher education on two dimensions. First, we argue that patents are one of the central forces in university planning for capitalizing on research efforts. Patenting figures prominently in the work of university research programs, technology transfer offices, and related national associations (e.g., the Association of University Technology Managers in the United States), as well as in state and national planning for economic development through higher education. Second, and of more direct concern to this study, university efforts to patent research products speak directly to the efficacy of the university in competition with others in the global knowledge economy. That is, university efforts to create, license, and enforce patents give evidence of their ability to compete in global markets for innovation dominated by multinational corporations. We begin from the standpoint that, with regard to patent activity at least, universities may desire to be "academic capitalists," but it is not at all clear that they are well positioned to do so. While Rhoades and Slaughter and other scholars have suggested that the aspirations of universities to compete for revenue through research in various arenas may be unrealistic, the study of the creation, licensing, and enforcement of patents offers empirical evidence of the challenge, and of universities' efforts to position themselves to participate and succeed.

To be clear, we do not argue that universities necessarily predicate efforts to create and capitalize on patents on the expectation of significant returns. While such expectancies no doubt inform planning, particularly in light of the many successful and lucrative patents some universities have obtained, prestige is a significant driver of university research activity, and the promise of patenting shapes research faculty and administrative decision making. This study examines what university decision makers say about their intentions for creating and enforcing patents as well as empirical evidence of actual patterns of university patent enforcement in the period 1973 through 2012. Our goal is to determine the degree to which universities are positioned to enforce patents under global competition, and under what conditions they are willing to do so. We aim to add empirical data to the conceptual model of academic capitalism in an effort to better understand the model and its implications for research universities in the United States and other nations.

Globalization, the University, and Intellectual Property

Just as the editors of this volume note that globalization permeates all social relations, we argue that the globalization of commerce and the commodification of intellectual property (IP) are fundamental drivers of contemporary university efforts to maximize the patenting of research. In turn, the economic development mission and the allure of revenue and prestige from technology transfer, patenting, and licensing are central drivers of efforts by research universities around the world to engage in academic capitalism. The postsecondary system in the United States is the acknowledged leader in commercializing IP, an essential component of models of twenty-first-century knowledge economies. In that pursuit, research universities rely on a variety of revenue streams, the support of international students and scholars, multinational financial and administrative partnerships, and legal agreements governing IP that must be established and enforced across borders (Rooksby 2012b). As with other aspects of globalization, the transnational pursuit of revenue, research power, and rankings has undeniable implications for the character of higher education in a variety of contexts, particularly with regard to the production of local, national, and global public goods (Marginson 2004; Pusser and Marginson 2012).

Commercializing Intellectual Property in Higher Education

Universities are inextricably linked to the creation and protection of IP. Innovating, creating, and disseminating knowledge is at the core of their missions. These activities that help define universities as centers of knowledge distribution and agents of the public good have long been subject to legal protections through the formal mechanisms of patent law. But universities have not always been permitted to claim an ownership interest in their faculty's inventions, as the federal government—as funder of faculty research—historically was the default owner of any patents flowing from such research.

The Bayh-Dole Act of 1980 changed this presumption. Motivated in part by growing concerns for the competitive threat posed by Japan's technological advances, policymakers in the late 1970s questioned whether the federal government's apparent inefficiency in licensing patents it owned was undermining the country's position as the world's leading innovator (Good 2004). Congress responded to these concerns by passing the Bayh-Dole Act. Universities and groups such as the American Council on Education lobbied heavily in support of the bill. The promotion of "collaboration between commercial concerns and nonprofit organizations, including universities" was one of the act's stated purposes (35 U.S.C. § 200 1980). Largely for that reason, it has been argued that the act "encouraged academic capitalism" (Slaughter and Leslie 1997, 46) and moved universities "into a new competitive arena characterized by commercial outputs that they were traditionally ill-equipped to manage" (Owen-Smith 2005, 93). Others have hailed Bayh-Dole as "a remarkably important piece of science policy legislation" (Cole 2009, 163), even calling it America's "most inspired piece of legislation" in over fifty years and one that allegedly helped reverse "America's precipitous slide into industrial irrelevance" (*Economist* 2002, 3).

Whatever its normative effect, the Bayh-Dole Act formalized a tripartite relationship between government, universities, and industry that many call "technology transfer," a broad term for what has become a favored method of product development and commercialization (Berman 2012; Matkin 1990). Patents—

which many believe incentivize industrial investment in technology transfer through the prospect of monopoly pricing—play a central role in the process of translating valuable breakthroughs in the laboratory to useful products in the marketplace. While critical for asserting ownership over IP, patents can create tensions for universities, as inherent in any patent is the potential to exclude and to profit (Slaughter and Rhoades 2010). The proprietary nature of innovations protected by patents challenges universities' historic charge to further the public good through distributing knowledge to society in an unfettered and undifferentiated manner (Slaughter and Rhoades 2004). University patenting, therefore, is in many ways a site of contest between the university's mission to disseminate knowledge and its countervailing need to seek revenues (Weisbrod, Ballou, and Asch 2008). As competitive pressures motivate research universities' ever-expanding search for revenues, many view patenting and technology transfer as potentially lucrative sources of revenue for cash-strapped universities (Etzkowitz and Webster 1998). Others suggest that most universities are far from generating surplus revenue from commercializing research (Slaughter and Rhoades 2004).

Patents and Licensing

The IP clause of the US Constitution establishes Congress's ability "to promote the Progress of Science and useful Arts, by securing for limited Times to Authors and Inventors the exclusive Right to their respective Writings and Discoveries" (US Const. art. I, § 8, cl. 8). While copyrights protect original expressions fixed in tangible media, and can exist without formal application or registration, patents are more arduous to obtain. An application must be filed with the US Patent and Trademark Office, and most are rejected for failing to meet statutory criteria. The process of obtaining a patent takes on average over three years, and applicants can spend anywhere from $10,000 to $50,000 in legal fees and costs during the process.

To be patent eligible, the claimed invention must be new, useful, and "nonobvious"—hurdles that can be difficult to overcome. While laws of nature, natural phenomena, and abstract ideas cannot be patented, "anything under the sun made by man" is patent eligible (*Diamond v. Chakrabarty*, 447 U.S. 303 1980). Inventions patented under this system include everything from the groundbreaking (life-saving pharmaceutical compounds) to the mundane (improved car parts) and inane (cat exercise methods).

Patents, which constitute rights in gross, are blunt instruments that have been likened to toll booths (Powell, Owen-Smith, and Colyvas 2007). They create a twenty-year limited monopoly during which their owners can exclude others from manufacturing, importing, using, selling, or offering for sale any product or process covered by the claims of the patent (35 U.S.C. § 154 271). As opposed to academic publications that act as funnels connecting knowledge sources, patents are more like "fences in the sense that they offer limited monopoly rights to the 'plot' of knowledge their claims demarcate" (Allison, Lemley, Moore, and Trunkey 2004). For most patent holders, patents are a means for producing a product that others may not produce without their permission. Universities are different, however, because they are not in the business of producing products. For universities, "patents are the product" (Geiger 2004, 216).

Classic innovation theory posits that firms seek patents in order to protect actual or anticipated business activities (Kitch 1977). When one firm's patents potentially block another firm from conducting an activity covered by a patent, a license opportunity exists for the patent holder. If the competitor company owns other patents that are of interest, the firms may decide to cross-license patents to one another, so both can exploit commercial opportunities without fear of an infringement lawsuit derailing business. But universities are different from firms in that they do not manufacture products. Accordingly, they "aren't going to trade their patents away in exchange for a cross-license, because they don't need a license to other people's patent rights. Instead, they want money" (Allison et al. 2004).

Licenses come in different forms. Patent holders may choose to license a patent nonexclusively—i.e., to more than one company for a minimal amount—or exclusively. Firms and patent holders often prefer exclusive licenses, which allow licensees more flexibility to capitalize on the patent premium through monopoly pricing. Time, geography, or field of use can limit exclusive licenses such that one patent may be subject to multiple exclusive licenses, whether simultaneously or over the length of its subsistence (Greene 2012).

Higher Education

Few would dispute that university involvement in patenting and technology transfer largely has "moved from a contested and peripheral activity among America's research universities to an accepted, indeed valued, part of core missions" (Feller 1991, 1). In fiscal year 2011 alone, American universities reaped over $1.8 billion in revenue from licensing patents, filed over 12,000 patent applications, and helped create over 600 start-up companies (Blumenstyk 2012). These activities offered the added benefits of increasing employment, building knowledge within local communities, and encouraging reinvestment into universities (Lowe and Quick 2005).

Substantial government funding of university research has helped facilitate the activity. In 2008, universities received $28.5 billion from the federal government, or roughly double what they received a decade prior (Committee on Management of University Intellectual Property 2010, 17). Federal funding accounts for around 60% of total university funding for research, compared to the 5% to 8% received by universities from industry (Etzkowitz and Webster 1998, 27; National Science Board 2012).

Despite the many beneficial attributes to university engagement in patenting and technology transfer, criticism of university engagement in these activities spans several grounds. A leading complaint is that taxpayers pay twice for products developed by universities—once through taxes that support government-funded university research, and again through the higher costs of patented products in the market (Ritchie de Larena 2007). Others believe that the Bayh-Dole Act improperly encourages universities to license their patents exclusively to only one company, thereby restricting dissemination of beneficial technology (Mowery, Nelson, Sampat, and Ziedonis 2004). A related concern is that increased patenting by universities has led to the creation of patent "thickets" that deter innovation and slow the speed with which new products reach consumers (Heller and Eisenberg 1998). Additional criticisms include that some universities' cutthroat approach to patenting has eroded the sense of community in academia (Bagley 2006), causing faculty to experience delays and difficulties in publishing their research (Durack 2006).

Although seeking patents has become a cost of doing research for most universities (Feller 1991), determining which patents will become commercially valuable is a speculative undertaking for any patent owner (Kitch 1977), as "it is difficult to identify blockbusters *ex ante*" (Powell et al. 2007, 128). The hit-or-miss nature of commercializing patents means that a small percentage of a university's patents generates the lion's share of revenues (Powers 2003), and many universities never reap significant financial returns from patent licensing (Bastedo and Harris 2009). This reality has led some scholars to argue that universities that aspire to "get rich quick" through patenting are likely to be disappointed in that "it is a game of almost all strike-outs and singles, but with a few home runs" (Cole 2009, 167).

To hit a home run appears to require quite a few at-bats. In a study of 101 universities and academic health centers over the period 1996 to 2005, Powers and Campbell (2009) found that twenty licenses per university per year was the optimization point for the chances of a net positive return on research and development investment. Universities licensing at that level had a 50% chance of net positive return, while the chance of net positive return fell off considerably for universities with more than twenty licenses per year. Data also indicated that no university exceeded a 65% chance of profitability in ten years, and that 35% of the universities never realized profitability over the ten-year period, no matter how much they invested.

Historically, the relatively low chance of achieving net positive returns with patents and technology transfer might have led some universities to view these activities "as loss-leaders, serving to induce additional sums of industrial support, or as public service undertakings" (Feller 1991, 34–35). It is certainly academic, but given the sustained lack of profit, one can argue that technology transfer is more akin to a subsidy of private economic development than to a postsecondary organizational foray into capitalism.

At the same time, public good does come from these activities, even if they do not prove lucrative for most universities that engage in them. Scholars have noted the positive impacts on local and regional economies, added employment, new firm development, and regional knowledge flows that often accrue from university engagement in patenting and technology transfer (Lowe and Quick 2005). Students also increasingly benefit from these activities and find that universities are keen to provide instruction, infrastructural support, and even financial backing to their entrepreneurial efforts (Mars, Slaughter, and Rhoades 2008).

Patent Infringement Litigation as an Enforcement Mechanism

Patents are not self-enforcing. Accordingly, companies and individuals are free to infringe patents unless and until a court orders the infringers to stop, or the infringers agree to cease infringing. To achieve either outcome—court order or out-of-court settlement—requires the patent owner to initiate patent infringement litigation, which is expensive for all involved. One party's legal bills are typically on the order of hundreds of thousands of dollars, if not millions of dollars, depending on the potential monetary recovery sought by the plaintiff in the lawsuit (American Intellectual Property Law Association 2013). "Even the threat of being forced to defend against patent infringement will, in many cases, compel companies to pay royalties or abandon particular products" (Jaffe and Lerner 2004, 76), which helps explain why most patent infringement cases never go to trial.

Scholars argue that the value derived from a patent "flows from patent litigation or, more typically, the threat of litigation" (Bessen and Meurer 2007, 205). "The threat of damages and, typically, injunctive relief, is a proverbial club useful in securing license fees and other payments from actual and potential infringers" (Sichelman and Graham 2010, 118–19). Failure to enforce could mean the loss of the premium conferred to a university from seeking and obtaining a patent, as "the efficacy of a patent depends on its owners' ability to police their property" (Owen-Smith 2005, 94). The felt need to protect one's investment leads to the inescapable conclusion that universities must enforce their patent rights if they want to generate more net revenue from research (Weisbrod et al. 2008). Doing so has risks, however, as a "significant percentage of litigated patents are held invalid, and a finding of invalidity is the death knell for a patent" (Allison, Lemley, and Walker 2011, 678).[1]

Even if they would like to, universities in many situations are unable to avoid the legal imperative that they participate as plaintiffs in any infringement lawsuit involving their patents. For example, for university-owned patents that are licensed nonexclusively, only the university has standing to sue for patent infringement (*Sicom Systems, Ltd. v. Agilent Technologies, Inc.*, 427 F.3d 971 [Fed. Cir. 2005]), so the decision to litigate rests entirely with the university. The same is true for university-owned patents that, for whatever reason, are not licensed. While situations where a university has granted an exclusive license to a company are more complex, there, too, universities often are unable to avoid involvement as a named plaintiff should the licensee pursue litigation (Greene 2012).

University Patents and the Public Interest

In addition to the often staggering out-of-pocket costs for universities involved with patent infringement litigation, the activity brings with it important indirect costs, including disruption to inventors and other university personnel in strategizing with attorneys, collecting and producing documents, testifying in depositions, and preparing for court appearances, as well as disruption to a university's licensure of patents not included in the litigation (Shane and Somaya 2007; Somaya 2003).

An additional indirect cost is the perception that the activity undermines universities' fundamental public-serving values (Duderstadt 2004; Rooksby 2012a). Involvement in patent litigation can lead to allegations that the university is behaving as a "patent troll"—a pejorative term for entities that choose to monetize patents through litigation (Lemley 2008)—or is even causing companies that are sued to cease hiring graduates from the university or funding their faculty's research. Others have argued that universities that are quick to initiate patent infringement lawsuits may find that such efforts undercut—in the court of public opinion, anyway—their defense to separate infringement lawsuits waged against their own researchers. Also, for-profit companies that otherwise would be hesitant to bring an infringement suit against a university may not be deterred if they view the university in question as a frequent plaintiff in infringement litigation. Numerous scholars have noted these tensions between mission and revenue generation in university research activities (Bok 2003; Rooksby 2012a; Slaughter and Leslie 1997; Weisbrod et al. 2008).

In view of these concerns, several leading universities have cautioned against enforcing patents for the purpose of extracting licensing revenues (Leland Stanford Junior University 2007). Other informed commentators, such as the National Academy of Sciences Committee on Management of University Intellectual Property, also have urged caution for universities contemplating patent enforcement (Committee on Management of University Intellectual Property 2010). But these pronouncements do not mean that all universities have shied away from litigating. Indeed, many have achieved notable public successes in this realm. Examples include Carnegie Mellon University, which in 2012 garnered a jury verdict of $1.17 billion in a case over alleged infringement of a semiconductor technology, and the University of California, which achieved both a high-profile victory against Microsoft (a $30.4 million settlement) and, when suing different companies over the same patent several years later, a high-profile defeat (a jury's invalidation of the patent).

Patent Enforcement and Historical Trends

Legal research across databases containing litigation records indicates that university participation as plaintiffs in patent infringement cases is on the rise. The year 2012 alone saw American universities bring forty-three patent infringement lawsuits—more than any other year since 1973, when reliable patent litigation records became available. A total of seventy universities (forty-one public, twenty-nine private) have participated as plaintiffs in 327 patent infringement lawsuits since that time.

Of these seventy universities, over half ($n = 38$, or 54.3%) have participated as a plaintiff in more than one patent infringement lawsuit. Over 84% ($n = 59$) are classified (or, in the case of university systems, have at least one campus within the system that is classified) by the Carnegie Foundation for the Advancement of Teaching as doctorate-granting research universities with very high research activity, and approximately 57% ($n = 40$) are members of the Association of

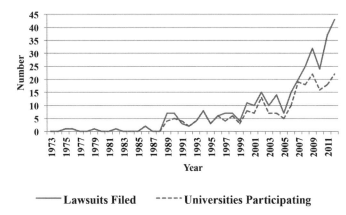

Figure 5.1. Number of patent infringement lawsuits filed in the United States since 1973 with universities as plaintiffs, as well as the number of different universities that participated in those lawsuits (some universities file multiple lawsuits in any given year).

American Universities. Patent licensing revenues for these universities generally have been robust. In 2011, most generated at least $1 million in licensing revenue, with twenty-six universities (37.1%) generating tens of millions of dollars in licensing revenue. For half of these universities, their endowments in 2012 were over $1 billion, placing them among the top seventy-five richest postsecondary institutions in the United States based on this metric.

Historical analysis of the population also is telling. The number of patent infringement lawsuits with universities as plaintiffs, as well as the number of individual universities that have participated as plaintiffs in such lawsuits, has risen substantially since the year 2000. Some of these increases are likely attributable to increased accuracy of the databases around this time, meaning that pre-2000 results are particularly underinclusive. Regardless, university involvement as plaintiffs in patent infringement litigation was at least as prevalent over the past forty years, as indicated in figure 5.1, with an average of 8.18 cases filed per year.

University Patent Enforcement:
Academic Capitalism's New Frontier?

Flowing from this legal background and history is a normative assumption that universities in the knowledge economy are likely to embrace patent enforcement for a variety of reasons. As academic capitalism pervades all corners of the modern university's research enterprise, decision makers are likely to find attractive the prospect of financial returns made available through patent litigation. Indeed, as patenting capacities and efforts by interstitial organizations increase, and university ties with intermediary organizations and service providers strengthen, participation in infringement lawsuits could be viewed as an inescapable eventuality for universities active in licensing. The significant budgetary constraints now facing universities only add a greater sense of inevitability to the story.

A Study of Universities That Litigate Patents

While the historical trends and data on incidence seem to support a normative story that universities are well positioned to litigate patent claims, the interest and ability of universities to succeed in litigation bear close examination. While the above data speak to end results—i.e., some dispute over IP led to a lawsuit— they reveal nothing concerning questions of institutional motivation, resources, agency, or considerations in the buildup to an institutional decision to litigate. That is, does the increase in cases speak to an increased willingness on the part of universities to litigate patents for financial returns, which would be consistent with the emerging model of academic capitalism in the research university, or are there other factors shaping this terrain?

Accordingly, in the fall of 2011, a mixed-method study was conducted, designed to build understanding of university efforts to enforce patents through litigation (Rooksby 2012b). As part of this study, leadership at twenty-two American universities (thirteen public, nine private) completed a survey intended to gather data concerning university approaches, goals, and decision making in patent infringement litigation.[2] The array of university participants included universities new to the activity and others more experienced.

Data from the study indicate that universities generally have not established formal institutional policies, frameworks, or guidelines intended to address their potential involvement as plaintiffs in patent infringement litigation. In fact, virtually no university budgets for the activity, yet leaders at most of the surveyed universities believed that future litigation was inevitable, viewing participation as a plaintiff to be an unavoidable consequence of engaging in patenting and technology transfer. When asked how much probable monetary return would make litigating "worth it," answers varied considerably, from $0 to $999 to upward of $9 million. Nearly a quarter of respondents indicated that projected monetary returns do not factor into their university's decision making at all. One interviewee in the study identified these diverging data as emblematic of the "philosophical dilemma" universities face in this realm: "Do you litigate because you're protecting your asset, or do you litigate for the homerun?"

Perhaps it is no surprise that considerations with direct financial implications (viz., potential monetary returns) were reported more frequently as influencing university decision making about patent enforcement than consider-ations with attenuated financial implications (such as diverted attention from faculty and professionals, emotional strain caused by the litigation, and public relations concerns). At the same time, no doubt in recognition of the high costs of patent litigation, most respondents indicated that their university is more likely to favor bringing an infringement lawsuit if a licensee pays for some of the university's legal fees.

Respondents were sharply divided as to whether defendant identity influ-ences their institution's decision making. As many as 41% of respondents said they view a defendant's identity as irrelevant in their university's decision mak-ing. But the same number indicated that a defendant's political influence and financial contributions to the university are considerations that their universi-ties weigh heavily in deciding whether to participate as a plaintiff in patent in-fringement litigation. Political influence is of particular sensitivity to decision makers at public universities, to a statistically significant degree.

While the opinions of many stakeholders are sought in university decisions to litigate patents, the actual or anticipated opinions of university licensees weigh heavily, often more so than opinions of the university's president or governing board. Actual or anticipated views of the public, students, and faculty play no substantial role. The university's contractual obligation to protect the rights of existing licensees is the consideration that typically drives decision making.

The question of whether enforcing patents in infringement litigation fur-thered university research missions drew sharp disagreement. Roughly half of respondents indicated that litigation does not further university research mis-sions, although more were comfortable with styling infringement litigation as a method of protecting the university's investment in research. Why should a university seek patents if it is not willing to enforce them? As one interviewee explained, "Is the act of litigation itself furthering a mission? No . . . but if you think about it in terms of whether it is a necessary part of protecting and ad-vancing our research, then you come up with a different answer . . . To me it's a necessary evil—I'll go ahead and use that word. If you're going to go forward and protect patents, the necessary follow-on to that is that you have to be willing to enforce them."

Summary of Findings

The study's findings suggest that universities may not be as well equipped to en-gage in patent enforcement as the theory of academic capitalism might otherwise suggest. Despite the growth and fortification of interstitial and intermediating organizations in the university technology transfer space, a uniform strategy, approach, or conceptualization of patent enforcement has failed to emerge among those institutions that engage in the activity. Indeed, these data show that many decision makers at universities that have participated in patent infringement litigation in the past are deeply conflicted about the activity's tie to their university's mission, and yet they are nearly certain that their institution will litigate again in the future. Despite this near-certainty of future participation in an activity that is costly, time consuming, and often controversial, essentially no universities profess to have developed frameworks, policies, or budgetary set-asides of the sort that would reflect mature preparation for deciding when and on what terms to engage in patent enforcement. Most profess to turn outward to industry instead of upward to presidential or board leadership for guidance on an activity of clear policy importance.

Data from the study do suggest that a minority of universities that litigate patents are comfortable with the concept of enforcing patent rights. At these universities, decision makers have accepted that ownership and enforcement of patents are intimately tied. Pursuing infringement litigation helps protect institutional investments into research and patenting. These universities seem committed to litigating their patents if the facts warrant, regardless of the infringer's identity and without undue concern for the activity's revenue-generating potential. These universities might be fairly regarded as willing to enforce their patent rights on principle.

But decision makers at most other universities in the study feel quite differently about the activity. At these universities, a potential defendant's identity, low projected monetary returns, and high legal costs may dampen enthusiasm for pursuing an infringement action. These universities are likely to see the activity as ancillary to, or even in direct conflict with, their mission as a research university, which causes them to be exceedingly cautious and reluctant actors when issues of infringement arise. Concerns for how others will view their involvement as plaintiffs in patent infringement litigation may hamper these universities' ability to effectively pursue the activity when the facts otherwise support their participation. Unwilling to take a uniformly strong stance against all infringers, the majority of universities that litigate patents are erratic in their decisions concerning patent enforcement, often hinging their approaches to patent infringement litigation on any number of idiosyncratic contingencies. These institutions have, to say the least, mixed feelings about fully endeavoring to capitalize on their patents, an activity that seems tailored to fit Rhoades and Slaughter's (2006) concept of "research and education products and services that commodify higher education's basic work" (104). Thus they may perhaps be best characterized as reluctant academic capitalists.

University Patenting and Academic Capitalism Reconsidered

A critical question that emerges from our findings concerns normative expectations for universities that litigate patents. What should success in this field of endeavor look like? Theories of academic capitalism would suggest that efforts to monetize IP developed in the sciences generally will appeal to research universities, and that coherent strategies of implementation naturally will develop to facilitate enforcement activity. Unencumbered by humanistic concerns for the potentially deleterious noneconomic effects of litigation involvement, the modern American research university presumably should embrace patent litigation as a revenue-generating activity that furthers research objectives for higher education in the new economy.

Our findings suggest a more complicated story, one that reveals more about universities' positioning to maximize commercialization of research than about their desires to do so. More than thirty years after the passage of the Bayh-Dole Act, most universities—instead of being seasoned players alert to patent enforcement opportunities—are still learning to litigate. They may be poorly equipped to pursue litigation and have mixed feelings about it. Yet for universities participating in an IP-driven, global knowledge economy, the activity may be evolving into a mandate. Nonetheless, university success with licensing patents already has proven to be uncertain, and the academy's facility at using patents as swords on the expanding frontier of patent enforcement is equally inchoate. The pressures and uncertainties universities face in obtaining and enforcing patents are consistent with those of global entrepreneurial capitalism in general, an arena increasingly dominated by exceptionally powerful firms whose success in litigation is often predicated on vast resources and resolute commitment. The importance of successful patent litigation in the global political economy is such that it is not unreasonable to think of patents as constructs conceived by inspiration, too often made real only by costly and prolonged litigation. On the basis of this research, it would thus be more accurate to frame university efforts to practice academic capitalism through enforcing patents as a license to try, not as a prescription to succeed. Patent enforcement is a particularly perilous space for organizations that are small, nonprofit, or dedicated to the public interest. Yet universities throughout the world aspire to capitalize on IP through patent litigation, in greater numbers nearly every year over the past decade.

The appropriate follow-on question is, should they be? This is, for the most part, *terra nova* for the leadership of research universities. Assertive litigation involvement is qualitatively different than the risk-minimizing prevention and defense of lawsuits that university counsel have managed for decades in non-IP realms. When litigation shifts from being a cost of doing business to a part of doing business—to, perhaps, *the* business of patent ownership—the frail conception of the university as disinterested agent for the public good arguably suffers yet another, perhaps irreversible, alteration. Even for institutions that can effectively compete for revenue under such intense market conditions (and not all can), the costs are high, including litigation dollars spent; challenges to mission, public image, and trust; and political and other capital lost amidst the backlash from companies sued by universities.

The uncertain and varied prospect for litigation success also should motivate university leaders to assess how serious their institutions will be in chasing infringers. The risks are severe. Few institutions have $10 million to spend on one case, or the capital to reimburse faculty stripped of funding when their university sues a research sponsor for patent infringement (Rooksby 2013a). In short, it becomes difficult to enforce patent rights on principle unless enforcing patent rights is considered principal to the mission of the university. Not all universities take such an approach, nor should they. Yet in the status hierarchy of global higher education (Pusser and Marginson 2012), rank-and-file universities will struggle to be realistic about their capacity to enforce patents, given the allure of financial rewards and the establishment of enforcement norms by elites in the field.

For those few institutions that have the financial and other resources to enforce effectively, unabashed pursuit and participation—on par with litigation norms of for-profit actors—appear to be the inevitable approach in light of what a patent is: a government-granted right to exclude. But patent enforcement reconciles awkwardly with the public good through higher education, which historically has included the use of knowledge for the public interest, locally, nationally, and globally (Marginson 2004). While the research mission in contemporary world-class universities may encompass significant patent litigation, the public that supports higher education might also expect full disclosure and transparency concerning such litigation. Market models for generating and protecting asset values inevitably run counter to traditional conceptions of the public interest in the creation and dissemination of knowledge through higher education. A similar case holds for the traditional approach to university decision making and the norms of litigation itself. These tensions were apparent in the initial phase of data collection in the study reported here, when three universities made a point of affirmatively expressing that they would not participate, for reasons suggesting hesitancy to expose thoughts about litigation to anyone other than favored market participants. Unfortunately, as more universities treat inputs and decision making about their traditional knowledge production and dissemination functions as privileged and impenetrable to informed academic inquiry—despite the knowledge's frequent genesis from public funding and its evident impact on the public good—undifferentiated knowledge withers (Marginson 2011).

Conclusion

In view of these consequences, as well as the university's important and persisting role in the public sphere (Pusser 2011), serious consideration should be given as to how best to calibrate university participation in patent enforcement in the global knowledge economy. These deliberations should encompass both whether universities should take an academic capitalist approach to creating and protecting patents, and whether they can succeed in doing so. Proposals for legislative solutions or other forms of collective action offer little clear direction, as some assume that universities are weak but appropriate agents for protecting IP (Rooksby 2013b; Vertinsky 2012), while others suggest that they are too ineffectual to succeed (Clements 2009; Litan and Cook-Deegan 2011; Moran and Warner 2011).

The problem with current policies is that they place universities adrift amidst a sea of possibilities that most institutions are ill suited to navigate. Our central finding—that universities are conflicted and perhaps even confused in their agency over IP—provides support for movement in either direction. We find it more than a little ironic that the concept of research universities building engines of academic capitalist economic development through patenting activities is, based on our research, bound to disappoint two groups: those who think it an unworthy or inadvisable endeavor for such essential institutions, and those who believe such institutions are likely to make it happen. Determining the highest utility of university knowledge production is certain to entail multiple paths forward for different institutional types and national contexts, depending on varying understandings and commitments to concepts of IP, commercialization, institutional identity, global responsibilities, and the public good through university research. In an era of academic capitalism, this is an important process, though not one that can be patented.

NOTES

1. Defendants of patent infringement lawsuits typically file counterclaims alleging that the patents asserted by the plaintiff(s) in the action are invalid. They make this allegation because a finding of invalidity necessarily means that the defendant cannot be found liable for infringing the patent. Accordingly, a decision to accuse an entity of patent infringement nearly always leads to the court's also being asked to evaluate the validity of the asserted patent.

2. The number of targeted universities was sixty at the time of data collection, yielding a response rate of 36.7%. See Rooksby (2012b) for further description of the study's design.

REFERENCES

Allison, J. R., M. A. Lemley, K. A. Moore, and R. D. Trunkey. 2004. "Valuable Patents." *Georgetown Law Journal* 92: 435–77.

Allison, J. R., M. A. Lemley, and J. Walker. 2011. "Patent Quality and Settlement among Repeat Patent Litigants. *Georgetown Law Journal* 99: 677–712.

American Intellectual Property Law Association. 2013. *AIPLA Report of the Economic Survey.* Arlington, VA: American Intellectual Property Law Association, Law Practice Management Committee.

Bagley, M. A. 2006. "Academic Discourse and Proprietary Rights: Putting Patents in Their Proper Place." *Boston College Law Review* 47: 217–73.

Bastedo, M. N., and N. F. Harris. 2009. "The State Role in Entrepreneurship and Economic Development: Governance, Oversight, and Public University Start-up Innovation." In *Advances in the Study of Entrepreneurship, Innovation & Economic Growth*, vol. 19, *Measuring the Social Value of Innovation: A Link in the University Technology Transfer and Entrepreneurship Equation*, edited by Gary D. Libecap, 215–35. Bingley: Elsevier.

Berman, E. P. 2012. *Creating the Market University: How Academic Science Became an Economic Engine.* Princeton, NJ: Princeton University Press.

Bessen, J., and M. J. Meurer. 2007. "Lessons for Patent Policy from Empirical Research on Patent Litigation." In *Intellectual Property and Information Wealth: Issues and Practices in the Digital Age*, edited by P. K. Yu, 199–226. Westport, CT: Praeger.

Blumenstyk, G. 2012. "Universities Report $1.8-Billion in Earnings on Inventions in 2011." *Chronicle of Higher Education*, August 28. http://chronicle.com/article/University-Inventions-Earned/133972/.

Bok, D. C. 2003. *Universities in the Marketplace: The Commercialization of Higher Education.* Princeton, NJ: Princeton University Press.

Clements, J. D. 2009. "Improving Bayh-Dole: A Case for Inventor Ownership of Federally Sponsored Research Patents." *IDEA: The Intellectual Property Law Review* 49: 469–516.

Cole, J. R. 2009. *The Great American University: Its Rise to Preeminence, Its Indispensable National Role, Why It Must Be Protected.* New York: PublicAffairs.

Committee on Management of University Intellectual Property. 2010. *Managing University Intellectual Property in the Public Interest*, edited by S. A. Merrill and A. M. Mazza. Washington, DC: National Academies Press.Duderstadt, J. J. 2004. "Delicate Balance: Market Forces versus the Public Interest." In *Buying in or Selling Out? The Commercialization of the American Research University*, edited by R. G. Stein, 56–74. New Brunswick, NJ: Rutgers University Press.

Durack, K. T. 2006. "Technology Transfer and Patents: Implications for the Production of Scientific Knowledge." *Technical Communication Quarterly* 15, no. 3: 315–28.

Economist. 2002. "Innovation's Golden Goose." *Economist*, December 12, 3.

Etzkowitz, H., and A. Webster. 1998. "Entrepreneurial Science: The Second Academic Revolution." In *Capitalizing Knowledge: New Intersections of Industry and Academia*, edited by H. Etzkowitz, A. Webster, and P. Healey, 21–46. Albany: State University of New York Press.

Feller, I. 1991. "Technology Transfer from Universities." In *Higher Education Handbook of Theory and Research*, vol. 7, edited by J. C. Smart, 7:1–42. New York: Agathon Press.

Geiger, R. L. 2004. *Knowledge and Money: Research Universities and the Paradox of the Marketplace*. Stanford, CA: Stanford University Press.

Good, M. L. 2004. "Increased Commercialization of the Academy Following the Bayh-Dole Act of 1980." In *Buying In or Selling Out? The Commercialization of the American Research University*, edited by R. G. Stein, 48–55. New Brunswick, NJ: Rutgers University Press.

Greene, T. D. 2012. "'All Substantial Rights': Toward Sensible Patent Licensee Standing." *Federal Circuit Bar Journal* 22: 1–51.

Heller, M. A., and R. S. Eisenberg. 1998. "Can Patents Deter Innovation? The Anticommons in Biomedical Research." *Science* 280, no. 5364: 698–701.

Jaffe, A. B., and J. Lerner. 2004. *Innovation and Its Discontents: How Our Broken Patent System Is Endangering Innovation and Progress, and What to Do about It*. Princeton, NJ: Princeton University Press.

Kitch, E. W. 1977. "The Nature and Function of the Patent System." *Journal of Law and Economics* 20, no. 2: 265–90.

Leland Stanford Junior University. 2007. "In the Public Interest: Nine Points to Consider in Licensing University Technology." Stanford, CA: Leland Stanford Junior University. www-leland.stanford.edu/group/OTL/documents/whitepaper-10.pdf.

Lemley, M. A. 2008. "Are Universities Patent Trolls?" *Fordham Intellectual Property, Media and Entertainment Law Journal* 18: 611–31.

Litan, R. E., and R. M. Cook-Deegan. 2011. "Universities and Economic Growth: The Importance of Academic Entrepreneurship." In *Rules for Growth: Promoting Innovation and Growth through Legal Reform*, 55–82. Kansas City, MO: Ewing Marion Kauffman Foundation.

Lowe, R. A., and S. K. Quick. 2005. "Measuring the Impact of University Technology Transfer: A Guide to Methodologies, Data Needs, and Sources." *Industry and Higher Education* 19, no. 3: 231–39.

Marginson, S. 2004. "Competition and Markets in Higher Education: A 'Glonacal' Analysis." *Policy Futures in Education* 2, no. 2: 175–244.

———. 2011. "Higher Education and Public Good." *Higher Education Quarterly* 65, no, 4: 411–33.

Mars, M. M., S. Slaughter, and G. Rhoades. 2008. "The State-Sponsored Student Entrepreneur." *Journal of Higher Education* 79, no. 6, 638–70.

Matkin, G. W. 1990. *Technology Transfer and the University.* New York: National University Continuing Education Association.

Moran, J., and M. Warner. 2011. "Sens. Moran and Warner Offer Bipartisan Job Creation Plan," news release, December 8, http://moran.senate.gov/public/index.cfm/2011/12/sens-moran-and-warner-offer.

Mowery, D. C., R. R. Nelson, B. N. Sampat, and A. A. Ziedonis. 2004. *Ivory Tower and Industrial Innovation: University-Industry Technology Transfer before and after the Bayh-Dole Act in the United States.* Stanford, CA: Stanford Business Books.

National Science Board. 2012. *Science and Engineering Indicators: 2012.* Arlington, VA: National Science Board.

Owen-Smith, J. 2005. "Trends and Transitions in the Institutional Environment for Public and Private Science." *Higher Education* 49: 91–117.

Powell, W. W., J. Owen-Smith, and J. A. Colyvas. 2007. "Innovation and Emulation: Lessons from American Universities in Selling Private Rights to Public Knowledge." *Minerva* 45, no. 2: 121–42.

Powers, J. B. 2003. "Commercializing Academic Research: Resource Effects on Performance of University Technology Transfer." *Journal of Higher Education* 74, no. 1: 26–50.

Powers, J. B., and E. G. Campbell. 2009. "University Technology Transfer: In Tough Economic Times." *Change: The Magazine of Higher Learning* 41, no. 6, 43–47.

Pusser, B. 2011. "Power and Authority in the Creation of a Public Sphere through Higher Education." In *Universities and the Public Sphere: Knowledge Creation and State Building in the Era of Globalization,* edited by B. Pusser, K. Kempner, S. Marginson, and I. Ordorika, 29–46. New York: Routledge.

Pusser, B., and S. Marginson. 2012. "The Elephant in the Room: Power, Politics, and the Global Rankings in Higher Education." In *The Organization of Higher Education: Managing Colleges for a New Era,* edited by M. N. Bastedo, 86–117. Baltimore: Johns Hopkins University Press.

Rhoades, G., and S. Slaughter. 2006. "Academic Capitalism and the New Economy: Privatization as Shifting the Target of Public Subsidy in Higher Education." In *The University, State, and Market: The Political Economy of Globalization in the Americas,* edited by R. A. Rhoads and C. A. Torres, 103–40. Stanford, CA: Stanford University Press.

Ritchie de Larena, L. 2007. "The Price of Progress: Are Universities Adding to the Cost?" *Houston Law Review* 43: 1373–444.

Rooksby, J. H. 2012a. "Sue U." *Academe* 98, no. 5: 24–28.

———. 2012b. *Universities That Litigate Patents.* Charlottesville: University of Virginia.

———. 2013a. "When Tigers Bare Teeth: A Qualitative Study of University Patent Enforcement." *Akron Law Review* 46: 169–205.

———. 2013b. "Innovation and Litigation: Tensions between Universities and Patents and How to Fix Them." *Yale Journal of Law and Technology* 15: 314–406.

Shane, S., and D. Somaya. 2007. "The Effects of Patent Litigation on University Licensing Efforts." *Journal of Economic Behavior and Organization* 63, no. 4: 739–55.

Sichelman, T., and S. J. H. Graham. 2010. "Patenting by Entrepreneurs: An Empirical Study." *Michigan Telecommunications and Technology Law Review* 17: 111–80.

Slaughter, S., and L. L. Leslie. 1997. *Academic Capitalism: Politics, Policies, and the Entrepreneurial University.* Baltimore: Johns Hopkins University Press.

Slaughter, S., and G. Rhoades. 2004. *Academic Capitalism and the New Economy: Markets, State, and Higher Education.* Baltimore: Johns Hopkins University Press.

———. 2010. "The Social Construction of Copyright Ethics and Values." *Science and Engineering Ethics* 16: 263–93.

Somaya, D. 2003. "Determinants of Decisions Not to Settle Patent Litigation." *Strategic Management Journal* 24, no. 1: 17–38.

Vertinsky, L. 2012. "Universities as Guardians of Their Inventions." *Utah Law Review* 4: 1949–2021.

Weisbrod, B. A., J. P. Ballou, and E. D. Asch. 2008. *Mission and Money: Understanding the University.* New York: Cambridge University Press.

CHAPTER SIX

Academic Capitalism and Practical Activity

Extending the Research Program

KEIJO RÄSÄNEN

> A practical philosophy in the classical sense sees theory as a moral
> and political inquiry involving a body of knowledge and a philoso-
> phy of practice engaging in reflection upon the nature of good life
> and the means to achieve it.
>
> —*Shapcott (2004, 1)*

Policies favoring academic capitalism are received differently across countries and actor groups. The same goes for the study of academic capitalism as practiced in the United States by Slaughter and Rhoades (2004) and their collaborators. Instead of proposing ways to apply this research approach in Finland, I explore some possibilities to complement and extend academic capitalism wherever it is used. I draw on two bases: a local, practice-based research approach and the literature on practical philosophy.

While studies of academic capitalism present empirically accurate descriptions of what is happening at universities and to academics, they leave in the shadows particular and important aspects of academic work and academics as subjects. In these studies, the academic is a political strategist, according to the traditions of political sociology (Slaughter 2001a; Slaughter and Rhoades 2005, 539). I propose that this emphasis on the political aspects of academic work can be complemented with other dimensions of human, social practice. To do this, we need a well-rounded concept of practical activity, which various strands of practice theory can help accomplish. Studies could focus not only on politics, but also on the morals, tactics, and subjects of academic work. This chapter is an attempt to articulate what these propositions could mean in research practice.

First, I outline the approach that our research group has developed for local needs. We conceptualize academic work as practical activity and potential praxis. Second, I relate this approach to a few basic ideas of practical philosophy.

One of them is that the only foundation that academic practitioners and researchers of academic practice can have is a moral-political vision (Bernstein 1982). In this sense, all research approaches come with a practical philosophy. These steps form a dual—comparative and philosophical—base for finally presenting ideas on how to complement studies of academic capitalism.

Studying Academic Practice: A Complementary Approach

The Management Education Research Initiative Group[1] has developed an approach with which it is possible frame academic work as a practical activity in four dimensions: tactics, politics, morals, and subjects (Räsänen 2010; Räsänen and Trux 2012). If it is true that studies of academic capitalism focus mainly on the political aspects of academic work, then this approach should be able to provide ideas on how to complement or expand the previous studies.

The group's approach is actually a tool of reflexivity: it provides a way of discussing what we, as academics, are doing and causing in our research work. Well-known practice theorists, including Pierre Bourdieu (Bourdieu 2003; cf. Gouldner 1970), have elaborated the call for reflexivity. For Bourdieu, theory is practice. If we take seriously practitioners' logics of action as different from the scholarly logic of thinking, we cannot assume that our (research practitioners') logics of action are reducible to our theoretical arguments. But how can we understand our own doings? One solution is to consider our work as practical activity in the four dimensions listed above.

I ask the researchers of academic capitalism to look at and question their own practice and its consequences, and not only specific concepts and knowledge claims. To be fair, I should enable a similar scrutiny of our own practice. Unfortunately, space limits prevent me from describing the practice itself here (see Räsänen 2009, 2010, 2012; Räsänen and Korpiaho 2011). Here I can only present an example of how the frame used and developed in our practice works and outline its basic ideas.

A Semifictional Example

An account of a semifictional situation in academia may partly express the intuition behind the frame of practical activity and its use.

> The manager of the department convenes a meeting. The three other participants are professors responsible for doctoral studies in their disciplines. The issue is new regulations concerning the selection and funding of doctoral students. The administrators of the school's doctoral program have

pushed through rules that require departments to fund each new student they admit, and for every four students the department funds, the school will fund one additional student. This is a change to the functions and commitments of the department, because each discipline has previously taken care of its own practices of doctoral education within the rules of the school's program, and students have been primarily responsible for arranging their own funding with the help of their advisors. According to the new rules, the more money the department invests in the doctoral studies, the more money it will receive from the school. The disciplines now have to negotiate quotas for student numbers, because the calculations are done at the departmental level. Moreover, as the department does not have all the money needed to fund this operation, it is up to individual professors to arrange the funding. Those who have large project portfolios and want to attract external money are able to take new students, whereas others have to disengage from doctoral student supervision. Here academic capitalism makes the department a business unit in one more respect by making the selection and supervision of doctoral students a matter of entrepreneurship. If not actual profits, successful players gain increased financial resources, and the selection and supervision of doctoral students become a money game.

From what stances do the participants approach the issue in the meeting? The professor of entrepreneurship starts to calculate how many students she can fund. Soon she says, "I can arrange this; the rules change often, but we just have to make the best out of them." The departmental manager says, "We are in a good position in this game; we can promise so many slots that we will get extra funding from the school." The professor of international business asks, "How does this affect the way we select and treat doctoral students; can we be fair and continue to allow access to diverse people?" The fourth professor thinks to himself, "This is the end of my career as advisor because only professors that keep applying and arranging project funding can employ new doctoral students as project researchers; what on earth can I do with the new regulations, and who am I if not an advisor?"

The four professors are engaged in one of the basic activities in academic work—administration. They ask different types of questions when confronting the new formal rules. They ask either *how* to do this, *what* to accomplish and achieve, *why* to do this and in this way, or *who* I am in doing this. In our terminology, the first professor takes a tactical orientation (how), the second a political orientation (what), the third a moral orientation (why), and the fourth a personal orientation with a concern about his professional identity (who). Altogether they cover the basic issues and orientations that are generic to practical activity, according to our way of framing it.

Individuals cannot necessarily deal with all the orientations at the same time, but they can switch orientations in a situation or across situations. The basic issues become resolved anyway, either consciously by the focal actors (professors in this story), other actors (like university managers), or by default through taken-for-granted practices. For instance, both the old and new rules may advance specific interests or express particular morals, but people do not necessarily pay attention to, or realize, their consequences in these respects.

Frame: Academic Work as Practical Activity

Practical activity is about resolving the four generic issues of how, what, why, and who. Natural language includes two additional questions: when? and where? We think that the four basic issues are confronted in their own time-frames and social frames. In other words, each orientation brings along its own type of nexus, ranging from the immediate here and now to political arenas, finite human life, and the experiential situation of the individual person across all these sites and times.

Table 6.1 presents the frame of practical activity in a schematic form. The columns after the questions summarize a substantive way of framing the generic issues. We speak about four (embodied) stances or, for simplicity, orientations. We further suggest a vocabulary that aims to hit a core aspect of each issue and to be usable to fellow academics and students. Hence "habits and means," "goals," "motives and justifications," and "identities" appear in the concretizations column. The issue of what to accomplish and achieve in academic work is a matter of goals, of the interests that come thereby to be interpreted and realized in this work, and of the practices by which goals come to be determined or chosen. The term "goal" is a shorthand version of what politics is about, and simultaneously a word used in everyday encounters. This minimal definition of the political stance to practice then opens up a stage for various practice theorists, like Bourdieu or Foucault, to illuminate our doings and self-reflections.

All four issues are present in any activity and at all times. They concern the same activity, and should not be taken as different spheres of activity. It is only that actors' orientations to what they are doing can vary. From each angle you can see all the issues, but they look different depending on your primary stance

TABLE 6.1
Frame of practical activity

Issue	Orientation	Concretization	Practice theorists
How?	tactical	habits and means	De Certeau, Goffman
What?	political	goals	Bourdieu, Foucault
Why?	moral	motives and justifications	MacIntyre, Taylor
Who?	personal	identities	Dreier, Harré, Holland

or concern. In addition, the order of issues in the table is not arbitrary. The order expresses the assumption that, contrary to many normative accounts, academics do not necessarily resolve the issues by starting from their identity and by affirming their moral motives, and then deducing suitable political goals and tactical means. We assume that ordinary action may be quite different in this respect, and that the primary concern occupying us most of the time is how to do something. We "make do" and improvise, being half-aware of our doings (de Certeau 1984).

The other orientations are likely to be evoked in special situations in which we are not immersed in performing a task and can act as subjects in a stronger sense. But here, by stating these assumptions, I arrive at the border between a theory and a practical philosophy. Different assumptions lead to different stances on our current condition and situation, and some of these assumptions cannot be deduced from other theories, induced from data, or tested by data. Yet we cannot avoid making these philosophical assumptions in our own academic practice, including research. The frame of practical activity, outlined above, reflects a practical philosophy of participatory research in the making.

Research Approaches as Practical Philosophies

Theoretically, the group's frame can be taken as an interpretation and way of using the concept of praxis (Räsänen 2009). For us, praxis is action that is morally motivated, politically conscious, goal oriented, tactically skillful, and expressive of identity. In this sense, we can envision a potentiality but seldom realize it in academic practice. Nevertheless, with the four-question frame we can study its dimensions and identify forms of praxis in emergence or decline.

The concept of praxis is central in the Aristotelian tradition of practical philosophy (Bernstein 1971, 1983; Gadamer 1975; Gramsci 1988 on "philosophy of praxis"). In a quest for a good life, people cannot avoid asking moral and political questions or avoid dealing with the feasibility of different lines of action. The current, prominent streams of practice theory—namely, praxeology, ethnomethodology, actor-network theory, and sociocultural or sociohistorical activity theory (Nicolini, Gherardi, and Yanow 2003)—do not explicitly use the concept. Nevertheless, it may be useful to return to ideas that were inspirational before neoliberalism started to dominate social visions. Critical reassessment of earlier ideas may suggest alternatives that are currently shadowed by the debate for or against one ideology. As Kezar (2004) claims, the study of higher education might also gain more generally from digging up weak or one-sided philosophical foundations.

Turns to Practice and Immanent Critique

Eikeland and Nicolini (2011) have presented an illuminating classification of the different ways of turning to practice in organization and management studies (see also Eikeland 2008, 458). They classify approaches to practice on two dimensions into four types. The two dimensions are researchers' knowledge interest and how they position themselves in relation to the practice studied. On the first dimension, "the interest of social scientists for practice can be motivated either by theoretical interests . . . according to the idea of detached research . . . or it can be stimulated and directed by broad practical interests . . . according to the model of 'engaged' inquiry" (Eikeland and Nicolini 2011, 166). As to the positions from which these interests are pursued, researchers can start either from above and outside or from within and below. In the former case, the researcher wants to stay "in a segregated spectator position" and approach practice through "explicitly theoretical lenses." In the latter case, the researcher wants to be "practically immersed in the practice being studied" (Eikeland and Nicolini 2011, 166).

Eikeland and Nicolini (2011) characterize four types of social research, which I label for the needs of this chapter as follows: (technically oriented) applied research, empiricist theorizing, developmental research, and immanent (dialogical) critique. The former two take an outsider position, the latter two an insider position. A practical interest is primary in applied and developmental research, whereas theoretical interest drives empiricist theorization and immanent critique.

How can one locate the study of academic capitalism and the practical activity approach in this scheme of research practices? I propose that the former represents empiricist theorization. The concept of academic capitalism is used to guide careful empirical studies, and it is revised to serve this task in light of the findings (Slaughter and Rhoades 2004). The latter research practice has mainly represented developmental research, but it has increasingly moved toward immanent critique. This movement has been necessary owing to new obstacles to autonomous developmental work in the local context.

Moral-Political Vision

What can immanent critique focus on and generate? Richard Bernstein's works provide an answer: in immanent critique, we construct or revise a moral-political vision for our practice. These visions can also be called forms of praxis. Moreover, Bernstein claims that philosophers have gradually acknowledged that they cannot identify a transcendental, universal foundation on which to build their philosophical systems or claims (Bernstein 1982, 332). All we can have as the ground is a moral-political vision. These visions suggest a better world and practice than we can observe and currently experience.

Bernstein (1982) has elicited and interpreted the kinds of visions on which a number of other philosophers and social theorists have built their work. In an article comparing the (in many respects different) views of Gadamer, Habermas, and Rorty, he says, quoting William James, "The common ground that emerges in the play of Rorty, Gadamer, and Habermas—their non-foundational pragmatic humanism—may yet serve as a vision that can move us, 'a mode of feeling the whole push, and seeing the whole drift of life,' that can enable us to cope with the darkness of our time and orient our *praxis*" (Bernstein 1982, 356). Bernstein thus identifies a possible vision, which he also shares with the three other authors. The quote expresses a key point. Bernstein is not talking about these visions as mere outcomes of intellectual exercises and creative imagination or as a matter of simple choice. Rather, the vision is what moves the researcher. It orients her work, making it (in principle) meaningful. It is in the work. It contains all that the researcher has learned of her situation and understands what is or could be good in (social) life. Paololucci's (2007) account of Sartre's humanism is an interesting example of how one can struggle with the construction and revision of a vision and how this all can be an experiential process with strong emotional turmoil and changing personal commitments. Another famous example is Edward Said's personal history and his democratic, secular humanism (Nixon 2006).

In a quest for a vision, one can possibly find inspiration from two sources: existing proposals on various forms of praxis or one's own practice. The latter option is more relevant to discuss here because it elaborates on the idea of immanent critique. But a few notes on praxis proposals or descriptions may be needed to show that the documented alternatives may not do the whole job.

Accounts of Praxis

Returning to decennia that predate the dominance of the neoliberal ideology, there are plenty of praxis accounts. It may be that this ideology has made the term unpopular, plagued with connotations of failure, ideological one-sidedness, and politicking. Yet praxis appears still in recent literature and has various meanings. We can omit accounts that use the term in a less precise sense, as referring to any practical activity contrasted to "theory" (e.g., Reckwitz 2002; Whittington 2007). Another typical feature of the recent literature is that authors seem to monopolize the classical term for their own line of political or moral action. They do not consider the possibility that people might prefer and rehearse different forms of praxis (for an exception, see Carp 2001). Examples of scholarship that considers praxis can be found in many fields, including education, social work, sociology, anthropology, social geography, and feminist studies.

A closer look at writings in the field of education shed light on this problematic. Words that were once meaningful to many may now sound hollow. One example is Lather's (1986) article "Research as Praxis." She discussed the methodological implications of feminist, empowering, and emancipatory research, and used the concept of praxis in a sophisticated sense. To some of us, terms like "struggle," "making change," and "emancipation" sound like empty signifiers in these times of "change management" and "employee empowerment." Those who make the best out of academic capitalism may think that they are the ones making a "revolution." In fact, Lather (2007) has herself suggested a different, poststructural conception of feminist praxis in her newer book *Getting Lost*. This is "a praxis of not being so sure." Certainty has turned into the lack of an explicit vision in her thinking and experience.

Kemmis's writings are especially interesting, because he has tried to connect his longtime interest in the idea of praxis to changing political currents. In the early 1980s, Kemmis, Cole, and Suggett (1983) named three political orientations to education with respective social visions: (1) the vocational/neoclassical orientation, (2) the liberal-progressive orientation, and (3) the socially critical orientation. They believed in the critical orientation and built on Habermas's (1972) more general ideas on critical social science (see also Carr and Kemmis 1983; Kemmis 2001).

The proposal of transition to the socially critical view of education was, however, "eclipsed" by neoliberalism and conservatism in the mid-1980s (Kemmis

2012). The aspiration to advance "pedagogy of emancipation from suffering, oppressions or domination" lost its resonance (Kemmis 2012, 93). Nevertheless, its proponents did not want to give it up, and in the most recent writings Kemmis is again seeing more positive prospects. He elaborates with his colleagues on what the original vision would mean in education and other professional practices. He has also done a lot of work to connect the idea of praxis to the more recent streams of practice theory (e.g., Kemmis 2011).

A problem in Kemmis's treatment of praxis is that it comes to highlight only one form of praxis or, more precisely, a knowledge interest, although he admits there may be multiple praxes in principle. This appears to be problematic for academics who are not yet committed to any praxis, find it hard to cultivate any, or cannot identify with these "older" interpretations of wise action. The purpose of an academic praxis, for instance, could be to emancipate from injustice by collective action, while another academic praxis might aim at something else— or would at least articulate the purpose in other terms.

Chaiklin (1996, 398) has added an interesting comment into this discussion. He summarizes his view in his thesis on Marx's eleventh thesis on Feuerbach: "The point is not to interpret nor change the world, but to live in it" (see also Eikeland 2007, 62). This statement questions nicely the grand rhetoric by which some moral-political visions have been expressed and simultaneously puts the academic in a humanly bearable position. There are mythical heroes and there are ordinary academics. The latter do not position themselves above those miserable people who are waiting for their emancipator. This emancipator identity is—to put it mildly—not anymore workable in academia. Now we are witnessing how some colleagues feel that they gain abundant resources by taking advantage of their new "freedoms" as entrepreneurs.

Articulating and Questioning "Working Attitudes"

Another route to examining moral-political visions, besides their explicit treatments in literature, is to articulate "working attitudes" in different, current research practices. One's own practice is a possible object of critical reflection, which is what Eikeland and Nicolini (2011) emphasize in their understanding of immanent critique.

What working attitudes are embedded in our group's approach to academic work as practical activity? Because I have to present this briefly and for the purpose of illustration, I can only list some stances that I consider crucial in our local practice:

- *Academic as practitioner.* We approach our own work and that of other academics as practical activity (in contrast to "life in theory").
- *Researcher as participant.* We accept and make use of the fact that we are participants in the worlds that we study.
- *Practice is eclectic.* The point is not to construct one theory, but to be receptive to various frames of interpretation used in practice.
- *No heroes assumed.* Tactical, half-aware action is taken as ordinary, while possibilities for political, moral, and expressive forms of action are not ignored either.
- *Suspending normativity.* While practice is unavoidably normative, for research, educational, and developmental purposes, it is wise to avoid taking too early a normative stance to the practice of others.
- *Quests for a vision.* Instead of assuming that all forms of practice are grounded on a moral-political vision, the approach aims to enable quests for a vision by providing questions and not answers.
- *Praxes.* We should be attentive to diverse praxes in emergence, and respect discontinuous, dispersed, and even failed attempts to rehearse good work or establish conditions for it.

Immanent critique can be rehearsed on two levels: Do we really act up to these lines of learned wisdom? Are these attitudes wise in the current conditions?

Leaving aside the extent of hypocrisy in our practice, it would be easy to argue that our practice is not feasible at the local university and in the field of higher education research. The most obvious problem is that participatory research does not easily result in publications (in "top journals") valued by higher education scholars and university managers. And without a stellar publication record, there is no employment relationship at universities, and consequently no "academic work" or emergent praxis. Moreover, university managers have good reasons to resist autonomous, "unmanaged" development work at universities (as elaborated by Räsänen 2012). But this problematization only repeats the more fundamental ideological issue motivating this piece of writing. Our practice may not fit well to academic capitalism, but it may still be worth continuing, against the odds, as it is after alternative visions.

A more fruitful, immanent critique would go into detail along the four dimensions of academic practice: (1) our working habits and means of action; (2) goal setting and interpretations of the political situation; (3) conception and realization of the internal and external goods of academic practice; and (4) our agency, consciousness, affects, and identity as subjects of work. A similar exercise could be done by the researchers who study academic capitalism and in the "empiricist theorization" mode. As an outsider I cannot demonstrate this exercise, but I can suggest a few ideas of how to complement the series of studies.

Complementing Studies of Academic Capitalism

Because the main intellectual root of studies of academic capitalism is in political sociology (Slaughter 2001a), these studies emphasize the political dimension of human action in constructing their research objects. The main object is called "regime of governance," which indicates that practical activity of various actors is not in the center of attention. But studies have also reported what various actors do under and with respect to changing and overlapping regimes (e.g., Slaughter, Archerd, and Campbell 2004). The approach avoids the typical sociological trap of totalism by not claiming an overall transformation in the university or science. Amongst the various accounts of change in universities, these studies represent a moderate stance, allowing for uneven development and resistance (Tuunainen 2005; Ylijoki 2003).

What if these studies took even more seriously dimensions of action other than the political? Below I try to determine what this might mean. As an amateur sociologist, I feel free to point out connections to other strands of sociological literature because I do not need to take into account internal divisions within the sociology field.

Taking seriously the tactical and habitual nature of ordinary action is the most important and most difficult task. If academics are only half-aware of their doings and cannot separate themselves from the context of their action, any claims on their intentional and conscious political acts are problematic. Tinkering, surviving, and improvising in given conditions differ from taking advantage of or resisting a regime of governance. This kind of activity surely has political consequences, but these are not outcomes of intentional political strategies or struggles. Moreover, the logics of tactical activity are difficult to identify, as de Certeau (1984) has argued. In his view, "the marginalized majority" is able to escape in various ways the disciplinary machineries, and to "make do" behind the appearance of conformity.

In US sociology, Goffman's (1991) dramaturgical approach and its later versions come close to appreciating these difficulties. For example, one could interpret academics' doings from the perspective of adaptation tactics, such as social withdrawal, colonization, conversion, and resistance (Goffman 1991; Räsänen and Trux 2012, 77–79). Perhaps researchers need to turn to what Abbott (2007) calls lyrical sociology to be able to recognize and express the subtle moods and modes of action in specific moments, which would require that the researcher is willing to report her own sentiments evoked by living among academics, students, managers, and their staff (cf. Reay 2005, on the psychic landscape of class). And, naturally, the tradition of pragmatic philosophy with its concept of habit is a huge source of resources for researching the academic "everyday." As a popular strand of practice theory, ethnomethodology provides tools and ideas for analyzing how people produce order in academic interactions.

What if the possibility of moral action was taken even more seriously, and not explained away as many sociologists have been inclined to do owing to their attachment to the concept of power as a counter to rational choice perspectives? Then we might notice cases in which academics act against their "interests" in a given game (cf. Bourdieu 1975). An academic may knowingly end up in a weaker, less respected position of the field because she does not want to act against her conception of good work. Not all academics necessarily fight to secure the best and most prestigious position, and one reason may be that they do not regard the means of rivalry to be ethically acceptable. Differences in habitus and social background may make particular moral stances understandable but do not determine them.

It is important to expand discussions on ethics from the mere focus on what is not ethically acceptable, typically expressed in the codes of professional conduct. Moral philosophers like MacIntyre (1985) and Taylor (1989) speak about the "goods" that are the motives of moral action and simultaneously central to identities. In MacIntyre's terminology, "internal goods" are what practitioners in a social practice aim to realize, and these goods are valuable in themselves, not mere means for other purposes. What may appear irrational to a university manager, for instance, may make sense to an academic. An academic may want to learn a new style of writing even though this style does not fit the "top" journals listed by the *Financial Times*. Some academics can, still today, believe that writing can be important in the realization of other good things beyond merely attending to externally defined success.

In the sociology of morals, there are interesting streams of studies that show how academic morals can be studied empirically. Michèle Lamont and her colleagues have studied how academics valuate other academics and their work (Mallard, Lamont, and Guetzkow 2009; Tsay, Lamont, Abbott, and Guetzkow 2003). Her collaborator Laurent Thévenot has discussed more generally what it would mean to bring the studies of morals back to sociology (e.g., Thévenot 2007). If Bourdieu was an expert in politics, these scholars want to broaden the agenda to include morals, at least in terms of justifications used in public arenas. And here we again meet Goffman, as "the morality of types" and "moral careers" have been a central interest in interactionism (Atkinson and Housley 2003, chap. 3, 4).

Another moral perspective comes from the philosophy of science. Instead of transcendental criteria, philosophers have tried to find other contextual and social criteria for evaluating research. Longino (1995) claims that even the Kuhnian set of criteria for making judgments concerning alternative theories should be questioned or at least complemented (see also Fuller's [1999] critique of the Kuhnian "paradigmitis" lacking political and ethical concerns). Kuhn claimed that the following values constitute objective grounds for theory choice: accuracy, simplicity, internal and external consistency, breath of scope, and fruitfulness. Longino's own work has elaborated on how "social or practical interests" function in determining what counts as good scientific judgment. She comes to suggest that we should consider also the moral qualities of theory, and not only its "objective"—i.e., cognitive—features. Longino (1995) says, "I want to think about a different set, drawing on work that has been done by feminist scientists and feminist historians and philosophers of science. Here one finds empirical adequacy (a.k.a. accuracy), but also novelty, ontological heterogeneity, complexity of interaction, applicability to human needs, diffusion or decentralization of power . . . Like the elements in Kuhn's list, they function as . . . [moral] qualities of theory . . . that are regarded as desirable and hence guide judgments between alternatives" (385). Studies of academic capitalism may thus be doing well in terms of the Kuhnian criteria. Nevertheless, one may question what these studies do in terms of an alternative set of criteria, as proposed by Longino.

There is an enormous literature on agency, subjectivities, and identities. Anthropologists have recently developed sophisticated concepts of identity in practice, once they had recovered from the shock caused by the Foucaultian wave (Holland and Lave 2001; Ortner 2005). Dorothy Holland and her coauthors present a frame that acknowledges the complications in authoring one's practice and identity in figured worlds (Holland, Lachiotte, Skinner, and Cain 1998). Another expanding, "post-discursive" stream of research focuses on affects, including in academia (e.g., Gregg 2010). There are also writings about particular moods in which people respond to changes in governance regimes (e.g., Brown 1999).

Finally, the frame of practical activity invites approaches that try to pay attention to the multiple dimensions of practice simultaneously. How do particular academics resolve the four basic issues (how, what, why, and who), and how do they deal with their interdependencies? This kind of work is certainly difficult and hardly doable, according to the standards of empiricist theorizing. One can expect accusations of eclecticism if one brings in too diverse orientations to practical activity. For instance, few scholars if any can honestly claim that the ideas of moral philosophers, taking morality as the primary stance to life, and the ideas of political sociologists, taking politics primarily, can be nicely integrated. But the ambition to synthesize can be avoided by accepting that both the focal and research practices are eclectic as to the frames of interpretation. The price is that the mainstreams of (publishing in) social studies are likely to exclude this kind of work.

How can I justify posing these demands of complementary perspectives to the studies of academic capitalism? My only justification is that academic practitioners live in figured worlds that ask all these questions. An academic has to respond every day to these calls: be skillful, goal oriented, morally motivated, and know who you are! The managerial regime of governance and its agents may work in a way that only the technical question of how is left to the academics, while managers and markets deal with the rest, but this regime is not the only one that puts demands on individuals in academia. If this regime were perfect, I would not write this text. Moreover, I am not suggesting that such empirical studies that the stream in question has generated can be expected to deal with all the aspects of practice. Other forms of research practice may also help the bewildered or angry practitioner.

Even if the accounts of academic capitalism could extend beyond a political perspective, it makes no sense to omit the politics of academic work. Quite the contrary, the point I am suggesting is that the tactical, political, moral, and personal perspectives are all important. One consequence of taking this agenda seriously would possibly be that "the political" would gain new meaning. To put it in simple terms: we know *what* to accomplish and achieve (politically) when we know *why* we engage in particular forms of academic work, *who* we want to become, and *how* we want to do this work. The substance of politics is to be found in the three other dimensions of practice.

Conclusion

This chapter suggests how appreciating the various aspects of academic work as practical activity could enrich the study of academic capitalism. My proposals are based on a version of participatory research and on ideas from the tradition of practical philosophy. The amendments might serve to strengthen the research program and make it even more relevant to people who struggle or try to live on under the new regime of governance.

The question is whether the program can provide academics with options and encouragement for meaningful action. The intellectual force of the political approach can have counterproductive effects: the studies "prove scientifically" that we are overpowered by the new regime. A richer concept of practice will open up a wider set of opportunities to those who resist the regime or unwillingly adapt to it in the lack of alternatives. Slaughter and her colleagues have also paid attention to the issue of ethics in academia, and not only to political games and strategies (e.g., Slaughter et al. 2004). Slaughter (2001b) says, "In the postmodern twenty-first century, the professional values that once marked the boundary between the corporate world and universities seem quaint, impossibly naive. Yet if professors and administrators want to continue to receive public trust and financial support, they must differentiate themselves from the corporate world and figure out a new social contract. Such a contract would not capitulate to the market, nor would it simply defend the older system" (26). "The new contract" mentioned in the quote above requires, in the terminology offered in this chapter, a new moral-political vision that is shared by multiple interest groups. But suggesting such a vision is surely beyond the purpose of this text. Instead, I have tried to write from a position where the lack of a livable and coherent vision is a deeply felt existential condition. Nevertheless, there are ways of approaching the quest for a vision also as an intellectual and collective task. Immanent critique focused on our own forms of research practice—on our solutions to the issues of who, why, what, and how—is one of these ways. The extended research agenda would indeed motivate the recruitment of a full army of researchers. This move would at least alleviate employment worries amongst critical scholars.

NOTE

1. The MERI researcher group was established in 2002 to do participatory research in higher education and to continue the renewal of local academic practices. The members of the group worked in the same discipline-based unit in the field of organization and management (in the former Helsinki School of Economics, which was merged in 2010 with the new Aalto University). In collaboration with a number of other colleagues, the group experimented with new educational, research, and self-governance practices and documented these efforts in academic publications. The original members of the group were Anne Herbert, Kirsi Korpiaho, Hans Mäntylä, Hanna Päiviö, and Keijo Räsänen. Susanna Kantelinen joined the group later. The group gradually developed a specific approach to practicing academic work and to framing it as practical activity. Some intellectual roots of this approach predate the MERI group because senior mem-

bers of the group had used similar practice-theoretical ideas since the early 1990s in studying managerial work and development work in different workplaces. See the group's website at: http://management.aalto.fi/en/research/groups/meri/.

REFERENCES

Abbott, Andrew. 2007. "Against Narrative: A Preface to Lyrical Sociology." *Sociological Theory* 25, no. 1: 67–99. doi:0.1111/j.1467-9558.2007.00298.x.

Atkinson, Paul, and William Housley. 2003. *Interactionism: An Essay in Sociological Amnesia.* London: SAGE.

Bernstein, Richard J. 1971. *Praxis and Action: Contemporary Philosophies of Human Activity.* Philadelphia: University of Pennsylvania Press.

———. 1982. "What Is the Difference That Makes a Difference? Gadamer, Habermas, and Rorty." *Proceedings of the Biennial Meeting of the Philosophy of Science Association* 2: 331–59.

———. 1983. *Beyond Objectivism and Relativism: Science, Hermeneutics, and Praxis.* Philadelphia: University of Pennsylvania Press.

Bourdieu, Pierre. 1975. "The Specificity of the Scientific Field and the Social Conditions of the Progress of Reason." *Social Science Information* 14, no. 6: 19–47. doi:10.1177/053901847501400602.

———. 2003. "Participant Objectivation." *Journal of the Royal Anthropological Institute* 9, no. 2: 281–94. doi:10.1111/1467-9655.00150.

Brown, Wendy. 1999. "Resisting Left Melancholy." *Boundary 2* 26, no. 3: 19–27.

Carp, Richard M. 2001. "Integrative Praxes: Learning from Multiple Knowledge Formations." *Issues in Integrative Studies* 19, no. 1: 71–121.

Carr, Wilfred, and Stephen Kemmis. 1983. *Becoming Critical: Knowing through Action Research.* Deakin: Deakin University Press.

Chaiklin, Seth. 1996. "Understanding the Social Scientific Practice of Understanding Practice." In *Understanding Practice: Perspectives on Activity and Context,* edited by Seth Chaiklin and Jean Lave, 377–401. Cambridge: Cambridge University Press.

De Certeau, M. 1984. *The Practice of Everyday Life.* Berkeley: University of California Press.

Eikeland, Olav. 2007. "Why Should Mainstream Social Researchers Be Interested in Action Research?" *International Journal of Action Research* 3, no. 1/2: 38–64.

———. 2008. *The Ways of Aristotle: Aristotelian Phrónêsis, Aristotelian Philosophy of Dialogue, and Action Research.* Bern: Peter Lang.

Eikeland, Olav, and Davide Nicolini. 2011. "Turning Practically: Broadening the Horizon." *Journal of Organizational Change Management* 24, no. 2: 164–74. doi:10.1108/09534811111119744.

Fuller, Steve. 1999. "Is Science Studies Lost in the Kuhnian Plot? On the Way Back from Paradigms to Movements." *Science as Culture* 8, no. 4: 405–35. doi:10.1080/09505439909526557.

Gadamer, Hans Georg. 1975. *Truth and Method.* New York: Seabury.

Goffman, Erving. 1991. *Asylums: Essays on the Social Situation of Mental Patients and Other Inmates.* New York: Doubleday.

Gouldner, Alvin Ward. 1970. *The Coming Crisis of Western Sociology.* New York: Basic Books.

Gramsci, Antonio. 1988. "Sociology and the Philosophy of Praxis." In *Interpretations of Marx,* edited by Tom Bottomore, 146–55. Oxford: Basil Blackwell.

Gregg, Melissa. 2010. "Working with Affect in the Corporate University." In *Working with Affect in Feminist Readings,* edited by Marianne Liljeström and Susanna Paasonen, 182–92. New York: Routledge.

Habermas, Juergen. 1972. *Knowledge and Human Interests.* London: Heinemann.

Holland, Dorothy, William Lachiotte Jr., Debra Skinner, and Carole Cain. 1998. *Identity and Agency in Cultural Worlds.* Cambridge, MA: Harvard University Press.

Holland, Dorothy, and Jean Lave, eds. 2001. *History in Person: Enduring Struggles, Contentious Practice, Intimate Identities.* Santa Fe: School of American Research Press.

Kemmis, Stephen. 2001. "Exploring the Relevance of Critical Theory for Action Research: Emancipatory Action Research in the Footsteps of Jurgen Habermas." In *Handbook of Action Research: Participative Inquiry and Practice,* edited by Peter Reason and Hilary Bradbury-Huan, 91–102. London: SAGE.

———. 2011. "What Is Professional Practice? Recognising and Respecting Diversity in Understandings of Practice." In *Elaborating Professionalism,* edited by Clive Kanes, 139–65. Dordrecht: Springer.

———. 2012. "Pedagogy, Praxis and Practice-Based Higher Education." In *Practice-Based Education,* edited by Joy Higgs, Ronald Barnett, Stephen Billet, Maggie Hutchings, and Franziska Trede, 81–100. Rotterdam: Sense.

Kemmis, Stephen, Peter Cole, and Dahle Suggett. 1983. *Orientations to Curriculum and Transition: Towards the Socially-Critical School.* Melbourne: Victorian Institute of Secondary Education.

Kezar, Adrianna J. 2004. "Wrestling with Philosophy: Improving Scholarship in Higher Education." *Journal of Higher Education* 75, no. 1: 42–55. doi:10.1353/jhe.2003.0052.

Lather, Patti. 1986. "Research as Praxis." *Harvard Educational Review* 56, no. 3: 257–77.

———. 2007. *Getting Lost: Feminist Efforts toward a Double(d) Science.* Albany: State University of New York Press.

Longino, Helen E. 1995. "Gender, Politics, and the Theoretical Virtues." *Synthese* 104, no. 3: 383–97. doi:10.1007/BF01064506.

MacIntyre, Alasdair. 1985. *After Virtue: A Study in Moral Theory.* 2nd ed. London: Duckworth.

Mallard, Grégoire, Michèle Lamont, and Joshua Guetzkow. 2009. "Fairness as Appropriateness: Negotiating Epistemological Differences in Peer Review." *Science, Technology, and Human Values* 34, no. 5: 573–606. doi:10.1177/0162243908329381.

Nicolini, Davide, Silvia Gherardi, and Dvora Yanow. 2003. "Introduction: Towards a Practice-Based View of Knowing and Learning in Organizations." In *Knowing in Organizations: A Practice-Based Approach,* edited by Davide Nicolini, Silvia Gherardi, Dvora Yanow, 3–31. Armonk, NY: M. E. Sharpe.

Nixon, Jon. 2006. "Towards a Hermeneutics of Hope: The Legacy of Edward W. Said." *Discourse: Studies in the Cultural Politics of Education* 27, no. 3: 341–56. doi:10.1080/01596300600838793.

Ortner, Sherry B. 2005. "Subjectivity and Cultural Critique." *Anthropological Theory* 5, no. 1: 31–52. doi:10.1177/1463499605050867.

Paololucci, Gabriella. 2007. "Sartre's Humanism and the Cuban Revolution." *Theory and Society* 36, no. 3: 245–63. doi:10.1007/s11186-007-9031-3.

Räsänen, Keijo. 2009. "Understanding Academic Work as Practical Activity—And Preparing (Business-School) Academics for Praxis?" *International Journal for Academic Development* 14, no. 3: 185–95. doi:10.1080/13601440903106502.

———. 2010. "On the Moral of an Emerging Academic Praxis: Accounting for a Conference Experience." In *Relational Practices, Participative Organizing*, edited by Chris Steyaert and Bart Van Looy, 155–76. Bingley: Emerald Group.

———. 2012. "'That's Dangerous': Autonomous Development Work as a Source of Renewal in Academia." In *Managing Reform in Universities: The Dynamics of Culture, Identity and Organizational Change*, edited by Bjørn Stensaker, Jussi Välimaa, and Claudia Sarrico, 179–97. Basingstoke: Palgrave MacMillan.

Räsänen, Keijo, and Kirsi Korpiaho. 2011. "Supporting Doctoral Students in Their Professional Identity Projects." *Studies in Continuing Education* 33, no. 1: 19–31. doi:10.108 0/0158037X.2010.515568.

Räsänen, Keijo, and Marja-Liisa Trux. 2012. *Työkirja: Ammattilaisen paluu* [Workbook: The Return of the Professional]. Helsinki: Kansanvalistusseura.

Reay, Diane. 2005. "Beyond Consciousness? The Psychic Landscape of Social Class." *Sociology* 39, no. 5: 911–28. doi:10.1177/0038038505058372.

Reckwitz, Andreas. 2002. "Toward a Theory of Social Practices: A Development in Culturalist Theorizing." *European Journal of Social Theory* 5, no. 2: 243–63. doi:10.1177/1368431022225432.

Shapcott, Richard. 2004. "IR as Practical Philosophy: Defining a 'Classical Approach.'" *British Journal of Politics and International Relations* 6, no. 3: 271–91. doi:10.1111/j.1467-856X.2004.00140.x.

Slaughter, Sheila. 2001a. "Problems in Comparative Higher Education: Political Economy, Political Sociology and Postmodernism." *Higher Education* 41, no. 4: 389–412. doi:10.1023/A:1017505525288.

———. 2001b. "Professional Values and the Allure of the Market." *Academe* 87, no. 5: 22–26.

Slaughter, Sheila, Cynthia Joan Archerd, and Teresa I. D. Campbell. 2004. "Boundaries and Quandaries: How Professors Negotiate Market Relations." *Review of Higher Education* 28, no. 1: 129–65. doi:10.1353/rhe.2004.0032.

Slaughter, Sheila, and Gary Rhoades. 2004. *Academic Capitalism and the New Economy: Markets, State, and Higher Education*. Baltimore: Johns Hopkins University Press.

———. 2005. "From Endless Frontier to Basic Science for Use: Social Contracts between Science and Society." *Science, Technology, and Human Values* 30, no. 4: 536–72. doi:10.1177/0162243905276503.

Taylor, Charles. 1989. *Sources of the Self: The Making of the Modern Identity*. Cambridge: Cambridge University Press.

Thévenot, Laurent. 2007. "The Plurality of Cognitive Formats and Engagements: Moving between the Familiar and the Public." *European Journal of Social Theory* 10, no. 3: 409–23. doi:10.1177/1368431007080703.

Tsay, Angela, Michele Lamont, Andrew Abbott, and Joshua Guetzkow. 2003. "From Character to Intellect: Changing Conceptions of Merit in the Social Sciences and Humanities, 1951–1971." *Poetics* 31, no. 1: 23–49. doi:10.1016/S0304-422X(03)00002-0.

Tuunainen, Juha. 2005. "Hybrid Practices? Contributions to the Debate on the Mutation of Science and University." *Higher Education* 50, no. 2: 275–98. doi:10.1007/s10734-004-6355-z.

Whittington, Richard. 2007. "Strategy Practice and Strategy Process: Family Differences and the Sociological Eye." *Organization Studies* 28, no. 10: 1575–86. doi:10.1177/0170840607081557.

Ylijoki, Oili-Helena. 2003. "Entangled in Academic Capitalism? A Case-Study on Changing Ideals and Practices of University Research." *Higher Education* 45, no. 3: 307–35. doi:10.1023/A:1022667923715.

Extending Academic Capitalism by Foregrounding Academic Labor

GARY RHOADES

In the US higher education literature, academic capitalism has been largely interpreted and applied to the orientation and practices of professors in research universities, particularly in STEM (science, technology, engineering, and math) fields (e.g., Mendoza 2012; Mendoza, Kuntz, and Berger 2012; Szelényi and Goldberg 2011). In the international literature, more attention has been devoted to the orientation and "moral order" of academic departments more generally (e.g., Ylijoki 2000, 2003) or to revenue structures and policy regimes of entire national systems (e.g., Fisher, Rubenson, Jones, and Shanahan 2009; Metcalfe 2010). In each of these literatures, academic capitalism is understood to be about professors, departments, universities, and systems structuring practices around revenue generation, and in the process engaging the private sector in ways that reshape the academy's values and move higher education away from its public good functions.

However, three dimensions of Slaughter's and my (2004) theory have been underexplored. One is the expansion of the nonacademic professional workforce of colleges and universities, so called "managerial professionals" (Rhoades 1998a). A second is the changing character and expanded managerial control of production workers that is embedded in a changing production process, evident in growth segments of an increasingly managed academic workforce (Rhoades 1998b). A third is the agency and collective dynamics by which the ongoing formation and (re)production of social relations between labor and management is (re)negotiated. Each of these three dimensions better enables us to see a deeper dimension of privatization that is reducing the public commons in higher education.

Academic capitalism is too often reduced in citation and application to revenue generation efforts. Far less common is an understanding that academic capitalism, like capitalism more broadly, is about power embedded in the social relations of production. It is about not just "extended managerial capacity" but also efforts to extend managerial control, and the collective contests surrounding those efforts (Slaughter and Rhoades 2004). When Slaughter and I wrote about colleges and universities engaging in market behaviors, we were foregrounding not just revenue generation efforts that commodify and commercialize higher education, but also political economic efforts that restructure and rationalize professional work.

In our view, the ascendance of the academic capitalist knowledge/learning regime requires us to rethink the centrality and dominance of the academic profession (Slaughter and Rhoades 2004). Thus we characterized academic capitalism as a reversal of the previous regime that had witnessed an "academic revolution": "Jencks and Riesman (1968) were conceptualizing the ascendancy of the national academic profession in the post–World War II era" (10n4). Academic capitalism is about political economic changes in professions in the academy. As part of the organizational changes that we theorized would accompany academic capitalism, we also theorized changes in the structure of professional employment.

In this chapter, I extend academic capitalism by returning to that insight and foregrounding academic labor. I also feature the constriction of the public commons, of an open space in which there is free pursuit and interplay of ideas in instruction, research, service, and deliberations about the future course of colleges and universities. The concept of a public commons is linked in the United States to a core value of the academic profession—academic freedom. It can and should be linked not simply to the changing conditions of professional work for individual professionals or segments of professions, but also to collective efforts and negotiations to (re)define that common, public space, and purpose of higher education.

The Rise of Managerial Professionals: Restructured Professional Employment, Reduced Professorial Prominence

Over the past three decades, the growth segment of professional employment in US colleges and universities is in nonfaculty "other" professionals. It is not executive, managerial positions that have increased the most; that is, positions at the level of dean or above (they have only slightly increased from about 11% to about 12% of professional employees from the 1970s to the 2000s). Rather, it is a range of professionals with advanced degrees (masters and PhDs) who serve in support positions throughout colleges and universities. The expansion and increased significance of these professionals relative to professors is part of what Slaughter and I (2004) identified as extended managerial capacity, through categories of employees over which management had greater control than of academics. Such professionals have not eclipsed the numbers of faculty (now slightly more than half of professional employees, compared to about one-third for support professionals), but they have reduced the prominence of professors.[1]

Although the phenomenon is most pronounced in the United States, the rise of other professionals is evident in Europe as well (e.g., see Rhoades and Sporn 2002a). Several European scholars have analyzed work in the interstices between academe and administration, focusing on the professionalization of new administrative workforces (Gornitzka and Larsen 2004; Schneijderberg and Merkator 2013). Some have characterized these employees as "blended" or "third space" professionals (Whitchurch 2009, 2013; Whitchurch and Gordon 2010).

Despite the increased importance of what I (1998a) have called "managerial professionals," there is little research on them, particularly in the United States, which is remarkable given that most graduate programs of higher education in the United States prepare significant numbers of such professionals, particularly in student affairs. It is also remarkable given the expansion of nonacademic offices and professional personnel in entrepreneurial realms like fund raising and technology transfer; in quality control and accountability realms like teaching centers and undergraduate assessment; and in realms of outreach, tutoring, and cultural center services to nontraditional students, as well as residence halls, student recreation centers, and high-end services for targeted, upper-middle-class students (Rhoades and Sporn 2002a).

The rise of each of the above types of managerial professionals can be linked to the rise of academic capitalism. Conceptually, the reason for labeling them professionals is that these categories of employees have masters and PhDs, signifying certain levels of expertise. They generally develop national professional associations, which spawn professional journals and bodies of knowledge and are part of articulating norms and best practices for the profession. They are in these senses professions (a concept distinctive to Anglo-American contexts, not being embedded in state civil service categories).

The reason for modifying the "professional" with "managerial" in coining this concept is that these professionals are more dependent on managers than are members of the academic profession. Managerial professionals are hired, evaluated, and either renewed or released by managers, with less peer influence than professors. Moreover, their daily work is less independent and more fully defined by managers than is the case for professors.

Several questions arise in relation to nonacademic professionals. Some relate to the shifts that are involved in the cost structure of higher education. It is worth tracking and describing the shift in higher education's cost structure. More than that, though, it is worth asking to what extent the rise of managerial professionals translates into or reflects a change in institutional priorities in higher education. One way of specifying that question is to ask to what extent and in what ways academic capitalism is driving priorities focused less on the production process (instruction and research) and more on marketing, assessment, and efforts to entrepreneurially engage and play in private sector markets. There is an irony here. We are in the midst of what could be called an austerity agenda that claims we are in a "new normal" of no new public resources for higher education and heightened concern about escalating tuition and student debt. Yet colleges and universities are investing in growing numbers of noninstructional employees, expanding costs in units and activities that lie outside the academy's core functions. To what extent is the periphery becoming the core?

In the United States, there has been some policy discussion of administrative costs. But conceptions of wasteful, bloated bureaucracy frame the discussion. The phenomenon is not explored as reflecting academic capitalist strategies for leveraging greater control over production processes and employees, as well as greater revenue from production and other activities. From this perspective, questions of why and how emerge regarding the reasons for which (why) and processes by which (how) the investment in nonacademic personnel, offices, and activities takes place. One example of such a study offers hypotheses about administrative costs (Leslie and Rhoades 1995). Similar hypotheses should be developed and explored for academic capitalism (e.g., Rhoades and Sporn 2002a, on managerial professionals). Yet with few exceptions there is little such work (see Powers 2003 and Powers and Campbell 2011, on technology transfer offices).

A second set of questions surround the social relations between the new managerial professions and professors. Professions are about establishing claims and control over domains of work (Abbott 1988). In the context of rising managerial professions, that raises the question of the extent to which segments of these professions lay claim to domains already claimed by professors.

One of the clearest examples of such a context surrounds classroom space. Various segments of nonacademic professionals have advanced claims of expertise in pedagogy and learning, leveraging the use of instructional and learning technologies in developing and justifying these claims. In US colleges and universities today, courses and classrooms are contested professional spaces, with managerial professionals in teaching centers, learning technologies centers, and more, challenging the prominence of professors in developing and delivering curricula (Rhoades 2011a; Smith and Rhoades 2006).

Similar analyses could be developed with regard to another core function of universities long controlled by professors—the realm of research. Consider the increased emphasis on technology transfer and the attendant rise of managerial professionals in offices devoted to getting knowledge out into the marketplace. To what extent and how are such professionals a part of redefining what sorts of knowledge creation get valued and prioritized in universities?

The above interprofessional contests over various production activities can best be understood if they are put in context of the relationship between managerial professionals and the executives who manage universities. The term I have coined speaks to that point, conveying a tighter linkage between their work and the aims of management than is found for professors. The extent to which that is the case as well as how managerial control is exercised over the work of these professionals are questions worth exploring, given that they have become such a significant segment of the workforce.

Managerial professionals can be understood as a mechanism by which managerial influence in the academic capitalist knowledge/learning regime is expanded. Managerial professionals are part of extended managerial capacity. That framing raises important questions. To what extent and how is the work of managerial professionals being invested in and utilized by management to redefine and evaluate the work of professors?

Implications for the Public Commons

Beyond the above issues, what are the implications of the changing structure and relations of professional employment in academic capitalism for the free and open exchange of ideas in the public commons? The question is all the more important because the rise of managerial professionals is in direct proportion to and in conjunction with the fall in the prominence of professors, and these professionals have fewer tools available to them to exercise an independent role in the academy. There are no embedded norms of academic freedom and tenure, for example, or of shared governance in their terms of employment.

In the area of instruction, one of the historical contributors to professors' academic freedom in their teaching has been the inherent privacy of the classroom. Yet that is changing, partly owing to technology. Students' cell phones make these spaces potentially open to public scrutiny. More than that, the introduction of various high technologies into instruction is also opening up the classroom space to external review. Most classes are run through course management systems, where notes and conversations can be posted and conducted, again opening them up to broader review from academic managers. Managerial professionals play a role in this process and are sometimes themselves "present" in the classroom—as assessors of quality in undergraduate education, as promoters of instructional technology to enhance student "engagement," and in some cases as having access to (and indeed in constructing and maintaining) the course management systems.

In the area of research, managerial professionals are involved in shaping research activities that were at one time largely within the sole purview of professors, in ways that shrink social critique and the public commons. Professionals have emerged in institutional review processes surrounding studies involving human subjects; these processes can affect teaching that involves students doing research as well as students' dissertations. Various discretionary judgments are involved in setting and applying standards surrounding human subjects research. Similarly, in technology transfer, managerial professionals are part of redefining what is considered valuable research, advancing a calculus centered in the commercial value of knowledge in the private sector.

Finally, the rise of managerial professions is linked to a shrinking public commons in public service and in decision making about universities' strategic direction. These professionals have no defined rights or responsibilities that would support their independent involvement in the defining public policy issues of the day. Nor do they enjoy a recognized role in governing the institution or in articulating stances at odds with those of management.

Contingent Faculty and Postdocs: Restructuring the Production of Teaching and Research

What is happening to the academic workforce amidst academic capitalism? In the United States, members of the academic workforce who are neither tenure eligible nor tenured professors are now doing an increasingly large share of production work in instruction and research. Yet, just as strategic planning (in universities and state systems as well as nationally) largely fails to consider these academics, the academic literature largely overlooks them. And it is not just the US academic workforce that is experiencing dramatic changes. In Europe and beyond there are significant changes that involve decreasing the power and independence of professors and increasing the power and independence of university managers (Enders and de Weert 2009; Kehm and Teichler 2013).

At the core of the academic capitalist knowledge/learning regime are new circuits of knowledge production and dissemination. Developing and (r)amping up such circuitry involves restructuring the production of teaching and research. Ironically, for all the public discourse from the media, policymakers, and academic managers about how resistant higher education is to change, the last three decades in US higher education (and the last few decades in Europe) have witnessed a fundamental transformation in the configuration of the academic workforce.

New Circuits of Producing Instruction

In the United States, a "new faculty majority" produces most of the undergraduate instruction.[2] Two-thirds of instructional workforce in the United States is "contingent"; they are not on the tenure track.[3] Contingent faculty lack many features of basic due process in hiring, evaluation, and continuing employment or "nonrenewal." Most are in part-time positions (49% of all faculty nationally, and 70% in community colleges).

Beyond part-time faculty, there are also full-time, non–tenure track faculty who now constitute nearly one-fifth of the academic workforce. Many are "teaching without tenure" (Baldwin and Chronister 2002), but many also work in grant-supported research positions. A majority of new hires in recent cohorts of faculty are not on the tenure track (Finkelstein, Seal, and Schuster 1998; Schuster and Finkelstein 2006). Despite their growing significance, we know little about this workforce. Some of the most important information about contingent faculty has come not from academic sources but from policy groups—most notably from the Coalition on Academic Work, which has conducted the largest-ever survey of contingent faculty.

The conditions of employment for contingent faculty substantially increase managerial discretion as compared to the conditions enjoyed by tenure track faculty. The dramatic expansion of this contingent instructional workforce has extended managerial discretion (Rhoades 1998b). For at the core of academic capitalism is a renegotiation of the social contract between organizations and professors, a fact captured in the Canadian term "contract staff," which refers to non–tenure track members of the academic workforce. They work on short-term contracts, affording extensive flexibility to managers in reorganizing the academic workforce.

In essence, part-time faculty are "at-will" employees, serving at the will of managers. Although full-time contingent faculty may have some measure of due process rights, extensive managerial discretion exists in not renewing these faculty at the end of their term contracts, even in unionized settings (Rhoades 1998b). Moreover, the contingent sectors of the academic workforce have experienced nonrenewal on a significant scale, a much less politically problematic measure than laying off faculty.

One set of empirical questions surrounding these developments has to do with the processes by which this transformation of the academic workforce has taken place. What are the decision-making processes by which the academic profession in the United States has gone from being a two-thirds tenure stream body to one that is two-thirds off the tenure track? It is common to hear in the public discourse, and to read in the academic literature, that the transformation has been in some sense natural. At the same time, others have suggested intentionality on the part of academic managers as well as of the tenured professoriate. But there is virtually no empirical work in this area.

Some recent work is suggestive, identifying exemplary practices in the employment conditions surrounding contingent faculty (Kezar and Sam 2013). Yet the examples are few and far between, and most likely to be found in unionized settings, seemingly suggesting that working conditions are negotiated terms of labor, with management seeking more discretion and flexibility, and labor seeking more autonomy and control over their work (Rhoades 1998b). Again, though, studies of academic administrators have not addressed these questions.

Much managerial flexibility in the delivery of education stems not simply from the contract terms of the staff, but also from managers having effectively bypassed tenured professors' conventional governance structures. Increasing portions of the curriculum in US colleges and universities are run through units that often lie outside the realm of academic governance. The establishment and expansion of such interstitial units, such as outreach, continuing, and extended education colleges, should be studied with an eye to the balance of influence between management and academic labor in shaping universities' curricular development and direction.

Moreover, new technological developments that are rapidly unfolding in the delivery of education represent yet further examples of new circuits of knowledge production and dissemination. The rise of distance, online education has certainly paralleled the expansion of part-time faculty, distanced from the creation of the curriculum that they are teaching. The massive open online courses that have emerged have profound implications for the stratification and structure of the academic profession that merit exploration.

Whatever the motivations and processes by which they were developed, the current terms of academic labor for contingent faculty express a "just-in-time" delivery model of instruction that maps easily onto the academic capitalist regime. A recent survey reveals that significant segments of the contingent academic workforce have their teaching assignments changed within two weeks before the academic semester starts (Street, Maisto, Merves, and Rhoades 2012). They also have limited or no access to key instructional resources, from library resources to course management systems. There is a fairly clear pattern of exploiting rather than embracing (Kezar 2012) and providing the new faculty majority with the tools to provide quality education.

Such working conditions raise the important question of what impact they have on various student outcomes and on educational quality. Several studies have been done on the relationship between proportions of part-time faculty and graduation rates, for example, among other outcomes (Eagan and Jaeger 2009; Umbach 2007). Such questions are worthy of further exploration, as are studies that probe more qualitatively into the connections between working and learning conditions.

Academic capitalism, it seems, is promoting a path in academic staffing that compromises educational quality and heightens social stratification. Lower-income students and students of color are most likely to be found in the least-resourced institutions with the highest proportions of part-time faculty. And here we return to an issue raised in discussing the rise of managerial professionals: there is a trend line in resource allocation away from investment in instruction and toward investment in nonacademic personnel and offices. The growth of contingent faculty as a proportion of the overall academic workforce is an expression of the changing priorities in academic capitalism, pushing production workers into the background and foregrounding various managerial professionals in marketing, enrollment management, student services, and entrepreneurial pursuits.

New Circuits of Producing Research

The new circuitry of academic capitalist knowledge creation is evident in at least two regards. One is a shift in what knowledge is prioritized. What was once "fundamental" or "basic" is now "curiosity driven," which is but a step from being "curious" or frivolous. What was once designated in a lesser category of "applied" is now seen as basic to revenue generation. Much of this was mapped out in *Academic Capitalism and the New Economy*, with the focus on technology transfer for enriching universities (versus the communities in which they are situated). Much of it can be seen in the heightened organizational focus on grant generation, a shift that has received some attention.

A second aspect of the new circuitry of knowledge creation has been overlooked. As with instruction, an emergent and subordinate segment of the academic workforce—postdoctoral researchers—is doing much of the research. From the late 1970s to the late 1990s, the number of postdocs at US universities doubled (National Academy of Sciences 2000). Significant growth continued in the 2000s (National Science Foundation 2011). For a good portion of the decade, postdocs were the fastest-growing category of employment for PhD graduates in science and engineering (Fiegener 2010).

Along with the growth came increasing policy concern as early as the late 1990s about the condition of postdoc labor, from institutional associations such as the Association of American Universities, federal agencies such as the National Institutes of Health and the National Science Foundation, and national committees (e.g., Nerad and Cerny 1999). In 2003, an advocacy group—the National Postdoctoral Association—was created with the aim of "enhanc[ing] the quality of the postdoctoral experience." Public policy discourse had come to recognize that postdocs were no longer steps on the educational ladder to a tenure track professorial position, but had become a long-term purgatory of exploitative working conditions (Stephan 2012; Zumeta 1985).

From the academic literature, we know little about postdocs, both in the United States and abroad. We know little about their working conditions. We know little about the relationship between these research production workers and another category of dependent researchers: graduate research assistants (for an exception, see Cantwell 2011). We know little about the impact on the independence, direction, and quality of research of having moved production to the most dependent segments of the workforce.

Academic Freedom in the New Circuitry of Academic Capitalism

At the core of academic freedom in the US academy has been tenure, partly because of the job security it brings, but also partly because of the due process it entails in employment and renewal decisions.[4] By contrast, at the core of the growth categories of academic employment is deep job *in*security and an almost total lack of due process, which fundamentally compromises academic freedom. Adjunct activists commonly articulate that contingent faculty members are one student complaint away from nonrenewal. Similarly, postdocs are one unhappy principal investigator away from nonrenewal.

Scholars too often overlook two types of academic freedom. One is the freedom to participate in organizational discussions about the university's strategic direction, and in conversations about its policies and practices. A second is the freedom to participate as experts in the broader public commons with regard to issues of the day.

Academic capitalism discourages both activities, directly and indirectly, in the restructuring of the academic workforce. When the defining logics are managerial control, revenue generation, and the public image of the enterprise, to raise questions about (let alone express objections or promote alternatives to) managerial direction is to raise a red flag. And when large segments of the academic workforce are in dependent, largely at-will positions, waving a white flag is structurally encouraged. The result is a severe narrowing of the public commons.

Negotiating a New Academy: Labor/Management Relations in Flux

Academic capitalism is a complex, powerful regime. It is a knowledge/learning regime borne and consisting of an elaborate and intersecting set of policies and practices. Yet, as Slaughter and I (2004) concluded, there are "alternatives within and beyond academic capitalism in the new economy . . . [Academic capitalism] is not inevitable, in its current configuration" (335). It is not inexorable.

Much of Slaughter's and my book focused on the ascendance of political economic structures that embed academic capitalism in higher education systems, institutions, and professions. We emphasized that it is not simply something done to higher education from the outside. Rather, various groups within the academy, including significant segments of the professoriate, are complicit and actively engaged in academic capitalism.

At the same time, at the core of our narrative was the recognition that academic capitalism is a negotiated set of policies and practices. The nature and outcomes of those negotiations can vary and change in different social and historical contexts. In short, amidst the systemic structures that express, perpetuate, and expand academic capitalism, there is also the possibility not just for resistance, but also for negotiating alternative arrangements.

Unfortunately, the higher education literature is lacking in studies of the struggles surrounding the definition of particular forms of academic capitalism and alternatives to them, particularly in relation to collective efforts to negotiate a different set of institutional and professional arrangements. There is no systematic attention devoted to the ways in which professors and new professionals are involved in collectivities, from unions to national professional and advocacy associations, to smaller local groups that are negotiating a new academy. To be sure, the players in this negotiation process are not on equal ground. But neither are professionals simply subject to domination by a managerial elite. Too little scholarship focuses on the contested relations between labor and management, as well as within academic labor that are involved in negotiating a new academy.

Our scholarship is not as rich as the collective moments and movements that are shaping the academy's future. Higher education as a policy realm is in a highly contested moment, both in the United States and globally. Academic capitalism as a knowledge/learning regime has been prevalent in the United States for over three decades; it has been ascendant for some time globally as well, to varying degrees in different regional, national, and local contexts. Yet the social relations defined by and expressed in that knowledge/learning regime are currently in flux, in ways that clarify the contest between labor and management.

Here I speak to four examples of how a new academy is being actively negotiated. One is the political contest at the state level in the United States of public employees' right to bargain collectively. A second is the extensive organizing activity among growth segments of the academic labor force in the United States. A third example is the role of academic labor organizations nationally working to defend the public mission of not-for-profit higher education. Finally, I speak to the role of managerial professionals in negotiating a new academy, independent of management.

After the US midterm elections of 2010, the country witnessed a series of assaults at the state level on the right of public employees to bargain collectively. So-called "right-to-work" legislation was introduced in several states, undermining professors' right to bargain collectively over their conditions of employment.[5] Two of the most remarkable battleground states are Wisconsin and Michigan. Wisconsin was the first state to pass legislation in the twentieth century that gave public employees the right to form unions. Michigan was the first state to pass legislation that specifically gave professors the same right. In Wisconsin in 2011, Governor Scott Walker and Republican state legislators successfully eliminated the bargaining rights of professors. In Michigan, state legislators in 2012 passed right-to-work legislation that eliminated "closed shops," meaning that people in the bargaining unit who are not union members cannot be charged an agency fee. By contrast, similar right-to-work legislation was repealed in Ohio by 60% of the popular vote in a ballot initiative.

Even as collective bargaining rights of professors in public institutions have been and are being challenged, there has been an extraordinary expansion in organizing academic employees, which has been the growth industry for major faculty unions. Most importantly, given the reconfiguration of the academic workforce, there has been dramatic growth in organizing postdocs in public universities and part-time faculty in private colleges and universities. In the middle to late 2000s, there were several efforts to organize postdocs into collective bargaining units. After an earlier organizing effort had failed in 2008, the California Employment Relations Board recognized the Postdoctoral Researchers Organization / International Union United Automobile, Aerospace, and Agricultural Implement Workers of America as the union representative for the entire University of California system, which includes roughly 10% of all academic postdocs nationally. Subsequently, new postdoc unions were also established at Rutgers University and the University of Massachusetts, Amherst.

Among part-time faculty, too, there has been a significant surge of organizing activity in the 2000s, although the unionization of faculty in part-time positions dates back decades. For the most part, these faculty members have been in bargaining units in which the dominant group is full-time tenure track faculty. "Until recently . . . the contingent-only units that existed were the exceptions that proved the rule and existed either for very particular historical reasons or because of particularly obdurate and hostile local full-time faculty leadership" (Berry 2005, 32). But two new adjunct units in Chicago at Roosevelt University and Columbia College, both private institutions, are examples of an emerging pattern: the independent organizing of part-time faculty, particularly in private colleges and universities.

Most dramatically, the changed organization of faculty (faculty in part-time positions in metropolitan areas often work in multiple institutions) has led to an emergent "metro strategy" of organizing citywide (Berry 2005). At present, the major promoter of this strategy is the Service Employees International Union, which is undertaking metro-wide campaigns organizing part-time faculty private colleges and universities in Boston, Seattle, and Washington, DC (Rhoades 2013). The ultimate goal is for these faculty to become part of one bargaining unit, with which institutions in a metropolitan area must contract.

Distinctively, given the concentration of part-time faculty in teaching, which is as much or more than any group of full-time faculty, the rallying cry of the "new faculty majority" is that their working conditions are students' learning conditions. Berry (2005) articulated what can be seen as a national-level campaign by unions as well as by advocacy groups like the organization New Faculty Majority. That campaign connects these faculty to goals of extending educational opportunity for lower-income students, running counter to patterns of heightened stratification embedded in academic capitalism (Berry 2005, 48). In short, amidst heightened attacks on faculty's collective bargaining rights, the least well-positioned and resourced faculty are reenergizing the academic labor movement and articulating a challenge to the path of academic capitalism (Rhoades 2008).

In addition to these organizing campaigns across the country, emergent national campaigns are also providing alternatives to the path of academic capitalism. The National Coalition for Universities in the Public Interest, dating to the 1980s, is one example (Noble 2001). Then, in 2000, David Noble, Ralph Nader, a number of major national locals (the California Faculty Association, the United University Professions, the Professional Staff Congress), as well as two national associations (the American Association of University Professors, or AAUP, and the Canadian Association of University Teachers, or CAUT) met to discuss a possible campaign.

More recently, the Campaign for the Future of Higher Education has emerged, holding a press conference at the National Press Club in May 2011, producing think-tank and working papers, and coordinating national actions seeking to shape public discourse and policy in ways that run counter to the course of academic capitalism (Campaign for the Future of Higher Education 2013; Rhoades 2011b).

Further, there are important examples of national associations taking actions to protect and extend the public commons in universities. That is a core function of the AAUP within the United States. The same is true for the CAUT, which in the past year successfully defended academic freedom in relation to corporate partnerships between universities and industry. In 2012, with the threat of potential censure, the CAUT successfully negotiated with two universities (Wilfrid Laurier and Waterloo) to rewrite a partnership agreement for the Balsillie School of International Affairs to de(limit) the ability of the donor to influence academic decisions in a partnership institute (CAUT 2012).

A fourth example of collective contest in negotiating a new academy is the case of managerial professionals. The rise of managerial professionals does not necessarily translate into greater managerial control of the academy. There are three ways we might expect and examine the active and independent involvement of these professionals in negotiating a new academy. One is that managerial professionals can organize at the campus or system level in collective bargaining units. A second is that as professional associations emerge around the work of these professionals, those associations may articulate goals and best practices that are counter to prevailing practices. A third way is that managerial professionals may be involved in negotiating a new academy at the local level, in initiatives that express a commitment to public functions of the academy rather than to increased privatization.

At the level of university governance, managerial professionals do not have the structural and normative independent involvement and voice held by tenured professors. Nevertheless, significant segments of these professional groups have some influence through being part of collective bargaining units. In some cases, such as the Academic Professionals of California, managerial professionals are organized in their own bargaining unit. In other cases, they are part of bargaining units with professors. Two staff unions in New York, which has one of the largest statewide and most significant citywide public university systems, are cases in point: the United University Professions of the State University of New York and the Professional Staff Congress of City University of New York represent managerial professionals as well as faculty.

In each of the above cases, professional staffs are part of collective bodies that articulate independent objectives that are contrary to those of management. Indeed, in championing the concerns of students in regard to access, tuition, and educational quality, these professionals are publicly engaging defining public policy issues of the day. They are important players in public policy debates surrounding higher education.

Another set of collective entities by which managerial professionals can exercise an independent voice in negotiating a new academy is their professional associations. Part of the professionalization process in the United States almost always involves the formation of national professional associations. These organizations help create, codify, and disseminate conceptions of "best practices," which can sometimes be at odds with prevailing practices in institutions. The National Academic Advising Association, for example, identifies a best-practices workload for advisors (i.e., number of students per advisor) that is inconsistent with what is happening in colleges and universities focused more on narrow conceptions of productivity, with student/advisor ratios that far exceed best practices (much like in the case of student faculty ratios).

Moreover, the professional associations of managerial professionals can sometimes be significant players in large public policy issues. A prominent example is NAFSA, formerly known as the National Association of Foreign Student Advisors (it was renamed the Association of International Educators in 1990, an example of their expanded role, shifting their identity from "advisors" to "educators," and from "foreign" to "international"). In the post–9/11 environment, this body pushed to retain open borders for the international exchange of students and faculty.

The point is, as these "managerial" employees become organized as "professionals," they develop structures and goals that can run counter to and be at odds with policy pushes for narrow efficiencies that come with academic capitalism and new public management. These large, sometimes global bodies can be important players in advancing certain dimensions of academic capitalism, from transforming higher education institutions into service providers to promoting forms of instruction that center high technology and decenter faculty. Yet these bodies can also play a role in countering certain aspects of academic capitalism.

Finally, an area worth considering in terms of research on academic capitalism is the extent to which managerial professionals at the local level resist certain organizational pressures or define alternative patterns of practice that advance more of a public good regime. One example in the literature is a study of enrollment management practices in an access university system. The study explores the ways in which local managerial professionals, despite a system directive to more actively recruit higher-income students, continued recruiting at the local, lower-income schools that have historically been the focus of their university's recruitment efforts (Luca 2010). Along similar lines, Kiyama, Lee, and Rhoades (2012) detail a progressive project at a public research university driven by a network of managerial professionals and faculty who are working at odds with academic capitalist goals and practices. It is important, then, in studying the extension of academic capitalism, to explore the ways in which professionals can construct alternative paths of practice.

Conclusion

The academic literature is not keeping up, neither empirically or conceptually, with changes in the structure of and relations among segments of the academic workforce. Patterns of academic capitalism globally have and continue to shape such changes. They extend to dimensions of academic capitalism that remain relatively unexplored in the academic literature.

This chapter identifies key dimensions of academic capitalism that have yet to be sufficiently explored in the literature. Each is suggestive of how we can extend our understanding of academic capitalism by foregrounding academic labor. Each enhances our understanding of how higher education's future is being negotiated through the collective agency of various groups, in this case between and among professional labor and management.

In closing, I speak to an additional set of considerations that should shape future research on academic capitalism. Thus far, academic capitalism has been conceptualized largely in terms of national systems of higher education. That was true of Slaughter and Leslie's (1997) comparison of the phenomena in Australia, Canada, and the United States. It was also evident in Slaughter and Rhoades's (2004) study of the United States. And it has been equally evident in Metcalfe's (2010) analysis of academic capitalism in Canada.

Yet just as capitalism is a global phenomenon that is embedded in and driven by multinational corporations that operate across national boundaries, so, too, it is with academic capitalism. Neither can be fully understood as staying within the confines of a single country. New models that address international organizations, activities of colleges and universities, and flows of students, professionals, and ideas are called for to fully understand academic capitalism. Three examples of a "glonacal" (Marginson and Rhoades 2002) consideration of global flows are considered.

In the realm of managerial professionals, and professional associations and policy bodies more generally, it makes sense to move beyond national boundaries to consider the international flows of key ideas embedded in academic capitalism. Consider the concept and practice of quality assurance, and the attendant heightened accountability processes that are aligned with greater managerial control of work processes and evaluation in universities internationally. Rhoades and Sporn (2002b) have traced the diffusion and adaptation of this concept through professional associations and international bodies, tracing a path that reaches across the Atlantic but then involves the active translation, adaptation, and promotion of such structures within continental Europe by Dutch institutions and entities, playing a longstanding historical mercantile role in circulating commodities—in this case, ideas, processes, and products in relation to quality assurance. The extent of the international translation is evident in the Organisation for Economic Co-operation and Development's Assessment of Higher Education Learning Outcomes initiative.

It is similarly important to examine global flows of professionals. European scholars have been more focused on such flows in academe (e.g., Enders 2005; Musselin 2005), perhaps because of efforts to shape a European academic labor market. One of the most compelling examples is the emergent and increasingly central segment of the academic workforce internationally: postdocs. In the life sciences, over half of postdocs in the United States, for instance, are international (Committee to Study the National Needs for Biomedical, Behavioral, and Clinical Research Personnel 2011). One important dimension to explore in the context of these flows is the structure of social relations between these professionals and principal investigators. For example, Cantwell and Lee (2010) offer a defining study of the neoracism and North/South dynamics embedded in these relations in US and UK universities. In the current global academic economy, First World science is conducted on the backs of Third World scientific labor. Postdocs are in a real sense the academy's international migrant workers, just as many part-time faculty are itinerant laborers in the fields of academe.

The implications of these flows and conditions of labor for academic freedom and the public commons in academe are profound. Particularly in the case of international postdocs, it is clear that these members of the academic workforce are structurally positioned in ways that doubly compromise academic freedom in science. They are highly dependent on their employing professors. Unless they are unionized, they enjoy little if any due process rights with regard to employment decisions. And they must understandably be concerned about their immigration status.

Finally, consider the flow of ideas and cross-border actions of professors' associations. In 2009, in recognition of employment rights and academic freedom issues surrounding contingent forms of academic employment at overseas campuses of North American universities, the CAUT and AAUP (2009) issued policy recommendations for conditions of employment in these global outposts. Notably, the cooperative statement defined principles of employment not just for faculty but for all employees, with a particular eye to the exploitation of foreign workers who build these campuses. Academic researchers would do well to study not just the cross-border initiatives of universities, but also the cross-border, international efforts to establish norms of policy and practice in the context of those initiatives.

In extending academic capitalism by foregrounding academic labor, it makes sense to examine the negotiation of a new academy not just locally, system- and statewide, or nationally, but also globally through the mechanisms, entities, and agency that extend like capitalism generically, within and across various political economic and professional boundaries.

NOTES

1. The terminology and percentages over time of professional employees in US postsecondary education are drawn from the National Center for Education Statistics' publication *The Condition of Education*.

2. The New Faculty Majority is a national advocacy group for full- and part-time contingent faculty. See their website: www.newfacultymajority.info/equity/.

3. The figures are drawn from the federal government's data on postsecondary faculty reported by institutions to the Integrated Postsecondary Data Analysis System and found in the National Center for Education Statistics' publication *The Condition of Education.*

4. That foundation is not what is central to academic freedom in various other countries, whether in continental Europe, where it historically has been grounded in the protected civil service status of professors, or in Canada, where due process protections are embedded in the collective bargaining agreements of colleges and universities.

5. Collective bargaining rights of professors in public colleges and universities, like those of state government public employees, are defined in the United States in state legislation and constitutions and are determined by state public labor relations boards. By contrast, the rights of professors and professionals in private-sector colleges and universities, like those of private-sector and federal government employees, are defined by the National Labor Relations Board.

REFERENCES

AAUP. American Association of University Professors. 2009. *On Conditions of Employment at Overseas Campuses.* Washington, DC: AAUP.

Abbott, Andrew. 1988. *The System of Professions: An Essay on the Division of Expert Labor.* Chicago: University of Chicago Press.

Baldwin, Roger G., and Jay L. Chronister. 2002. *Teaching without Tenure: Policies and Practices for a New Era.* Baltimore: Johns Hopkins University Press.

Berry, Joe. 2005. *Reclaiming the Ivory Tower: Organizing Adjuncts for Change in Higher Education.* New York: Monthly Review Press.

Campaign for the Future of Higher Education. 2013. http://futureofhighered.org/.

Cantwell, Brendan. 2011. "Academic In-Sourcing: International Postdoctoral Employment and New Modes of Academic Production." *Journal of Higher Education Policy and Management* 33, no. 2: 101–14. doi:10.1080/1360080X.2011.550032.

Cantwell, Brendan, and Jenny J. Lee. 2010. "Unseen Workers in the Academic Factory: Perceptions of Neoracism among International Postdocs in the United States and the United Kingdom. *Harvard Educational Review* 80, no. 4: 490–516.

CAUT. Canadian Association of University Teachers. 2012. "CAUT Withdraws Consideration of Censure of University of Waterloo and Wilfrid Laurier University." Ottawa: CAUT. www.caut.ca/news/2012/11/26/caut-withdraws-consideration-of-censure-of-university-of-waterloo-and-wilfrid-laurier-university.

Committee to Study the National Needs for Biomedical, Behavioral, and Clinical Research Personnel. 2011. *Research Training in the Biomedical, Behavioral, and Clinical Research Sciences.* Washington, DC: National Academy of Sciences, National Academy of Engineering, and the Institute of Medicine.

Eagan, M. K., and A. J. Jaeger. 2009. "Part-Time Faculty at Community Colleges: Implications for Student Persistence and Transfer." *Research in Higher Education* 50, no. 2: 168–88.

Enders, Jürgen. 2005. "Border Crossings: Research Training, Knowledge Dissemination, and the Transformation of Academic Work." *Higher Education* 49, no. 1–2: 119–33. doi:10.1007/s10734-004-2917-3.

Enders, Jürgen, and Egbert de Weert, eds. 2009. *The Changing Face of Academic Life: Analytical and Comparative Perspectives.* Houndsmill: Palgrave.

Fiegener, Mark K. 2010. "Number of Doctorates Awarded Continues to Grow in 2009: Indicators of Employment Outcomes Mixed." InfoBrief, NSF 11–305. Washington, DC: National Science Foundation.

Finkelstein, Martin J., Robert K. Seal, and Jack H. Schuster. 1998. *The New Academic Generation: A Profession in Transition.* Baltimore: Johns Hopkins University Press.

Fisher, Donald, Kjell Rubenson, Glen Jones, and Theresa Shanahan. 2009. "The Political Economy of Post-Secondary Education: A Comparison of British Columbia, Ontario, and Quebec." *Higher Education* 57, no. 5: 549–66. doi:10.1007/s10734-008-9160-2.

Gornitzka, Åse, and Ingvild Marheim Larsen. 2004. "Towards Professionalization? Restructuring of Administrative Work Force in Higher Education." *Higher Education* 47, no. 4: 455–71. doi:10.1023/B:HIGH.0000020870.06667.f1.

Kehm, Barbara M., and Ulrich Teichler, eds. 2013. *The Academic Profession in Europe: New Tasks and New Challenges.* Dordrecht: Springer.

Kezar, Adrianna, ed. 2012. *Embracing Non-Tenure Track Faculty: Changing Campuses for the New Faculty Majority.* New York: Routledge.

Kezar, Adrianna, and Cecile Sam. 2013. "Institutionalizing Equitable Policies and Practices for Contingent Faculty." *Journal of Higher Education* 84, no. 1: 56–87. doi:10.1353/jhe.2013.0002.

Kiyama, Judy Marquez, Jenny J. Lee, and Gary Rhoades. 2012. "A Critical Agency Network Model for Building an Integrated Outreach Program." *Journal of Higher Education* 83, no. 2: 276–303. doi:10.1353/jhe.2012.0009.

Leslie, Larry L., and Gary Rhoades. 1995. "Rising Administrative Costs: On Seeking Explanations." *Journal of Higher Education* 66, no. 2: 187–212.

Luca, Sandra Guillen. (2010). "Formal Policy and Enacted Practices at Regional Public Universities: The Orientation and Practices of Recruitment Professionals at the California State University." PhD diss., University of Arizona.

Marginson, Simon, and Gary Rhoades. 2002. "Beyond National States, Markets, and Systems of Higher Education: A Glonacal Agency Heuristic." *Higher Education* 43, no. 3: 281–309. doi:10.1023/A:1014699605875.

Mendoza, Pilar. 2012. "The Role of Context in Academic Capitalism: The Industry Friendly Department Case." *Journal of Higher Education* 83, no. 1: 26–48. doi:10.1353/jhe.2012.0002.

Mendoza, Pilar, Aaron M. Kuntz, and Joseph B. Berger. 2012. "Bourdieu and Academic Capitalism: Faculty 'Habitus' in Materials Science and Engineering." *Journal of Higher Education* 83, no. 4: 558–81. doi:10.1353/jhe.2012.0025.

Metcalfe, Amy Scott. 2010. "Revisiting Academic Capitalism in Canada: No Longer the Exception." *Journal of Higher Education* 81, no. 4: 489–514. doi:10.1353/jhe.0.0098.

Musselin, Christine. 2005. "European Academic Labor Markets in Transition." *Higher Education* 49, no. 1–2: 135–54. doi:10.1007/s10734-004-2918-2.

National Academy of Sciences. 2000. *Enhancing the Postdoctoral Experience for Scientists and Engineers: A Guide for Postdoctoral Scholars, Advisers, Institutions, Funding Organizations, and Disciplinary Societies.* Washington, DC: National Academies Press.

National Science Foundation. 2011. "NSF/NIH Survey of Graduate Students and Postdoctoral Researchers in Science and Engineering." Washington, DC: National Science Foundation. https://webcaspar.nsf.gov/.

Nerad, Maresi, and Joseph Cerny. 1999. "Postdoctoral Patterns, Career Advancement, and Problems." *Science* 285, no. 5433: 1533–35.

Noble, David F. 2001. *Digital Diploma Mills: The Automation of Higher Education.* New York: Monthly Review Press.

Powers, Joshua B. 2003. "Commercializing Academic Research: Resource Effects on Performance of University Technology Transfer." *Journal of Higher Education* 74, no. 1: 26–50. doi:10.1353/jhe.2003.0005.

Powers, Joshua B., and Eric G. Campbell. 2011. "Technology Commercialization Effects on the Conduct of Research in Higher Education." *Research in Higher Education* 52, no. 3: 245–60. doi:10.1007/s11162-010-9195-y.

Rhoades, Gary. 1998a. "Reviewing and Rethinking Administrative Costs." In *Higher Education: Handbook of Theory and Research,* vol. 13, edited by John C. Smart, 11–47. New York: Agathon Press.

———. 1998b. *Managed Professionals: Unionized Faculty and Restructuring Academic Labor.* Albany: State University of New York Press.

———. 2008. "The Centrality of Contingent Faculty to Academe's Future." *Academe* 94, no. 6: 12–15.

———. 2011a. "Whose Educational Space? Negotiating Professional Jurisdiction in the High-Tech Academy." In *The American Academic Profession: Transformation in Contemporary Higher Education,* edited by Joseph C. Hermanowicz, 92–110. Baltimore: Johns Hopkins University Press.

———. 2011b. "A National Campaign of Academic Labor: Reframing the Politics of Scarcity in Higher Education." *New Political Science* 33, no. 1: 101–18. doi:10.1080/07393148.2011.544482.

———. 2013. "Disruptive Innovations for Contingent Faculty: Common Sense for the Common Good." *Thought & Action* 29: 71–86.

Rhoades, Gary, and Barbara Sporn. 2002a. "New Models of Management and Shifting Modes and Costs of Production: Europe and the United States." *Tertiary Education and Management* 8, no. 1: 3–28. doi:10.1080/13583883.2002.9967066.

———. 2002b. "Quality Assurance in Europe and the U.S.: Professional and Political Economic Framing of Higher Education Policy." *Higher Education* 43, no. 3: 355–90. doi:10.1023/A:1014659908601.

Schneijderberg, Christian, and Nadine Merkator. 2013. "The New Higher Education Professionals." In *The Academic Profession in Europe: New Tasks and New Challenges,* edited by Barbara M. Kehm and Ulrich Teichler, 53–92. Dordrecht: Springer.

Schuster, Jack H., and Martin J. Finkelstein. 2006. *The American Faculty: The Restructuring of Academic Work and Careers.* Baltimore: Johns Hopkins University Press.

Slaughter, Sheila, and Larry L. Leslie. 1997. *Academic Capitalism: Politics, Policies, and the Entrepreneurial University.* Baltimore: Johns Hopkins University Press.

Slaughter, Shelia, and Gary Rhoades. 2004. *Academic Capitalism and the New Economy: Markets, State, and Higher Education.* Baltimore: Johns Hopkins University Press.

Smith, Vernon C., and Gary Rhoades. 2006. "Community College Faculty and Web-Based Classes." *Thought & Action* 22: 97–110.

Stephan, Paula. 2012. *How Economics Shapes Science.* Cambridge, MA: Harvard University Press.

Street, Steve, Maria Maisto, Esther Merves, and Gary Rhoades. 2012. "Who Is Professor 'Staff' and How Can This Person Teach So Many Students?" Policy Report 2. LOCATION: Campaign for the Future of Higher Education. http://futureofhighered.org /policy-report-2/.

Szelényi, Katalin, and Richard A. Goldberg. 2011. "Commercial Funding in Academe: Examining the Correlates of Faculty's Use of Industrial and Business Funding for Academic Work." *Journal of Higher Education* 82, no. 6: 775–802. doi:10.1353/ jhe.2011.0040.

Umbach, Paul D. 2007. "How Effective Are They? Exploring the Impact of Contingent Faculty on Undergraduate Education." *Review of Higher Education* 30, no. 2: 91–123. doi:10.1353/rhe.2006.0080.

Whitchurch, Celia. 2009. "The Rise of the Blended Professional: A Comparison between the United Kingdom, Australia, and the United States." *Higher Education* 58, no. 3: 407–18. doi:10.1007/s10734-009-9202-4.

———. 2013. *Reconstructing Identities in Higher Education: The Rise of "Third Space" Professionals.* Society for Research into Higher Education. New York: Routledge.

Whitchurch, Celia, and George Gordon, eds. 2010. *Academic and Professional Identities in Higher Education: The Challenges of a Diversifying Workforce.* New York: Routledge.

Ylijoki, Oili-Helena. 2000. "Disciplinary Cultures and the Moral Order of Studying: A Case-Study of Four Finnish University Departments." *Higher Education* 39, no. 3: 339–62. doi:10.1023/A:1003920230873.

———. 2003. "Entangled in Academic Capitalism? A Case-Study on Changing Ideals and Practices of University Research." *Higher Education* 45, no. 3: 307–35. doi:10.1023 /A:1022667923715.

Zumeta, William Mark. 1985. *Extending the Educational Ladder: The Changing Quality and Value of Postdoctoral Study.* Lexington, MA: Lexington Books.

PART TWO

ACADEMIC CAPITALISM
AND GLOBALIZATION

CHAPTER EIGHT

The Global Enterprise of Higher Education

ILKKA KAUPPINEN AND BRENDAN CANTWELL

In the first part of this book, contributors dealt with many theoretically and empirically challenging questions in order to update and challenge our ways of approaching academic capitalism as a theory and studying it as a phenomenon. A number of the chapters also included references to one particular topic, namely, globalization. One of the key tasks for further studies on academic capitalism is to analyze how globalization and academic capitalism are interrelated. This relationship was recognized already by Slaughter and Leslie (1997) as well as by Slaughter and Rhoades (2004), and we believe this relationship deserves further analysis, for instance, in terms of methodological implications of globalization for studies on academic capitalism. The chapters that follow concentrate specifically on the topic of academic capitalism and globalization.

There is a growing consensus that higher education is a global enterprise. Strong evidence underpins this assumption. The Organisation for Economic Co-operation and Development (OECD) finds that the number of students who study outside of their country of citizenship or permanent residence exceeds four million and grows each year (OECD 2012). Numerous league tables and ranking schemes compare university organizations on a worldwide basis, each using similar standardized sets of criteria, and normalize global-level competition (Cantwell and Taylor 2013). Policy coordination now occurs at the supranational level, and organizations with regional and global mandate—e.g., the Asian Development Bank, European Commission, OECD, UNESCO, and World Bank—have increasing influence over higher education (Bassett and Maldonado-Maldonado 2009; King 2009; Shahjahan 2012).

In short, the specter of globalization in higher education reigns large. As Musselin (2011) put it, "it is probably impossible to nowadays find a policy statement on higher education that does not start with a sentence close to 'In a globalized world . . . higher education plays a critical role'" (461). This statement is undoubtedly correct. Policymakers and university leaders often cite globalization as a motivation for reform. But what is perhaps most telling about Musselin's comment is that globalization, which is a relatively new term in the study of higher education, has too often come to be understood, by policymakers and scholars alike, as a singular megaprocess pressing down on higher education, simultaneously increasing the importance of higher education organizations in the global political economy and compelling them to respond strategically to a new global environment (Cantwell and Maldonado-Maldonado 2009).

This does not mean that research on globalization and higher education should be dismissed. To the contrary, much if this work demands serious consideration. But we should also be critical about the way globalization is understood in the study of higher education. Additional research is needed to develop more complete, textured, and nuanced understandings of how higher education— and more specifically academic capitalism—is transforming in an era of globalization, as well as how higher education might be advancing at least some dimensions of globalization.

Globalization Defined

Globalization, as set of processes including cross-border flows of capital, people, and ideas as well as the ascendance of a post-Fordist production model, has transformed (albeit unevenly) social, political, cultural, and economic relations worldwide. Given the enormous complexities related to globalization, it remains a concept subject to intense scrutiny and debate. A number of questions about globalization remain contested. For example, how old of a phenomenon is globalization? Is the core of globalization economic, political, or cultural, and how are these aspects interlinked? What is the relationship between globalization and nation-states? What are the implications of the transnationalization of social relations for individual identity, and for society? Is globalization about quantitative or also qualitative change? (See Robinson [2007] for a review of these debates.)

Nevertheless, social scientists from a wide range of perspectives agree that the study of globalization is paramount in understanding contemporary social arrangements (e.g., Castells 1996; Held and McGrew 2007; Robinson 2007; Sassen 2007; Scholte 2005). Many social scientists also agree on the following points: (1) the pace of social change and transformation seems to have quickened dramatically in the latter decades of the twentieth century, with implications for many dimensions of social life and human culture; (2) these social changes and transformations are related to increasing connectivity among peoples and countries worldwide (an objective dimension), together with an increased awareness worldwide of these interconnections (a subjective dimension); (3) the effects of globalization and, more precisely, of those more specific economic, social, political, cultural, and ideological processes to which the term refers are felt everywhere, albeit unevenly, and that different dimensions of globalization are interrelated (see Robinson 2007).

Of particular interest to the contributors to this book is the transformed role of knowledge in the global political economy. As transnational flows of people, goods, capital, and information intensify, and if economic growth relies on innovation more than manufacturing efficiency, the production and application of knowledge appear to have become key drivers in social and economic organization (Cowan and van de Paal 2000). Because higher education is heavily involved in knowledge production and transmission, universities are organizations of central importance in the global economy. But it is debatable whether universities should be seen as guiding social change, or whether they are becoming subordinate to a capitalist value system that reduces knowledge into measurable and transferable commodity (Patrick 2013).

Scholars of higher education clearly recognize the significance of globalization on the transformation and governance of academic systems, individual colleges and universities, academic work, and student markets. Thus there is an established and growing body of literature on higher education and globalization (e.g., Altbach and Balán 2007; Clark 1998; Currie and Newsom 1998; King, Marginson, and Naidoo 2011; Marginson and van der Wende 2006). Despite the development of this rich and sophisticated literature, the most common understanding in the field of higher education renders globalization as an exogenous megaprocess and internationalization as higher education's (often strategic) response to globalization. This Newtonian concept of a force (globalization) causing a reaction (by higher education organizations) is insufficient because it assumes that globalization is inevitable, and that universities respond in a way that is at once reflexive and intentional (Cantwell and Maldonado-Maldonado 2009).

While we wish not to offer too specific a definition for globalization, it is nonetheless important to review what we see as the processes' key dimensions in order to provide a basis for the subsequent chapters. As stated above, globalization in this book is seen as a set of processes that have contributed to the transnationalization of social relations. Globalization is further characterized by attributes described below that distinguish it from such phenomena as Americanization and Westernization.

First, globalization is multiscalar. It originates from a variety of activities on many geographical scales (Jessop 2003), implying that globalization cannot be studied by solely focusing on global scale. Instead, those actors and processes that originate on local and national scales also need to be studied if we are to develop concrete understanding on globalization (Sassen 2007). In terms of higher education, the implication is that globalization of higher education originates through activities on local, national, and transnational scales (Marginson and Rhoades 2002). The multiscalar dimension of globalization further implies that there is a need to study strategies and activities of a wide variety of actors ranging from individual actors such as academics and administrators in different universities, to collective actors such as entire universities and higher education systems, national ministries, and other governmental agencies, private corporations, and international organizations such as the OECD and UNESCO. In other words, it is important to examine how these different actors operate in different scales and network with each other in an increasingly competitive global field of higher education.

Second, globalization is multicentric. Globalization originates, though unevenly, from activities in many places (Jessop 2003). Immigration and foreign direct investments are good examples of those activities that do not originate only in some particular nation-state or even region. Thus globalization of higher education is not a process that can be explained, for instance, in terms of how US higher education institutions have aimed to expand their activities around the globe. While prominent institutions in countries with advanced higher education systems are no doubt influential, they do not alone shape global higher education. A central assumption of this book is that there are valid and compelling reasons for studying actors, networks, and processes that originate in multiple places across the continents, while at the same time recognizing that globalization of higher education has been, and is, an uneven process.

Third, globalization is thematically a wide set of processes. That is, globalization is affected by the economy, politics, culture, religion, and so forth (Jessop 2003). This is the commonly accepted starting point of globalization studies (e.g., Scholte 2005), but at the same time it is a much debated topic whether it is plausible to claim that globalization is primarily driven by some particular social force. In the context of this book, it can be asked whether the globalization of higher education should be explained by concentrating on the causal effects of some specific social system or systems, or whether it should be accepted that there is not any particular social system (e.g., capitalism) that can explain how the globalization of higher education is currently proceeding.

Fourth, globalization is multitemporal; it involves both time-space distancia-tion, or the stretching and increased control of social relations over time and space, and compression. The latter refers to technologies that have increased the speed of material and immaterial flows (Jessop 2003). For instance, informa-tion and transport technologies have facilitated such activities that have made possible the transnational securing of external revenues in the form of online education and transnational mobile students, as well as research and development (R&D) collaboration with transnational corporations.

Fifth, globalization is multicausal, meaning that multiple causal mechanisms lead to globalization. Globalization in itself does not cause anything. Rather, causation lies in those subprocesses that constitute globalization (Jessop 2003), implying that causal explanations should not be based on such overgeneraliza-tions as "globalization forces nation states to cut public spending." In the case of higher education, one example of a sufficiently specific causal mechanism (that simultaneously characterizes globalization) would be the establishment of transnational R&D networks that involve both private corporations and research universities and that are often promoted by nation-states (Kauppinen 2012). Such causal mechanisms sustain transnational academic capitalism.

Sixth, globalization is multiform. Capitalist globalization is not the only possible form of globalization (Jessop 2003). In the context of this book, the predominant form of the globalization of higher education is an empirically open question, the answer to which is likely contingent upon context. Capitalist globalization surely affects how the globalization of higher education is cur-rently advanced—which is assumed by the use of academic capitalism as a point of departure—but it is nevertheless important to understand that there is not any necessary reason why it always should be that way. Thus the future path of academic capitalism is also an empirically open question. Such an approach al-lows for the identification of the limits of academic capitalism as well as alterna-tives to academic capitalism.

This rather abstract definition of globalization is well suited for this part be-cause it leaves sufficient room for a variety of more concrete understandings under which authors will approach their specific topics. Our definition does not involve any a priori assumption regarding which social sphere is causally most important for the emergence of globalization, for example. Moreover, our defi-nition does not require the adaptation of methodological transnationalism (e.g., Robinson 1998) in any strong sense. Actually, the opposite is the case because we hold that globalization emerges from activities on different geographical scales. The chapters that follow take up a variety of units of analysis from individuals, institutions, national systems, and transnational processes. This heterogeneity of analysis permits a broad and deep understanding of the way academic capitalism interacts with other globalization processes as well as how academic capitalism plays out around the world in different national contexts.

Given all this complexity, it is plausible to claim that "the overall course of globalization will be the largely unintended, relatively chaotic outcome of inter-action among various strategies to shape or resist globalization . . . It follows that any account of globalization is likely to be partial and incomplete, exag-gerating some features, missing others, and risking neglect of events and processes on other scales" (Jessop 2003, 4). We believe that this complexity also applies to the globalization of higher education and related theoretical frameworks.

The Globalization of Academic Capitalism

As mentioned above, all theories of globalization of higher education involve a likely risk that, while shedding light on some dimensions of globalization of higher education, they also neglect some other events and processes that would be important to other dimensions of the globalization of higher education. In other words, we recognize that this book, just like any other, is not capable of doing justice for all the relevant and important dimensions of globalization of higher education. One simple reason is that the concept of academic capitalism is not meant to capture all the layers of higher education, as higher education cannot be reduced to market and market-like activities (see Marginson 2004). It is also plausible to assume that how the globalization of higher education is evolving is not reducible to any conscious design even if a vast number of organ-izational actors have been involved in facilitating the globalization of higher education.

We argue that by recognizing that nation-states are not the exclusive contain-ers of the networks and activities that characterize academic capitalism, a better understanding of the globalization of higher education can be achieved. But what do we actually mean when we speak about globalization of academic capi-talism? It can have at least two following meanings. First, it can refer to the global spread of academic capitalism in the sense that some aspects or layers of higher education in different nation-states involve, to different degrees, such networks and activities that characterize academic capitalism. But this does not necessarily imply that these networks and activities would be identical in differ-ent nation-states, but can be identified as concrete examples of the academic capitalist knowledge/learning regime (e.g., Kauppinen and Kaidesoja 2013).

Here the latter is understood as an abstract theoretical model, and this sort of understanding leaves it for empirical research to demonstrate how academic capitalism has been brought about in different economic, historical, cultural, and political contexts (see chap. 10 in this volume). In other words, this understanding remains open to the possibility that causal mechanisms explaining the emergence of academic capitalism in different nation-states may have both similarities and differences. Slaughter and Cantwell (2012), for example, support this latter point.

The second meaning is related to the first meaning, and at an empirical level there are overlaps, but it is nevertheless useful and feasible to separate them analytically. The globalization of academic capitalism thus may also refer specifically to those networks and activities that characterize academic capitalism but are organized and operate across nation-state borders and integrate both individual and collective actors operating in the spheres of higher education, states, and markets (e.g., chap. 9 in this volume; see Kauppinen 2012, 2013). Using this meaning, we can argue that academic capitalism has entered a transnational phase while acknowledging that it does not imply the end of such forms of academic capitalism taking place within the borders of different nation-states. This emergence of transnational academic capitalism is an ongoing process and, just like the emergence of global capitalism in a broader sense (see Robinson 2004), this process may take unforeseen turns and may have unintended consequences for higher education institutions.

Thus academic capitalism should be studied also in the context of transnationalization of social relations. This recognition opens up a new space to explore both methodological and theoretical questions while at the same time exposing an obvious need to identify and study empirical markers of transnational academic capitalism. These tasks are obviously so demanding that in this book we will be able to provide just the first steps toward this new set of methodological, theoretical, and empirical topics. But we believe that these steps are highly important and will offer many fruitful insights for future studies (see also Shahjahan and Kezar 2013).

By conceptualizing academic capitalism in a way that goes beyond methodological nationalism, we are not only able to develop an understanding of how various subprocesses of globalization (such as deregulation) affect higher education, but also the ways in which actors related to higher education have contributed—and are contributing—to globalization. In this way this book has the potential to contribute not only to higher education studies, but also more broadly to scholarly literature on globalization. Examining how higher education interacts with other globalization processes may help to better understand both the changing role of higher education as well as broader social and economic changes.

Part II of this book begins with chapter 9, by Ilkka Kauppinen and Brendan Cantwell. They argue that academic capitalism is enacted as a transnational process through the establishment of and participation in global production networks. They maintain that, analogous to industrial production, academic production is now unbundled over time and space and occurs through complex transnational networks that link colleges and universities with other actors in the global political economy.

Tuukka Kaidesoja and Ilkka Kauppinen in chapter 10 theorize the causal foundations of a shift toward academic capitalism in various places around the world. Rather than describing how academic capitalism works in linking universities with states and corporations, they identify social mechanisms that may explain what has caused a policy and institutional shift to academic capitalism. They argue that the shift toward academic capitalism can be observed in many places around the world. While the shift is heterogeneous, it can be explained by four generic social mechanisms: (1) global competition, (2) coalition formation, (3) legislation, and (4) organization design and redesign that encourage academic capitalism.

Chapter 11, by Alma Maldonado-Maldonado, evaluates the relevance of academic capitalism in the context of developing countries and emerging economies. She explains, in way similar to Jussi Välimaa (chap. 3 in this volume) but for different reasons, that the theory of academic capitalism, which was developed through research in the United States and other wealthy English-speaking countries, is not able to fully explain higher education in much of the world. Maldonado-Maldonado also offers a set of revisions to make academic capitalism more globally applicable.

In chapter 12, Hei-hang Hayes Tang provides an account of academic capitalism in greater China. Tang demonstrates that China, Hong Kong, Macao, and Taiwan have all made, to varying extents, a shift toward academic capitalism. As Tang shows, however, these higher education systems that share a common cultural heritage have taken divergent routes to academic capitalism.

Roger P. King argues in chapter 13 that risk management is now an essential consideration for universities. For example, globalization processes have created opportunities for universities to engage in academic capitalism by establishing branch campuses abroad. But King explains that such opportunities are fraught with risk.

Finally, in chapter 14, Ilkka Kauppinen, Charles Mathies, and Leasa Weimer consider what academic capitalism means for students. They develop a framework for understanding international students as commodities. Their work helps to identify how the globalization of academic capitalism is transforming the status of students.

REFERENCES

Altbach, Philip G., and Jorge Balán, eds. 2007. *World Class Worldwide: Transforming Research Universities in Asia and Latin America*. Baltimore: Johns Hopkins University Press.

Bassett, Roberta Malee, and Alma Maldonado-Maldonado, eds. 2009. *International Organizations and Higher Education Policy: Thinking Globally, Acting Locally?* New York: Routledge.

Cantwell, Brendan, and Alma Maldonado-Maldonado. 2009. "Four Stories: Confronting Contemporary Ideas about Globalisation and Internationalisation in Higher Education." *Globalisation, Societies and Education* 7, no. 3: 289–306. doi:10.1080/14767720903166103.

Cantwell, Brendan, and Barret J. Taylor. 2013. "Global Status, Intra-Institutional Stratification and Organizational Segmentation: A Time-Dynamic Tobit Analysis of ARWU Position among US Universities." *Minerva* 5, no. 2: 195–223. doi:10.1007/s11024-013-9228-8.

Castells, Manuel. 1996. *The Rise of the Network Society*. Vol. 1, *The Information Age: Economy, Society, Culture*. Oxford: Blackwell.

Clark, Burton R. 1998. *Creating Entrepreneurial Universities: Organizational Pathways of Transformation*. Issues in Higher Education. New York: Emerald Group.

Cowan, Robin, and Gert van de Paal. 2000. *Innovation Policy in a Knowledge-Based Economy*. Luxembourg: Commission of the European Communities.

Currie, Jan, and Janice Newsom, eds. 1998. *Universities and Globalization: Critical Perspectives*. London: SAGE.

Held, David, and Anthony McGrew. 2007. *Globalization/Anti-Globalization: Beyond the Great Debate*. 2nd ed. Cambridge: Polity Press.

Jessop, Bob. 2003. "Globalization: It's about Time Too!" *Reihe Politikwissenschaft* 85: 1–23.

Kauppinen, Ilkka. 2012. "Towards Transnational Academic Capitalism." *Higher Education* 64, no. 4: 543–56. doi:10.1007/s10734-012-9511-x.

———. 2013. "Towards a Theory of Transnational Academic Capitalism." *British Journal of Sociology of Education*. doi:10.1080/01425692.2013.823833

Kauppinen, Ilkka, and Tuukka Kaidesoja. 2013. "A Shift towards Academic Capitalism in Finland." *Higher Education Policy*. doi:10.1057/hep.2013.11

King, Roger. 2009. *Governing Universities Globally: Organizations, Regulation and Rankings*. London: Edward Elgar.

King, Roger, Simon Marginson, and Rajani Naidoo, eds. 2011. *Handbook on Globalization and Higher Education*. London: Edward Elgar.

Marginson, Simon. 2004. "Competition and Markets in Higher Education: A 'Glonacal' Analysis." *Policy Futures in Education* 2, no. 2: 175–244.

Marginson, Simon, and Gary Rhoades. 2002. "Beyond National States, Markets, and Systems of Higher Education: A Glonacal Agency Heuristic." *Higher Education* 43, no. 3: 281–309. doi:10.1023/A:1014699605875.

Marginson, Simon, and Marijk van der Wende. 2006. "Globalization and Higher Education." Paris: Organisation for Economic Co-operation and Development. www.oecd.org/innovation/research/37552729.pdf.

Musselin, Christine. 2011. "Convergences and Divergences in Higher Education Systems." In *Handbook on Globalization and Higher Education*, edited by Roger King, Simon Marginson, and Rajani Naidoo, 454–68. London: Edward Elgar.

OECD. Organisation for Economic Co-operation and Development. 2012. *Education at a Glance*. Paris: OECD.

Patrick, Fiona. 2013. "Neoliberalism, the Knowledge Economy, and the Learner: Challenging the Inevitability of the Commodified Self as an Outcome of Education." *ISRN Education*. doi:10.1155/2013/108705.

Robinson, William I. 1998. "Beyond Nation-State Paradigms: Globalization, Sociology, and the Challenge of Transnational Studies." *Sociological Forum* 13, no. 4: 561–94. doi:10.1023/A:1022806016167.

———. 2004. *A Theory of Global Capitalism*. Baltimore: Johns Hopkins University Press.

———. 2007. "Theories of Globalization." In *Blackwell Companion to Globalization*, edited by George Ritzer, 125–43. Oxford: Blackwell.

Sassen, Saskia. 2007. *A Sociology of Globalization*. New York: W. W. Norton.

Scholte, Jan Aart. 2005. *Globalization: A Critical Introduction*. 2nd ed. Basingstoke: Palgrave Macmillan.

Shahjahan, Riyad A. 2012. "The Roles of International Organizations (IOs) in Globalizing Higher Education Policy." In *Higher Education Handbook of Theory and Research*, vol. 27, edited by John C. Smart and Michael B. Paulsen, 369–407. Dordrecht: Springer. doi:10.1007/978-94-007-250-6_8.

Shahjahan, Riyad A., and Adrianna J. Kezar. 2013. "Beyond the 'National Container' Addressing Methodological Nationalism in Higher Education Research." *Educational Researcher* 42, no. 1: 20–29. doi:10.3102/0013189X12463050.

Slaughter, Sheila, and Brendan Cantwell. 2012. "Transatlantic Moves to the Market: Academic Capitalism in the United States and European Union." *Higher Education* 63, no. 5: 583–603. doi:10.1007/s10734-011-9460-9.

Slaughter, Sheila, and Larry L. Leslie. 1997. *Academic Capitalism: Politics, Policies, and the Entrepreneurial University*. Baltimore: Johns Hopkins University Press.

Slaughter, Sheila, and Gary Rhoades. 2004. *Academic Capitalism and the New Economy: Markets, State, and Higher Education*. Baltimore: Johns Hopkins University Press.

CHAPTER NINE

Transnationalization of Academic Capitalism through Global Production Networks

ILKKA KAUPPINEN AND BRENDAN CANTWELL

In taking stock of universities' cross-border activities, scholars have argued that there is a growing a trend toward "transnational" higher education (e.g., Altbach 2004; McBurnie and Ziguras 2001; Wilkins and Huisman 2012). Examples include, but are not limited to, cross-border research networks, branch campuses and multinational joint ventures, dual or multicampus university degree programs, and the development of massive online course consortia. While accounts of transnational higher education have always included trends such as cross-border student mobility, they have recently focused on multicampus universities that operate in more than one country. From a broader perspective, transnational higher education also includes participation in transnational research and development (R&D) networks linking universities with each other and market actors such as transnational corporations.

Multinational universities are important organizational markers of transnational higher education, but describing these organizations does not help to understand how we should theorize transnational higher education, nor identify what sorts of concepts would be useful in this respect. We approach the question of how to theorize the development of transnational higher education from the point of view of academic capitalism. In doing so, we argue that the concept of global production networks is useful for extending our understanding of academic capitalism as a phenomenon that is not exclusively nation-state bound.

In terms of analogy, as recent decades have witnessed the emergence of the global economy (e.g., Castells 1996; Robinson 2004; Sklair 2002), academic capitalism also has become an increasingly global phenomenon. We intentionally use the term "transnational academic capitalism" because empirical evidence does not allow us to speak more ambitiously about global academic capitalism. In other words, we feel it is not plausible to claim that academic capitalism operates all over the world, connecting a huge variety of actors into one single system that covers every corner of the earth. We further argue that the concept of global production networks helps to partially reveal the distinctive features of transnational academic capitalism (TAC) when compared to academic capitalism bound within a particular state. We also argue that TAC manifests itself in heterogeneous organizational forms. One such organizational form is an emerging multinational university. Multinational universities contribute to a shift toward TAC by participating, for instance, in global production networks in which the academic production processes are unbounded across space and connected to actors across nation-state borders.

TAC refers to such activities, practices, networks, and processes that cross nation-state borders and contribute to transnational flow of ideas, innovations, capital, goods, and people. Transnational R&D networks are composed of a variety of actors from different countries, for example, and these networks link higher education organizations to transnational corporations through different forms of research collaboration (Kauppinen 2012, 2013a). The concept of TAC also holds that individual researchers, research teams, and higher education organizations have increased the possibilities of securing external transnational funding (e.g., through the European Union's funding mechanisms). Overall, the concept of TAC holds that the nation-state is not the basis of all market and quasi-market activities and that these activities are not bound within national borders (see Kauppinen 2012, 2013a; Shahjahan and Kezar 2013).

In this chapter we evaluate the uses and limitations of the concept of global production networks to advance research into TAC. We further assess the types of organizations that may indicate the emergence of TAC through global production networks. Our focus is on building a conceptual framework, but we also draw on empirical examples to illustrate our argument. We begin by discussing TAC and global production networks—building on the concept of globalization outlined in chapter 8 in this volume—before considering how different organizational forms are contributing to a shift toward or are constitutive parts of TAC. We conclude by considering the advantages and limitations of the concept of TAC and global production networks.

Transnational Academic Capitalism

According to the theory of academic capitalism, policymakers, administrators, as well as some researchers, research teams, and departments increasingly understand knowledge as an object of commodification (Kauppinen 2013b; Slaughter and Rhoades 2004). As a commodity, knowledge can be transferred from one location to another, and between organizations, in order to establish a competitive advantage and to generate profits in (quasi)markets. Nation-state borders do not exclusively restrict these flows; nation-states are not absolute containers of the flows, circuits, networks, and practices that characterize academic capitalism.

We define TAC as an ongoing and open-ended integration of transnational dimensions into teaching, research, and service in a way that enhances integration between universities and globalizing knowledge capitalism. TAC increases opportunities for universities and individual academics to diversify external funding sources across nation-state borders. Thus our point of departure is the explicit assertion that the practices, networks, and circuits of knowledge that academics and universities use to diversify sources of economic as well as other forms of capital are increasingly transnational. This assertion enjoys indirect support by many others (Altbach and Knight 2007; King, Marginson, and Naidoo 2011; Marginson 2008; Marginson and Rhoades 2002; Naidoo 2003; Slaughter 2001; Slaughter and Cantwell 2012).

We do not claim that academic capitalism has become a worldwide phenomenon that occurs in all historically, economically, culturally, and politically specific national contexts. The concept of TAC is thus not synonymous with the idea of a single "global script." Instead, it refers to geographically uneven cross-border integration between higher education and knowledge capitalism. Examples include the formation of transnational innovation networks that link universities and corporations that are regional rather than global in extent but that have implications for the global political economy. One such example is the Universities of Applied Sciences Network (UASnet). UASnet links technological institutes in ten European countries with firms and government agencies and aims to shape Europe's position in the global economy. The stated objective of UASnet (2012) is "to strengthen the contribution of the Universities of Applied Sciences sector to the research and innovation strategy of Europe" in order to enhance the region's global competitiveness (para. 1). This and other examples show how higher education is integrating with transnationally mobile capital and those transnational corporations that are heavily involved in knowledge-intensive transnational economic practices (see Kauppinen 2012, 2013a). Transnational corporations are seen as key collective actors in global capitalism (see Robinson 2004; Sklair 2002), and we argue that these corporations are important actors (along with universities, governments, and nongovernmental organizations) in global production networks.

By discussing the concept of TAC specifically with reference to cross-border flows, networks, and activities, instead of referring to it as a sort of global convergence of national higher education systems and their respective organizations, we leave room for the possibility of "cross-societal institutional heterogeneity" (Beckert 2010, 154). In this way we are open to the possibility that "the existing institutional regulation is reinforced by the prevailing institutional logics" (Beckert 2010, 154) in each national context. This is the main reason why the idea of a global script is incompatible with the concept of TAC.

Furthermore, the concept of TAC does not suppose that the production of knowledge would take place within the boundaries of each nation-state, and that only the dissemination or distribution of knowledge commodities (whether patentable research results or educational products) would take place in international markets. Similar to the idea of the global economy (Robinson 2004), TAC is characterized by the transnationalization of production networks, implying that our definition of TAC is based more on ongoing changes within the realm of production rather than changes within distribution and consumption markets. From this perspective, the key collective actors of TAC are complex higher education organizations with production networks that stretch beyond nation-state borders and that also tend to operate (more or less) on global scales. But how should we conceptualize these production networks, which require us to step beyond methodological nationalism?[1] To address this question, we turn to work on the concept of global production networks, developed primarily by economic geographers.

Global Production Networks

The shift toward transnational academic capitalism is a multicentric process similar to globalization. In other words, TAC does not originate from any single country or region but involves actors from different countries and regions. That said, it is also safe to assume that some nation-states and universities have more significant roles in shaping TAC than do others. TAC is not an American- or European-led process, but some actors in these areas are clearly central to the process. The concept of global production networks provides a fruitful starting point to further develop the idea of multicentric TAC.

Our basic premise underlying the emergence of TAC is that universities are similar to "multiproduct firms" that operate on a transnational basis.[2] As multiproduct firms, universities generate a variety of outputs (Cohn, Rhine, and Santos 1989; Leslie, Slaughter, Taylor, and Zhang 2012), including student instruction, research, public service, and technology transfer. Traditional political economists, neoclassical and Marxian alike, theorize that the production of goods and services is a function of three factors: (1) land, (2) labor, and (3) capital. In industrial production, these factors are mobilized by firms and bounded organizations, which are run by managers on a local or national basis on behalf of owners, shareholders, or "stakeholders" (Davis 2009). The higher education analogue is of local or national universities run by the faculty and administration on behalf of various stakeholders with an interest in higher education, including students, trustees, the state, and corporations.

In addition to the classical factors of production, we also consider knowledge as the fourth factor of production. Retrievable information; research results; individuals' knowledge, skills, and "know-how"; and social capital (which helps to hold production networks together) are, similar to the classical production factors, raw ingredients in the production process. In other words, we see knowledge not only as a commodity output, but also as an input in the production process. It is assumed that knowledge inputs shape production processes.

Multisite production concepts have been developed to explain production that occurs in remote sites linked through the process of generating a good or service. Michael Porter (1985) has famously cast economic production as occurring through a "value chain" in which raw materials are converted into goods that are ultimately consumed at the conclusion of a multistep, multifirm process. Departing from value chain views, which emphasize linear processes and deemphasize politics and power, we draw from the work of economic geography (Coe, Dicken, and Hess 2008; Coe, Dicken, Hess, and Yeung 2010; Henderson, Dicken, Hess, Coe, and Yeung 2002), management (Levy 2008), and research policy scholars (Ernst and Kim 2002), who describe global production networks. A production network is a "nexus of interconnected functions, operations and transactions through which a specific product or service is produced, distributed or consumed" (Coe et al. 2008, 274).

We consider production networks to be "global" when they span national borders. For us, global does not imply that production networks cover every corner of the globe. Unlike value chains, which are linear and closed systems, global production networks are dynamic and interface with states, firms, public, and nonprofit and nongovernmental organizations. We argue that in order to understand global production networks concretely, there is a need to go beyond the corporate realm, and to also include noneconomic actors in the analysis of production (see Coe et al. 2010, 145). Unlike Coe et al. (2010), however, we include higher education institutions in our analysis. In this way we add a new element to the concept of global production networks. The term "production" in turn does not refer here only to economic activities (i.e., production of goods and services) but also other social processes such as the (re)production of knowledge, discourses, capital, and labor power (Henderson et al. 2002; Jessop 2008; Levy 2008).

Our understanding of the concept of TAC aims to take into account a wide variety of actors. The range of actors we consider probably goes beyond the traditional set of actors commonly included in higher education studies. We argue that, given the extensive involvement of actors, it is now plausible to conduct analysis that examines extensive political pressures and incentives to develop links between higher education, markets, and quasi-markets, as well as state-sponsored development and competitiveness projects in order to produce innovations to increase competitiveness of nation-states (see Slaughter and Cantwell 2012). In some respects, global production networks can be understood as similar to the "new circuits of knowledge" described by Slaughter and Rhoades (2004) in their theory of academic capitalism. Yet we extend this concept by emphasizing that these "new circuits of knowledge" operate transnationally because there is no inherent reason why these circuits should be contained by nation-state borders.

Global production networks shape the strategies of higher education actors. But higher education actors are also players in the global political economy. In other words, higher education organizations—and their constituents—not only react to their environment but also shape the global environment in which they reside (see Cantwell and Maldonado-Maldonado 2009). The idea that global production networks are dynamic sets of economic, political, and social relations though which the production process is unbounded across national and organizational boundaries supports this assertion. As Levy (2008) explains, global production networks are "integrated economic, political, and discursive systems, in which market and political power are intertwined" (2). We also assume that political and market power are tightly connected in these networks.

A variety of actors who may wish to assert governance claims or capture a larger share of the distributed benefits usually contest the stability of these networks. Hence the term "network" refers to the idea that there are multiple relational forms and directions (Coe et al. 2010). The study of global production networks does not assume that the production processes are linear and monodirectional (in contrast to supply-chain or core-periphery analysis; see Altbach 2004). Because global production networks are dynamic, their durability and predictability vary. Numerous actors exert influence and shape power relations between (and within) universities in the networks, which are constantly subject to change. Just as states can be understood as sites of contest between multiple interests, universities and the academic social sphere are also sites of contest and struggle (Pusser 2008), meaning that the shape and extent of global production networks are not inevitable or unchangeable. One example of within-university struggle with implications for global production networks is the contest at Yale University between faculty and administration over Yale's partnership with the National University of Singapore (the GlobalHigherEd blog edited by Kris Olds and Susan Robertson is a good source of information; see http://globalhighered.wordpress.com).

Given their multicentric nature (see chap. 8 in this volume), global production networks span multiple geographic locations, requiring that actors involved in these networks be able to coordinate their production circuits and integrate a variety of activities needed to efficiently produce the end products and services. "Production circuit" (Dicken 2007) refers in this case to production processes at individual universities that depend on a variety of factors, such as technological inputs (e.g., quality control), service inputs (e.g., human resources, insurance, advertising, and marketing), logistical systems (e.g., movement of people and information/knowledge), and financial (e.g., credit and banking), regulation, coordination, and control systems (e.g., laws regarding intellectual property rights). Each production circuit is in turn "enmeshed in broader production networks" (Dicken 2007, 15), including relationships between universities, governmental agencies, private corporations, and nongovernmental organizations. Following Holton's (2008) typology, these networks embrace elements of business, knowledge, and policy networks, further complicating the nature of these production networks in addition to their geographically multicentric nature. At the same time, however, these networks, which embrace elements of business, knowledge, and policy networks, exemplify the nature of academic capitalism, namely, the blurring boundaries between economic, academic, and state spheres.

Take for example the production of transnational education. Large-scale education of international students requires, among other things, coordination between universities and organizations such as recruitment firms that link universities with students, along with organizations that translate academic transcripts and verify language proficiency, states that regulate international student mobility through immigration policy, and an international banking system that facilitates currency exchange and wire transfers so that students can pay tuition and meet living expenses. Moreover, given the complex nature of these networks, they are subject to complicated governance structures at multiple levels (Levy 2008), such as organizational and disciplinary norms, laws, contracts, and other actors with market and political power. In other words, we assume that the norms that shape academic work, national and local law, and existing and new contracts are not subsumed by global production networks but rather interact complexly in the governance and maintenance of these networks.

Multiple Ways to Get Involved in Global Production Networks

It would be rather easy to state that emerging multinational universities, given their resources to stretch activities across the nation-state borders, are the only key organizational actors in the field of higher education when it comes to transnational academic capitalism. But we believe concentration only on multinational universities fails to fully understand the nature of this complex and open-ended process. For this reason, we provide an initial overview about the sort of actors that may have contributed and are contributing (intentionally or unintentionally) to the emergence of TAC through global production networks. First we discuss emerging multinational universities, as they are among the higher education organizations most capable of conducting transitional activities and participating in networks that both contribute to a shift toward and characterize TAC.

We are not the first to describe multinational universities as an emerging organizational form. Lane and Kinser's (2011) recent edited volume addresses multinational universities, for example, and their work identifies international branch campuses as central to the development of multinational colleges and universities. In doing so, multinational universities are defined as "institutions that have extended their academic operations outside of their home country with a combination of research sites, outreach offices, joint degree programs, and branch campuses" (Lane 2011, 5). Gallagher and Garrett (2012) further refine our understanding of multinational universities by differentiating them from international universities. International universities' activities extend beyond the nation-state in which they are located, for example, by enrolling international students. But international universities maintain production in bundled organizations, whereas multinational universities unbundle their production processes through global networks much like multinational corporations.[3]

We find the emergence of multinational universities as indicative of a transnationalization of academic capitalism through global production networks and therefore not simply a reproduction of the old hierarchical order through more complex organizations. These emerging organizations may rely on developing countries as inexpensive sites of doing research and may design degrees to match culturally and politically specific market demands in different nation-states instead of relying on a one-size-fits-all approach (Gallagher and Garrett 2012). This type of university organization departs from traditional concepts of "core" and "periphery" academic relations in which periphery organizations rely on the core (see Altbach 2004).

Universities may be taking multinational forms as a strategic measure to solidify their position and to capture a larger share in an increasingly competitive global higher education market (Gallagher and Garrett 2012). A related possible reason for taking a multinational form is the acknowledgment of shrinking funding in home countries. In other words, universities may recognize the importance of trying to secure revenue from other countries because available nationally based funding sources are either in decline or not expanding sufficiently to meet organizational goals. For this reason, the emerging multinational universities can be seen as organizational forms that contribute directly to a shift toward TAC. In advancing this argument, we build on the existing work on multinational universities by integrating this concept with the work of global production networks described above.

Gallagher and Garrett (2012) argue that the internationalization of higher education has reached, or is currently reaching, a third phase.[4] The first phase of internationalization involved international graduate student recruitment and the development of short-term study abroad exchanges. Phase two included the development of export education through fee-paying international students and branch campuses. During the third, more radical, phase of internationalization, "offshore activities and international partnerships are poised to play a leading role as universities come more closely to resemble higher education analogues of multinational corporations" (Gallagher and Garrett 2012, 2). We further assert that this third phase does not only imply that universities are adopting some of the characteristics of multinational corporations, but also that collaboration between universities and multinational corporations is intensifying, which in turn means that universities are becoming increasingly important organizations when seeking to understand and explain how globalizing knowledge capitalism operates (Kauppinen 2012a, 2013a).

Prestigious universities like Stanford and Yale are likely to have the greatest presence and most influence in global production networks. As Gallagher and Garrett (2012) note, these universities would "maintain their historic headquarters in the US" and "most of their highest value added work, including governance and strategy, will continue to be done at [the headquarters], and most global revenues will be returned there and remain controlled there" (6). Those universities able to slice up "the global value chain" (Gallagher and Garrett

2012, 6) present a threat to more traditional forms of international higher education. Instead of "seeking to teach large numbers of international students at competitive prices, multinational universities are designing education and research at home, using cheap but high quality labor and infrastructure abroad for their production, selling directly into the markets of their offshore operations, and reinvesting the returns in even more innovative products or cross-subsidizing the research programs" (Gallagher and Garrett 2012, 6).

The emergence of multinational universities will likely be disruptive to many tertiary institutions but is unlikely to upturn existing university hierarchies. If already prestigious and well-resourced universities become multinational and command, even indirectly, a larger share of available resources, in our assessment the result will be increased stratification and inequality among higher education organizations (Cantwell and Taylor 2013; Slaughter and Cantwell 2012). Thus the emergence of multinational organizational forms, and by extension the transnationalization of academic capitalism, may strengthen the position of already prominent North American, European, and Asian universities.

But does this mean that the United States or US citizens will benefit, for example? Assuming that public goods, such as pure knowledge, are generated alongside private goods that can be monopolized (see Marginson 2007), then it is reasonable to assume that US citizens will benefit but perhaps not more than anyone else. And even if the private goods accumulated through production networks by multinational universities are concentrated in the United States, we see no reason to assume that these goods will be distributed in a way that ameliorates current patterns of inequality and wealth concentration. At the most basic level, access to elite universities remains highly stratified in the United States, and groups of students who have been historically excluded from these intuitions have made little headway in gaining access (Bastedo and Jaquette 2011). We see no reason to assume that TAC will profoundly alter access inequality. Moreover, similar to global capitalism, transnationally operating corporations have gained more power within global production networks through foreign direct investments (Dicken 2007), which may also happen over time in the globalizing field of higher education.

We agree that Gallagher and Garrett's (2012) model well describes a type of multinational university but add that there may be other types of multinational universities as well. Further, there are also other ways more traditional higher education organizations might become involved in global production networks. For instance, the University of Helsinki in Finland is part of a set of knowledge and innovation communities (KICs) that operate under the European Institute of Innovation and Technology (EIT). KICs are specifically European-based transnational networks that are constituted by higher education organizations, private corporations, and public actors that originate from different European countries (EIT 2013). Additionally, globally oriented corporations seek partners around the world, and universities with whom these corporations have research collaborations may be both multinational and more traditional universities. In all of these cases, universities, regardless of their organizational structure, are drawn into global production networks and generate potentially patentable research results (e.g., Kauppinen 2012, 2013a). Such networks do not necessarily involve industrially funded research, but rather publically financed research findings are often channeled into industrial production through links with universities in global production networks (see also chap. 5 in this volume; Slaughter and Rhoades 2004).

Universities may be multinational not only in their roles as educational producers but also as knowledge producers. Involvement in TAC by executing "their research and teaching all around the globe" (Gallagher and Garrett 2012, 1) provides possibilities to leverage new sources of academic talent (i.e., to increase their academic capital transnationally), new sources of funding and financial support (i.e., to increase their economic capital transnationally), and new student markets (i.e., to increase their economic and academic capital transnationally). For multinational universities, at least in some cases, circuits of knowledge and accumulation of various forms of capital take place transnationally through global production networks. For multinational universities, academic production does not occur in organizations that are either autonomous or state directed and tidally situated within a particular nation-state. Rather, the means of production are embedded in a transnationally networked set of relationships that potentially include a variety of actors, including private corporations, governmental institutions, and nongovernmental organizations in addition to universities.

Universities that are involved in global production networks and the people who govern and control these organizations clearly do not see their respective nation-state as their sole field of action. Rather, their orientation is beyond the borders of their nation-state in a way similar to how the CEOs of globally oriented corporations orientate and identify themselves (see Robinson 2004; Sklair 2002). For instance, New York University "envisages a world in which the best students from all over the global [sic] can move seamless [sic] among its network of campuses spanning all the major continents" (Gallagher and Garrett 2012,

21). Moreover, it is likely that those who govern and control multinational universities do not identify themselves solely with their country of origin, or at least are developing other layers of identity for themselves (whether they fully acknowledge it or not). For instance, the administration and governance board of a university involved in establishing a research center or branch campus in another country must necessarily understand their role as actors who operate on a transnational, rather than strictly national, basis.

There seem to be tentative signs of some universities starting to evolve, at least in certain respects, into organizations that resemble multinational corporations. Such developments may also have implications for those who govern and rule multinational universities. Evidence from the short-lived ouster of the University of Virginia's president demonstrated that board members there closely identified with multinational corporations engaged in "winner-take-all" competition (Pusser 2012). And research by Sheila Slaughter and her colleagues shows that board members' industrial affiliations are predictive of the areas in which universities are generating commercial knowledge through patents (e.g., Mathies and Slaughter 2013).

Two Examples of Global Production Networks

We now turn to two examples of how higher education organizations are involved in global production networks. In presenting these empirical examples, we assess how they are indicative of a transition to transnational academic capitalism. The first example we consider is the Skolkovo Institute of Science and Technology (Skoltech), a recently established private research university located in a suburb of Moscow. The second example we consider is Coursera, a Silicon Valley–headquartered for-profit firm that is composed of nonprofit university consortia established to produce and distribute massive open online courses (MOOCs). We selected these examples because they may be involved in different aspects of global production networks and TAC. Skoltech is a single-site university formed by a transnational partnership and is primarily focused on research and technology transfer. Coursera is not a university but rather a for-profit firm that links many universities located in a number of countries in a network with global reach that produces and distributes products in the form of online courses.

Skoltech

The designers of Skoltech see it as an international university whose mission is to create educational, scholarly, and economic impacts both in the Russian Federation and around the world (Skoltech 2013). The development of Skolkovo into the Russian Silicon Valley is a government-led scheme (*Economist* 2012) that aims to integrate market actors and universities in order to boost the Russian knowledge economy as well as to have an impact also outside Russian borders.

Skoltech is organized into five clusters: information technologies, energy-efficient technologies, nuclear technologies, biomedical and space technologies, and telecommunications. Skoltech collaborates with foreign transnational corporations—including Alstom, Boeing, Cisco, Dow Chemical, EADS, Ericsson, IBM, Intel, Johnson & Johnson, Microsoft, Nokia, SAP, and Siemens Network—whose counties of origin are Finland, France, Germany, Sweden, and the United States. University partners include Ariel University Center (Israel), Ural Federal University (Russia), and Skolkovo Open University (Russia; see Skoltech 2013).

In addition to the transnational links described above, Skoltech has entered into a major partnership with the Massachusetts Institute of Technology, known as the MIT Skoltech Initiative. Given that MIT has made "the agreement to collaborate in building capacity in education, research and entrepreneurship programs at Skoltech" (MIT Skoltech Initiative 2012), and considering its other transnational links, we argue that that Skoltech can be considered an example of a university that has been established through transnational circuits of knowledge and whose aim has been to participate in global production networks under the assumption that it would benefit the Russian Federation's national innovation system. Skoltech's aim, with help from MIT and other public and private partners, is to become a unique, world-class graduate research university. Skoltech's strong economic orientation is demonstrated by the fact that as of December 2012 there were over 700 private companies collaborating with Skoltech in various ways (Skolkovo 2012).

As the institute explains, "Cooperation with international companies at all levels naturally integrates our project into the international innovation environment [and] plays a role of a link to products and services created by global players" (Skolkovo 2012, 1). In other words, Skoltech is engaged with a variety of transnational corporations in terms of research collaboration, and through these collaborative ties Skoltech is drawn into global production networks, specifically global R&D networks. Skoltech is a strong organizational example demonstrating how higher education can be integrated into global production networks through TAC.

Coursera

Coursera is a Silicon Valley firm that partners with universities to produce and distribute MOOCs. Andrew Ng, a former Stanford University computer science professor, founded Coursera in 2012. As of May 2013, sixty-three educational organizations had partnered with Coursera to offer MOOCs. While most of the partners are research universes like the National University of Singapore, Stanford, University of Tokyo, and University of Toronto, other educational organizations such as the Museum of Natural History in New York and the UK-based Commonwealth Education Trust have also partnered with Coursera. English is the primary language of instruction, but Coursera also offers courses in Chinese, French, Italian, and Spanish. As of mid-2103, approximately 2.7 million students had enrolled in a Coursera course. Coursera is a good example of the role of global production networks in the transnationalization of academic capitalism because it links universities, nonprofit organizations, and for-profit firms in a globally extensive network that is at once clearly related to knowledge capitalism and part of the traditional academic process of disseminating knowledge to students through noncapitalist exchange. Moreover, although individual universities reside within various national contexts, the network itself is not contained or controlled by any state.

Coursera courses are free for students to take, with no entrance requirements, no applications, and no fees to enroll. In this way, Coursera, like other MOOC platforms, reflects its roots in the open educational resources and open-source software movements (Weiland 2012). In expressing its corporate vision—"We believe in connecting people to a great education so that anyone around the world can learn without limits"—Coursera frames itself as transnationally accessible by eliminating the constraints of space, time, and social and financial exclusivity that have heretofore limited access to higher education. But Coursera (as well as other MOOC providers) differs from other open technology movements in important ways. Coursera does not offer technology platforms like LUnix or applications like Firefox but rather offers content-rich online courses. Exclusive (as opposed to creative commons) copyright protects the content, which cannot be tinkered with, added to, or modified in any way. Rather, the MOOCs produced and disturbed by Coursera are widely available and free at the point of consumption (and reconsumption) but not "open" in the sense that the underlying intellectual property may be modified and used by others for whatever noncommercial activities they see fit (Weiland 2012).

Like Facebook and Google before it, Coursera attracted substantial interest by tech investors even before it was clear if, when, or how it would generate positive net revenue. But Coursera clearly intends to make a profit. It is, after all, a business firm. As of July 2012, venture capitalists had invested $22 million in Coursera. It is not clear how Coursera will be monetized, but there are a number of possibilities. One is that it will sell advertising similar to Google, Facebook, Twitter, YouTube, and other Internet services that are free at the point of consumption. Another possibility is to charge students for certification of course completion (a sort of back-end tuition). Partner universities could charge tuition to their own students for taking the Coursera courses produced by their own faculty, or third-party universities might contract to offer Coursera courses with credit and for a fee (Young 2012).

We do not assume that profit is the primary motivation, at least in the short term, for the universities that partner with Coursera. So far as we can tell, there is not yet a substantial revenue flow associated with Coursera MOOCs, and universities only stand to capture a small share (6–15%) of the revenue that is generated from the individual MOOCs they produce (Young 2012). Then why have universities from around the world rushed to participate in Coursera? One possibility is that university administrators are afraid of "missing the boat" on MOOCs and a share of potential future revenue. Clearly there are longer-term possibilities for global revenue streams. Another possibility is that universities enter Coursera and other MOOC consortia because they yield access to information and technology that flow through the network. Participating in these and similar global course production networks also raises visibility and, like global university rankings, is a marker of global or world-class status that may afford access to other resources like top students and faculty. In other words, involvement in Coursera may provide universities opportunities to accumulate various forms of capital.

Conclusion

Global production networks offer actors in the field of higher education opportunities to operate across nation-state borders, and in this way these networks contribute to the transnationalization of academic capitalism. The spatial complexity of these networks suggests that the transnationalization of academic capitalism must be studied at multiple spatial scales, as its traces can be found at local, national, and transnational scales.

By integrating with multinational or transnational corporations through global production networks (e.g., global R&D networks), higher education organizations are not only contributing to a shift toward TAC, but also enhancing an ongoing shift toward global capitalism. In this chapter we have suggested that the emergence of multinational universities is not just about a new organizational form and the sorts of challenges these organizations will likely face, but also about how this new organizational form is connected to global production networks that are constitutive elements of global capitalism and act as complex nonlinear channels through which the transnationalization of academic capitalism has taken place.

We further propose that universities are playing a new, or at least expanded, role in the global political economy in which multiple actors seeking to accumulate advantage and shape the means of production produce commodified and monopolized knowledge or access to the transmission of nonproprietary knowledge. In this respect, the establishment of TAC can be seen as a strategic moment in these private players' attempts to secure and advance their accumulation of capital in knowledge capitalism. Also, we expect that universities have begun to establish themselves as multinational organizations in the interests of extending their own status, power, and resource base. In other words, universities enter global production networks in order to accumulate different forms of capital through their transnational activities by expanding the reach of their production networks beyond the boundaries of the respective nation-state, strongly implying that a need exists to continue work on methodological implications of globalization to higher education studies.

NOTES

1. See also Shahjahan and Kezar (2013) on methodological nationalism in higher education.

2. A key difference between business firms and universities is that universities, even those that are increasingly revenue seeking, do not seek to maximize profits or share prices on behalf of their owners. That is, even as we make the comparison between universities and capitalist corporations in the way they operate, we claim that universities are actually becoming businesses.

3. We use terms "multinational corporations" and "transnational corporations" as synonyms depending on the original source.

4. We find Gallagher and Garrett's strategy to draw certain analogs/parallels between multinational corporations and multinational universities quite interesting, but also think that in certain cases these analogs/parallels are clearly exaggerated and not plausible. In this chapter we do not focus on these problematic aspects given limitations of space.

REFERENCES

Altbach, Phillip G. 2004. "Globalisation and the University: Myths and Realities in an Unequal World." *Tertiary Education and Management* 10, no. 1: 3–25. doi:10.1080/1358 3883.2004.9967114.

Altbach, Phillip G., and Jane Knight. 2007. "The Internationalization of Higher Education: Motivations and Realities." *Journal of Studies in International Education* 11, no. 3–4: 290–305. doi:10.1177/1028315307303542.

Bastedo, Michael N., and Ozan Jaquette. 2011. "Running in Place: Low-Income Students and the Dynamics of Higher Education Stratification." *Educational Evaluation and Policy Analysis* 33, no. 3: 318–39. doi:10.3102/0162373711406718.

Beckert, Jens. 2010. "Institutional Isomorphism Revisited: Convergence and Divergence in Institutional Change." *Sociological Theory* 28, no. 2: 150–66. doi:10.1111/j.1467-9558.2010.01369.x.

Cantwell, Brendan, and Alma Maldonado-Maldonado. 2009. "Four Stories: Confronting Contemporary Ideas about Globalisation and Internationalisation in Higher Education." *Globalisation, Societies and Education* 7, no. 3: 289–306. doi:10.1080/14767720903166103.

Cantwell, Brendan, and Barret J. Taylor. 2013. "Global Status, Intra-Institutional Stratification and Organizational Segmentation: A Time-Dynamic Tobit Analysis of ARWU Position Among US Universities." *Minerva* 51, no. 2: 195–223. doi:10.1007/s11024-013-9228-8.

Castells, Manuel. 1996. *The Rise of Network Society: The Information Age: Economy, Society, and Culture.* Vol. 1, 2nd ed. Oxford: Blackwell.

Coe, Neil M., Peter Dicken, and Martin Hess. 2008. "Global Production Networks: Realizing the Potential." *Journal of Economic Geography* 8, no. 3: 271–95. doi:10.1093/jeg/lbn002.

Coe, Neil M., Peter Dicken, Martin Hess, and Henry Wai-Cheung Yeung. 2010. "Making Connections: Global Production Networks and World City Networks." *Global Networks* 10, no. 1: 138–49. doi:10.1111/j.1471-0374.2010.00278.x.

Cohn, Elchanan, Sherrie L. W. Rhine, and Maria C. Santos. 1989. "Institutions of Higher Education as Multi-Product Firms: Economies of Scale and Scope." *Review of Economics and Statistics* 71, no. 2: 284–90.

Davis, Gerald F. 2009. *Managed by the Markets: How Finance Re-Shaped America.* Oxford: Oxford University Press.

Dicken, Peter. 2007. *Global Shift: Mapping the Changing Contours of the World Economy.* 5th ed. SAGE: London.

Economist. 2012. "Can Russia Create a New Silicon Valley?" Economist, July 14. www.economist.com/node/21558602.

EIT. European Institute of Innovation and Technology. 2013. "Knowledge and Innovation Communities: What Are Knowledge and Innovation Communities (KICs)?" Budapest: European Institute of Innovation and Technology. http://eit.europa.eu/kics/.

Ernst, Deiter, and Linsu Kim. 2002. "Global Production Networks, Knowledge Diffusion, and Local Capability Formation." *Research Policy* 31, no. 8: 1417–29. doi:10.1016/S0048-7333(02)00072-0.

Gallagher, Sean, and Geoffrey Garrett. 2012. "From University Exports to the Multinational University: The Internationalization of Higher Education in Australia and the United States." Sydney: United States Studies Centre. http://ussc.edu.au/ussc/assets/media/docs/publications/1301_GarrettGallagher_HigherEd_Final.pdf.

Henderson, Jeffrey, Peter Dicken, Martin Hess, Neil Coe, and Henry Wai-Chung Yeung. 2002. "Global Production Networks and the Analysis of Economic Development."

Review of International Political Economy 9, no. 3: 4436–64. doi:10.1080/ 09692290 210150842.

Holton, Robert J. 2008. *Global Networks*. New York: Palgrave MacMillan.

Jessop, Bob. 2008. "Cultural Political Economy of Competitiveness and Its Implications for Higher Education." In *Education and the Knowledge-Based Economy in Europe*, edited by Jessop, Bob, Norman Fairclough, and Ruth Wodak, 13–40. Rotterdam: Sense.

Kauppinen, Ilkka. 2012. "Towards Transnational Academic Capitalism." *Higher Education* 64, no. 4: 543–56. doi:10.1007/s10734-012-9511-x.

———. 2013a. "Academic Capitalism and the Informational Fraction of the Transnational Capitalist Class." *Globalisation, Societies and Education* 11, no. 1: 1–22. doi:10.10 80/14767724.2012.678763.

———. 2013b. "Multiple Meanings of 'Knowledge as Commodity' in the Context of Higher Education." *Critical Sociology* 39, no. 4: 1–17. doi:10.1177/0896920512471218.

King, Roger, Simon Marginson, and Rajani Naidoo, eds. 2011. *Handbook on Globalization and Higher Education*. London: Edward Elgar.

Lane, Jason E. 2011. "Global Expansion of International Branch Campuses: Managerial and Leadership Challenges." *New Directions for Higher Education* 2011, no. 155: 5–17. doi:10.1002/he.440.

Lane, Jason E., and Kevin Kinser. 2011. "Editor's Notes." *New Directions for Higher Education* 2011, no. 155: 1–4. doi:10.1002/he.439.

Leslie, Larry L., Sheila Slaughter, Barrett J. Taylor, and Liang Zhang. 2012. "How Do Revenue Variations Affect Expenditures within US Research Universities?" *Research in Higher Education* 53, no. 6: 614–39. doi:10.1007/s11162-011-9248-x.

Levy, David L. 2008. "Political Contestation in Global Production Networks." *Academy of Management Review* 33, no. 4: 943–63. doi:10.5465/AMR.2008.3442.

Marginson, Simon. 2007. "Global University Rankings: Implications in General and for Australia." *Journal of Higher Education Policy and Management* 29, no. 2: 131–42. doi:10.1080/13600800701351660.

———. 2008. "Global Field and Global Imagining: Bourdieu and Worldwide Higher Education." *British Journal of Sociology of Education* 29, no. 3: 303–15. doi:10.1080/ 01425690801966386.

Marginson, Simon, and Gary Rhoades. 2002. "Beyond National States, Markets, and Systems of Higher Education: A Glonacal Agency Heuristic." *Higher Education* 43, no. 3: 281–309. doi:10.1023/A:1014699605875.

Mathies, Charles, and Sheila Slaughter. 2013. "University Trustees as Channels between Academe and Industry: Toward an Understanding of the Executive Science Network." *Research Policy* 42, no. 6–7: 1286–300. doi:10.1016/j.respol.2013.03.003.

McBurnie, Grant, and Christopher Ziguras. 2001. "The Regulation of Transnational Higher Education in Southeast Asia: Case Studies of Hong Kong, Malaysia and Australia." *Higher Education* 42, no. 1: 85–105. doi:10.1023/A:1017572119543.

MIT Skoltech Initiative. (2012). "Skolkovo Foundation and MIT to Collaborate on Developing the Skolkovo Institute of Science and Technology." Cambridge, MA: MIT Skoltech Initiative. http://web.mit.edu/sktech/news-events/pr1.html.

Naidoo, Rajani. 2003. "Repositioning Higher Education as a Global Commodity: Opportunities and Challenges for Future Sociology of Education Work." *British Journal of Sociology of Education* 24, no. 2: 249–59. doi:10.1080/01425690301902.

Porter, Michael. 1985. *Competitive Advantage: Creating and Sustaining Superior Performance.* New York: Free Press.

Pusser, Brian. 2008. "The State, the Market and the Institutional Estate: Revisiting Contemporary Authority Relations in Higher Education." In *Higher Education Handbook of Theory and Research,* vol. 23, edited by John C. Smart, 105–39. Netherlands: Springer. doi:10.1007/978-1-4020-6959-8_4.

———. 2012. "Mr. Jefferson, Meet Mr. Friedman: Governance, Markets, and the University as a Public Sphere." Paper presented at the annual meeting of the Association for the Study of Higher Education, Las Vegas, Nevada.

Robinson, William I. 2004. *A Theory of Global Capitalism: Production, Class, and State in a Transnational World.* Baltimore: Johns Hopkins University Press.

Shahjahan, Riyad A., and Adrianna J. Kezar. 2013. "Beyond the 'National Container' Addressing Methodological Nationalism in Higher Education Research." *Educational Researcher* 42, no. 1: 20–29. doi:10.3102/0013189X12463050.

Sklair, Leslie. 2002. *Globalization: Capitalism and Its Alternatives.* New York: Oxford University Press.

Skolkovo. 2012. "Investors." http://community.sk.ru/net/investors/.

———. 2013. "Partners." http://community.sk.ru/net/partners/.

Skoltech. 2013. "Home Page." www.skoltech.ru/sites/default/files/.

Slaughter, Sheila. 2001. "Problems in Comparative Higher Education: Political Economy, Political Sociology and Postmodernism." *Higher Education* 41, no. 4: 389–412. doi:10.1023/A:1017505525288.

Slaughter, Sheila, and Brendan Cantwell. 2012. "Transatlantic Moves to the Market: Academic Capitalism in the United States and European Union." *Higher Education* 63, no. 5: 583–603. doi:10.1007/s10734-011-9460-9.

Slaughter, Shelia, and Gary Rhoades. 2004. *Academic Capitalism and the New Economy: Markets, State, and Higher Education.* Johns Hopkins University Press: Baltimore.

UASnet. Universities of Applied Sciences Network. 2012. "About UASnet." www.uasnet.eu/about-uasnet.

Weiland, Steve. 2012. "Open Educational Resources: American Ideals, Global Questions." Paper presented at the annual meeting of the Association for the Study of Higher Education, Las Vegas, Nevada, November 14–17.

Wilkins, Stephen, and Jeroen Huisman. 2012. "The International Branch Campus as Transnational Strategy in Higher Education." *Higher Education* 64, no. 5: 627–45. doi:10.1007/s10734-012-9516-5.

Young, Jeffrey R. 2012. "Providers of Free MOOCs Now Charge Employers for Access to Student Data." *Chronicle of Higher Education,* December 4. http://chronicle.com/article/Providers-of-Free-MOOCs-Now/136117/.

CHAPTER TEN

How to Explain Academic Capitalism

A Mechanism-Based Approach

TUUKKA KAIDESOJA AND ILKKA KAUPPINEN

Empirical studies on academic capitalism have mostly described the changing relations and blurring boundaries between universities, markets, and states in different contexts. This chapter asks whether it is possible to take one step further, to develop systematic causal explanations of this restructuring of the systems of higher education. Our goal is to propose an affirmative answer to this question by outlining a mechanism-based approach to social explanation and applying it to the phenomenon of academic capitalism. We also suggest that when we are explaining the emergence of academic capitalism, there is a need to investigate how globalization and academic capitalism are interrelated.[1]

Previous studies on academic capitalism have aimed to provide not only descriptions but also explanations. For example, in their book *Academic Capitalism and the New Economy*, Slaughter and Rhoades (2004) write: "we present a theory of academic capitalism that *explains* the processes by which colleges and universities are integrating with the new economy, shifting from a public good knowledge/learning regime to an academic capitalist knowledge/learning regime" (7; emphasis added). They also identify several "processes by which universities integrate with the new economy" (14) as well as explicate an array of "*mechanisms* and behaviors that constitute an academic capitalist knowledge/learning regime" (15; emphasis added). Slaughter and Leslie (2001, 155) accordingly discuss various external and internal mechanisms through which concrete actors and organizational units have enacted or adapted to academic capitalism. They also write that, in comparison to competing theories that seek to explain recent changes in higher education, a theory of academic capitalism "focuses more clearly on mechanisms, enabling the identification of strategic points of change around which resistance can be mobilized" (156). Slaughter and Cantwell further extended this theory in 2012. One could thus argue not only that the explanatory theory of academic capitalism has already been developed, but also that this theory cites a number of social mechanisms and processes that are either constitutive of the academic capitalist knowledge/learning regime or have contributed to its emergence in various national contexts.

Though we do not deny that the research literature on academic capitalism contains important sketches of those processes and mechanisms that have contributed to the shifts toward the academic capitalist knowledge/learning regime in various national contexts, we nevertheless suggest that the theory of academic capitalism can be further developed as an explanatory theory because Slaughter and Rhoades (2004) do not specify in what sense the theory of academic capitalism should be considered as explanatory, nor do they specify their concept of explanatory mechanism. It is also unclear what exactly is the phenomenon or range of phenomena of which this theory is supposed to explain. As we indicate below, there are also some conceptual ambiguities in this theory.

The aim of this chapter is to advance explanatory research on academic capitalism by outlining a methodological framework for that purpose. The framework we go on to develop is based on the concepts of social mechanism and the model of mechanism-based explanation. We do so by building on some recent methodological discussions on mechanism-based explanations in the philosophy of social sciences and historical sociology. Drawing on the existing research literature, we also illustrate how this framework could be applied to the phenomenon of academic capitalism. Before addressing these methodological issues, we take a closer look at some aspects of the theory of and empirical studies on academic capitalism.

The Need for Explanatory Studies

In many recent studies on academic capitalism (e.g., Slaughter and Leslie 2001; Slaughter and Rhoades 2004), the concept of academic capitalism performs a double role. First, it is used to refer to a collection of empirically identifiable behaviors, activities, practices, mechanisms, and processes that are conceived as objects of empirical study. Second, it functions as a name of the theory that aims to explain the emergence of these empirically identifiable phenomena that characterize the academic capitalist knowledge/learning regime. In our view, this ambiguity in the concept of academic capitalism involves a risk of confusing explanandum (a phenomenon to be explained) and explanans (factors that are cited in the explanation of the phenomenon) in explanatory studies on this topic. Such ambiguity is one of the reasons we believe that more precise and explicit articulation of the methodological ideas that could provide guidance for building of causal explanations is needed.

In addition, though Slaughter and Rhoades (2004, 1) claim that the theory of academic capitalism is meant to provide an explanation for the recent restructuring of systems of higher education as well as for the blurring boundaries between universities, states, and markets, we nevertheless argue that research literature on academic capitalism has so far been mostly descriptive. It has focused on identifying and characterizing recent trends and changes in universities and in their relations to other social systems. Some studies have also examined how these institutional changes have given rise to increasingly contradictory demands experienced by various groups of academic workers in universities (e.g., Ylijoki 2003). As a result, relatively few efforts have been made to provide causal explanations to these phenomena. In addition, while the theory of academic capitalism provides a set of interconnected theoretical concepts that are useful in conceptualizing the recent restructuring of higher education systems, it nevertheless does not provide methodologically conscious causal explanations for the emergence of academic capitalist knowledge/learning regimes in various contexts.

There is nothing wrong with descriptive (in contrast to explanatory) studies in social sciences. Descriptive studies not only provide useful information for various practical purposes (e.g., policy making), but they are also often indispensable in identifying and specifying empirical phenomena that are worth explanatory studies as well as in providing empirical evidence that can be used in evaluations of the proposed explanations. Descriptive studies may also offer useful cues for the construction of tentative theoretical ideas and models about the explanatory mechanisms that have brought about empirically identified phenomena. Nevertheless, given the numerous descriptive studies that have addressed the phenomenon of academic capitalism in different contexts, we believe that the time is right to start developing more specific causal explanations to these empirically documented changes in higher education. As mentioned above, we acknowledge that there are some important explanations in the relevant research literature, but argue that these sketches can be fruitfully elaborated by using some fresh methodological ideas.

Because our point of departure is the mechanism-based model of explanation, something should said about the uses of the concept of mechanism in the academic capitalism literature (e.g., Slaughter and Leslie 2001; Slaughter and Rhoades 2004). In contrast to the notion of social mechanism developed below, the meaning of the term "mechanism" is typically left unspecified in the academic capitalist literature. It is also used rather ambiguously, as it refers to social entities and processes of various kinds. Slaughter and Leslie (2001), for example, specify a number of "external and internal mechanisms"—such as market contraction, increased competition, privatization, commercialization, deregulation of public entities, and interstitial organizational emergence—that involve "the enactment or adaptation of academic capitalism by concrete actors and organizational units" (155). Just like the concept of academic capitalism, these mechanisms have a double role in that some of them appear to constitute the phenomena that characterize the academic capitalist knowledge/learning regime while others could be seen as causal processes that have contributed to the emergence of this regime. Furthermore, Slaughter and Cantwell (2012) state that narratives, discourses, and social technologies are mechanisms that explain the emergence of academic capitalism. As we show below, our understanding of what constitutes an explanatory mechanism is different and more specific.

In this chapter we try to disentangle the social mechanisms that constitute the academic capitalist knowledge/learning regime from the social mechanisms that have brought about the restructuration of higher education and universities, resulting in the rise of this regime. In order to do so, we first specify the nature of mechanism-based explanations and social mechanisms.

Mechanism-Based Explanations and Social Mechanisms

Recent decades have witnessed discussions on social mechanisms and mechanism-based explanations in many contexts in the methodology and philosophy of the social sciences (for a review, see Hedström and Ylikoski 2010). These ideas have nevertheless received relatively little attention in the field of higher education studies (for an important exception, see Bastedo 2012). Here we try to change this situation by briefly introducing some of the ideas that we consider promising in the context of explanatory studies on academic capitalism.

Sociologist Peter Hedström (2005) states that "the core idea behind the mechanism approach is that we explain not by evoking universal laws, or by identifying statistically relevant factors, but by specifying mechanisms that show how phenomena are brought about" (24). Mechanism-based explanations are thus different from covering-law explanations, as the former do not typically involve any general law statements, nor is the deductive form necessary to mechanism-based explanations (Hedström 2005, chap. 2; Hedström and Ylikoski 2010, 54–55; see also Bastedo 2012; Tilly 2001). Because social mechanisms are typically assumed to consist of interacting social actors and their activities, mechanism-based explanations are also regarded as alternatives to functionalist and structuralist explanations, which either abstract from the social actions of concrete social actors or see these actions as inevitable consequences of the larger social structures or systems.

In addition, the model of mechanism-based explanation in the context of the social sciences is often connected to the Mertonian idea of middle-range theory (e.g., Hedström 2005), meaning that the mechanism-based approach is distinguished not only from "grand" social theories—which are often deemed too general, abstract, and conceptually ambiguous for explanatory purposes—but also from the tradition of correlation-based statistical "causal modeling," which is criticized for its eclectic empiricism and tendency to replace real social actors with statistical variables (e.g., Hedström 2005, chaps. 1 and 5). Nevertheless, the usefulness of statistical analysis in empirical testing of theories and models about social mechanisms cannot be denied. But what exactly are these social mechanisms that are said to bring about social phenomena?

Drawing on Machamer, Darden, and Craver's (2000) influential paper on mechanism-based explanations in biology, Hedström (2005) answers: "A social mechanism, as here defined, describes a constellation of entities and activities that are organized such that they regularly bring about a particular type of outcome" (25). Elsewhere, Hedström (2005, 2) makes it clear that in the case of social mechanisms the key entities and activities are social actors and their actions. Though this view is not included in his definition of social mechanism, as an advocate of methodological (or structural) individualism, Hedström makes an additional assumption that social actors in social mechanisms are always individual human beings. Mario Bunge's account of social mechanisms rejects this methodologically individualist view.

For Bunge (1997), a social mechanism is "a mechanism in a social system" (447). He also writes, "a social mechanism is a process involving at least two agents engaging in forming, maintaining, transforming, or dismantling a social system" (447). Social systems are in turn "composed of people and the artefacts they use to communicate" (Bunge 1998, 311), or, in the case of more complex social systems, they are composed of social subsystems. Furthermore, Bunge (1996) holds that all social systems are ultimately "held together (or torn asunder) by feelings (e.g., of benevolence or hatred), by beliefs (e.g., norms and ideals), by moral and legal norms, and above all by social actions such as sharing and cooperating, exchanging and informing, discussing and commanding, coercing and rebelling" (21; see also Bunge 2003; Kaidesoja 2013; Wan 2011). According to his CESM model of systems, every social system can be analyzed in terms of its Composition, Environment, (relational) Structure, and Mechanisms (e.g., Bunge 2003, 35–36). He thus ties the concept of social mechanism to that of social system.

Four things in Bunge's (1996, 2003) view on social systems (see also Kaidesoja 2013; Wan 2011) should be emphasized: (1) social systems have ontologically emergent properties that their individual members lack and that are not mere ontological aggregates (or resultants) of the properties of the systems' parts; (2) social systems are concrete and dynamical entities ultimately composed of people and their artifacts; (3) social systems are inherently dynamical entities that continuously interact with their changing social (and natural) environments (including other social systems), meaning that the members, structures, environments, boundaries, and functions of social systems tend to change over time; and (4) social systems not only interact with but also intersect each other, in the sense that most people living in modern societies are members of more than one social system at the same time.

Examples of emergent properties of social systems include the relational structure, norms, institutions, and cohesion of a system. According to Bunge (2003), emergent properties of this kind are not unexplainable mysteries because they are dependent on the properties of the parts of these systems as well as their mutual relations and interactions. They therefore can be explained in terms of the properties, relations, and interactions of the components of the system as well as, at least in some cases, in terms of their relations and interactions with their environment. But explanations of this kind do not eliminate the properties that have been explained from our social ontology, as "explained emergence is still emergence" (Bunge 2003, 21). Hence Bunge advocates a weak (or rationalist) variety of the concept of emergent property that should be distinguished from the strong forms of this concept because the latter deny the possibility to scientifically explain emergent properties of social systems.

What is more important in this chapter is that there are two points separating Bunge's understanding of social mechanisms from that of Hedström's. Bunge holds that (1) every social mechanism exists in some social system and (2) there are social mechanisms not just at the level of interacting individual human beings but also at the level of interacting collective actors, such as organizations (see Wan 2011). Both of these views run counter to the methodological individualism advocated by Hedström (2005).

Bunge's (1997) ideas on mechanism-based explanations suggest that, from the viewpoint of theory development, the most interesting social mechanisms recur in many social systems. Hence, though he tends to equate mechanisms with concrete processes, Bunge's (2004) concept of social mechanism is meant to explicate the causal interaction structures that a certain class of social systems shares and that drives systems of this kind—or "makes them tick." Furthermore, it can be expected that in all complex social systems composed of social subsystems there are many interacting and intersecting mechanisms operating at different levels of organization (Bunge 1997, 431; 2004, 193). According to Bunge (1997), it follows that "the mechanism of every major social change is likely to be a combination of mechanisms of various kinds coupled together" (417) and that "all unifactorial (in particular unicausal) explanations of social change are at best partial" (417–18).

We believe that the best way to understand the concept of social mechanism is to combine some ideas from both of these views. Like Hedström (2005), we emphasize that social mechanisms consist of interrelated and interacting social actors and their activities in certain contexts, but deny his view that these actors should always be individual human beings. In addition to social mechanisms that are composed of interacting individuals, we maintain that there are important social mechanisms in which the core actors are concrete social systems (in Bunge's sense), such as formal organizations.² Hence social mechanisms can be said to exist at different levels of organization in the social world depending on what type of entities they consist of. Following Bunge, we admit that many social mechanisms could be usefully construed as mechanisms of social systems (i.e., the interaction structures of social processes that result in the formation, sustenance, transformation, or dismantling of social systems) but deny that this point applies to all social mechanisms. In our assessment, his view that ties all social mechanisms to some social system is too limited for the purposes of developing mechanism-based explanations of social phenomena, as there appear to be interesting social mechanisms that are not necessarily connected to any specific (kind of) social system (Maynzt 2004, 243).

Drawing selectively on both Hedström's (2005) and Bunge's ideas, we thus maintain that social mechanisms could be best understood as structures of interlinked actions or organized interactions of many social actors (either individuals or organized collectives) that drive social processes, and that these mechanisms may (but do not have to) be connected to some systemic context. Sometimes it is also necessary to pay attention to the artifacts that mediate the actions and communications between these social actors. In addition, unlike what is sometimes assumed in the social mechanism literature, we believe that the concept of social mechanism does not imply a commitment to any specific theory of action even though it highlights the importance of environmentally embedded social action in explanations of social phenomena (Kaidesoja 2012;

Maynzt 2004). This understanding entails the possibility of utilizing conceptual resources of different action theories for different explanatory purposes and that, for some explanatory purposes, collectives (e.g., formal organizations) may be regarded as social actors.

Social Mechanisms Contributing to the Emergence of Academic Capitalism

There are some plausible candidates for social mechanism that have contributed to the emergence of the academic capitalist knowledge/learning regime in the United States and elsewhere. Here we focus on social mechanisms that (1) are compatible with the previous characterization of this concept; (2) have been mentioned in, or assumed by, the existing research literature on academic capitalism (though not always termed social mechanisms); and (3) can be considered as explanatory mechanisms in the sense that they have participated in the causal generation of the academic capitalist knowledge/learning regime by restructuring higher education and universities in the United States as well as in other contexts. We suggest that there are at least four generic mechanisms that meet these requirements: global economic competition, coalition formation, legislation, and organization design (and redesign).

Here we view narratives, discourses, and social technologies as components of social mechanisms of different kinds rather than as distinct social mechanisms (cf. Slaughter and Cantwell 2012) because we like to stress that interacting social actors of various kinds always (re)produce, circulate, and use these entities in order to achieve certain objectives or to pursue their interests—regardless of whether they are successful. It is also methodologically important to emphasize that narratives and discourses are often embedded in artifacts like strategy papers, reports, policy programs, university rules, and legislative texts generated and circulated by various social actors for various purposes. Insofar as we are interested in mechanism-based explanations of social phenomena, it is not enough to focus only on the abstract contents of these texts, but they should be rather seen as artifactual components of social systems and mechanisms of various kinds.

Global Economic Competition

The rise of the neoliberalist ideology promoted by the Reagan and Thatcher administrations (among others), the collapse of the Soviet Union and its satellite countries, the end of Cold War, the deregulation of capital flows in and between many countries, as well as the invention and diffusion of new information and communication technology tools and infrastructures have all contributed to a new round of globalization of the capitalist economy that accompanied the intensification of the global economic competition. Intensified global economic competition in turn characterizes the social environment of higher education systems throughout the world. But how exactly should we understand the mechanism of global economic competition?

In general terms, competition can be seen as a process whereby two or more social actors pursue the same scarce resource in mutually exclusive ways that over time result in the uneven distribution of this resource between the competing actors and the increased efficiency (in some respect) of the most successful actors (i.e., the winners of the competition). It is then possible to apply this abstract mechanism scheme to more concrete processes of competition, such as global economic competition between companies for market shares and profits in global markets or competition between states for drawing new investments and mobile economic capital to a country by means of creating institutional environments (e.g., in terms of a national innovation system and low taxation) that advance the competitiveness of companies in a country. These competition mechanisms could be further specified, for example, by relying on theories of global capitalism (e.g., Centeno and Cohen 2010; Robinson 2004; Sklair 2002). But all processes of competition are regulated by moral or legal norms (or both), which is what separates competition from war or violence. The processes of global economic competition related to global capitalism thus presuppose a historically created institutional framework. Though different mechanisms of global economic competition could be further theoretically specified, here we nevertheless rely on more intuitive understandings of these mechanisms and consider their relation to academic capitalism.

The mechanisms of economic competition between private companies (both national and transnational), regional industries, and national economies can be considered one of the key drivers of the development toward academic capitalism. Increasing economic competition between companies in global markets accompanied by the recent crises of global capitalism have created serious fiscal problems for rich industrial states, resulting in cuts to public spending as well as searches for new sources of revenues. Given the intensified global economic competition, current political climate, massification of higher education, and decreased budget funding, universities have been forced to search for new sources of external funding to cover their operational expenditures. They have also faced intensified expectations to contribute to the new knowledge-driven economy by means of more efficient commodification and commercialization of the results of scientific research and education services (see Rhoades, Maldonado-Maldonado, Ordorika, and Velásquez 2004; Slaughter and Cantwell

2012; Slaughter and Leslie 1997; Slaughter and Rhoades 2004). As discussed below, neoliberalist ideology and the related competitiveness narrative are essential elements in understanding how various social actors—who are responsible for science and education policy, university legislation, university administration, as well as applied research—responded to the outcomes of the increasing global economic competition.

There are also competition mechanisms that characterize (or constitute) the academic capitalist knowledge/learning regime, including competition between universities for wealthy and bright students as well as for external funding and rankings, competition between departments for budget funds and external funding, and competition between research teams and individual researchers for prestige and external funding. Also, many of these competition mechanisms are by nature transnational or even global (e.g., student markets; see chap. 14 in this volume).

Creation, diffusion, and intensification of these types of competition mechanisms and respective markets that constitute the academic capitalist knowledge/learning regime, however, can be seen as consequences of the workings of the explanatory mechanisms that we have identified here rather than as generators of the institutional restructuring of higher education. For example, not only new legislation and regulation policies produced by powerful political coalitions but also designing (and redesigning) of both intermediating and interstitial organizations by academic and nonacademic actors have enabled universities to act more smoothly in various types of markets as well as to create new types of "academic quasi-markets" (e.g., building new kinds of funding mechanisms of universities that are based on the competition between departments in terms of their academic production). Nonetheless, for other explanatory purposes, these types of competition mechanisms may well be seen as explanatory.

Coalition Formation

Coalition formation can be defined generally as a process in which a temporal alliance or union between two or more individuals or groups is established for some specific purpose. Coalition formation between individuals or groups thus requires the creation of a shared representation of the aims of the coalition, which often demands compromises between parties. In order to achieve its intended aims (such as certain kind of new legislation), a coalition often draws upon the expertise (e.g., to identify the problem and to provide information) and framing skills (e.g., to translate some specific issue into an instrument of policy making) of its members (see Sell and Prakash 2004).

In the US context, Slaughter and Rhoades (1996, 2004, chap. 2) have analyzed the formation of the political competitiveness coalition that, according to
their view, followed and partially intersected the Cold War / health war coalition.
The competitiveness coalition was gradually formed during 1970s. Its aims
were to: "(1) win control of global markets through privatization and commodification of intellectual property; (2) establish government subsidies for high-
technology and producer services industries; and (3) move R&D, including
university R&D, toward commercial science and technology" (Slaughter and
Rhoades 1996, 314). According to their analysis, this coalition was composed
not only of the Republican Party and most Democrats but also of state and local
governments, universities (or certain groups within universities), and certain
corporations (Slaughter and Rhoades 1996, 308). Profound changes in defense,
health, agricultural, and insurance industries that facilitated the interests of
companies to promote the new competitiveness coalition in R&D policy pre-
ceded the formation of this coalition (Slaughter and Rhoades 1996).

In order to pursue these goals, the coalition rewrote "the narrative that privileged basic science" in a way that promoted "a more commercial science and technology" (Slaughter and Rhoades 1996, 307) in order to secure the competitiveness
of the private companies in the United States. In the new competitiveness narrative, "knowledge was valued not for its own sake, or for what it might someday
contribute to economic development, but for its contribution to the creation of
products and processes for the market of the moment" (Slaughter and Rhoades
1996, 317). The coalition then employed this narrative as a source of reasons to
publicly justify new legal reforms and university policies. As we shall see, the
mechanism of coalition formation is tightly interconnected to that of legislation.

At the transnational level we can identify a formation of a similar competitiveness coalition within Europe in the 1980s. In crude terms, the key actors of this
European-wide coalition were the transnational policy-making group European
Round Table of Industrialists (ERT) and European political leaders (especially the
European Commission). This coalition successfully promoted the competitiveness agenda and, more broadly, the Single European Market project (e.g., Bradanini 2009; van Apeldoorn 2000, 2002). And, just like in the case of US-based
business leaders (see Slaughter and Rhoades 1996), the ERT was also reacting in
many ways to destabilizing events, external threats, and perceived problems and
challenges. In the European context, these included the advantages of both the
United States and Japan in terms of university-industry collaboration, threats
posed by the emerging East Asian economic competitors, and the fragmentation
of European higher education. One of the aims of this coalition was to restructure

European higher education in a way that would strengthen linkages between higher education and industry between and in European national states (Kauppinen 2014). This example nicely illustrates how a shift toward academic capitalism in Europe cannot be explained by referring only to the social mechanisms that take place within nation-state borders. Rather, we should remain open to the possibility that at least some of these social mechanisms are constituted across nation-state borders. The same applies to legislation.

Legislation

The legislation process proceeds somewhat differently depending on the context even though in most cases it has an identifiable interaction structure. In parliamentary democracies, legislation usually involves the following steps: (1) preparation of the legislation proposal; (2) a parliamentary process that leads to either acceptance or rejection of the proposal; and (3) implementation of the accepted law. It also typically involves state agencies, political parties, and lobbyists (e.g., interest organizations) of various kinds.

As emphasized by Slaughter and Rhoades (1996, 2004), many of the laws that enabled and created new opportunities for academic capitalist activities and practices in US universities were supported by a bipartisan coalition in the Congress that was receptive to the competitiveness narrative. They also importantly indicate that, although the congressional coalition that "legislated the privatization and commercialization of federal research" was "bipartisan, it was political" (Slaughter and Rhoades 2004, 229). "The coalition drew together Democrats and Republicans who worked with the business class . . . to develop neoliberal policies that fostered privatization, deregulation, and commercialization under state auspices and with state support" (Slaughter and Rhoades 2004, 229). So there is an important connection between the mechanisms of coalition formation and legislation.

In general, empirical studies on academic capitalism have focused on "national and international legislation, treaties, and trade agreements that create opportunities for academic capitalism in postsecondary education" (Slaughter and Rhoades 2004, 35) as well as in research universities (Slaughter and Rhoades 2004, chaps. 2 and 3). For example, legislation that pertains to US academic capitalism at federal, state, and international scales includes the following laws (for a more complete list, see Slaughter and Rhoades 1996, 317):

- 1980 Public Law 65–517, the Bayh-Dole Act, and Reagan's 1983 memo on government patent policy;
- 1984 Public Law 98–462, National Cooperative Research Act;

- 1988 Public Law 100–418, Omnibus Trade and Competitiveness Act;
- 1993 Public Law 103–182, North American Free Trade Agreement; and
- 1994 Public Law 103–465, General Agreement on Tariffs and Trade.

Similar legislative changes have been discussed in other national contexts. As already noted, however, it is not only national legislation that has contributed directly or indirectly to the shift toward academic capitalism, but also international legislation. For instance, the Trade-Related Aspects of Intellectual Property Rights agreement of the World Trade Organization (WTO) facilitated universities' patenting activities, and hence a shift toward academic capitalism, in WTO member countries because it strengthened the protection of intellectual property (IP) and broadened the category of IP (Kauppinen 2012). Various studies have revealed how the promotion of this agreement was a transnational process and that some of the main actors in this respect were transnational corporations (e.g., Braithwaite and Drahos 2000; Kauppinen 2012; Sell 2003). Also, this example suggests that methodological nationalism is an inadequate framework to explain a shift toward academic capitalism both in some particular nation-state and a region (e.g., Europe).

As Slaughter and Rhoades (1996, 323–24) indicate, the legislation mechanism is related to the mechanisms of organization design and redesign: new legislation that promoted the competitiveness of US companies by removing the barriers of fluid capital from the boundaries between private, nonprofit, and public organizations enabled the emergence of new types of intermediating organizations between universities and markets, which in turn blurred the boundaries between universities, markets, and states (see Slaughter and Rhoades 2004, chap. 2). Legislation may thus be understood as one of the most important social mechanisms contributing to academic capitalism in the United States as well as at the transnational scale (e.g., restructuring European higher education), as new legislation enabled and stimulated the emergence of novel organizations, activities, and practices that characterize academic capitalism.

Organization Design and Redesign

The creation of intermediating and interstitial organizations is one of the key elements of the theory of academic capitalism. These organizations promote and create policies, practices, and activities that characterize the academic capitalist knowledge/learning regime, as well as blur the boundaries between markets, state, and universities (Slaughter and Rhoades 2004). Here we emphasize that intermediating and interstitial organizations have been all designed in the sense that they did not emerge spontaneously. Rather, they were intentionally established by means of design plans, policies, and blueprints developed by specific social actors in order to secure and increase external resources of their universities in competition against other universities. Some of these organizations were also generated by redesigning previously existing organizations within universities.

Though we regard design and redesign of organizations as important social mechanisms contributing to the emergence of the academic capitalist knowledge/learning regime, we emphasize that the implementation of the plans, policies, and blueprints of designers tend to produce both intended and unintended consequences. In other words, it is an empirical matter to what extent the designed organizations have succeeded to meet their designers' objectives and what kind of unexpected side effects the workings of these organizations have brought about. In addition, particular aims and plans of designers do not come out of the thin air, but institutional and cultural environments have a rather heavy influence. For this reason, we also address some mechanisms that mold the entire organizational field through affecting the activities and plans of organization designers.

Social mechanisms operating at the level of organizational fields have been discussed under the institutional isomorphism literature. They are typically invoked in explanations of why organizations of certain kind, such as universities, tend to become structurally similar to each other within a particular organizational field (e.g., DiMaggio and Powell 1983). These well-known mechanisms can be labeled as mechanisms of coercion, mimesis, and attraction (Beckert 2010; DiMaggio and Powell 1983). In the case of European and Latin American higher education systems, for example, many designers of new higher education organizations (and redesigners of the old systems) imitated the organizations and policies of US universities (cf. mimesis) that they considered successful as well as tried to translate them to meet the requirements of local institutional contexts (cf. coercion; see Rhoades et al. 2004; Slaughter and Cantwell 2012). We do not assume that these mechanisms necessarily push higher education organizations toward homogenization; however (following Beckert 2010), those same mechanisms (depending on conditions) may also lead toward divergence and, in this case, divergent organizational ways to adopt and participate in those networks and activities that characterize academic capitalism. This assumption is in line with the idea that there is not just one but many types of academic capitalism (e.g., Slaughter and Leslie 1997; Slaughter and Rhoades 2004). Furthermore, we assume this divergence can be found both between and within nation-states.

We also include a fourth mechanism to the previous list—competition between organizations (see Beckert 2010)—that may or may not contribute to academic capitalism in various contexts, as competitive pressures can lead either to the homogenization or diversification of organizations in a field depending on the interpretations of the designers (and redesigners) of the organizations in different contexts. It may also contribute to the hybridization of academic capitalism in various national contexts because the competition may lead to the (re)design of "diverse political-legal rules and organizational models that allow for niches" (Beckert 2010, 160) in which universities may specialize.

The key here is that mechanisms operating at the level of organizational fields can trigger and influence organization design and redesign.[3] The questions of under which conditions these mechanisms would contribute to the homogenization and when heterogenization would occur are fundamentally empirical. Organizations that are developed in some African, Asian, or European countries do not have to be exact copies of the organizations found in the United States in order to qualify as organizational examples of academic capitalism. Just as it makes sense to speak about various capitalist economic systems, it makes sense to consider varieties of academic capitalism and respective organizations for numerous reasons (e.g., differences in regulatory environment).

Moreover, social technologies, such as European-level benchmarking (e.g., Slaughter and Cantwell 2012) and global university rankings, can help produce structural similarity by advancing competition through identifying what types of universities are successful in global competition over prestige. As far as these university types are successful not only in terms of how prestigious they seem but also in terms of operating in markets or interacting with market actors (either nationally or transnationally), one might suggest that there are regionally or even globally affective mechanisms (e.g., competition and "soft" coercion) that tend to encourage academic capitalism at organizational levels in different countries and regions. In such cases, organizational (re)designers are both pushed and pulled toward certain types of solutions. Furthermore, as has been well documented by empirical research on academic capitalism (e.g., Rhoades et al. 2004; Slaughter and Cantwell 2012), international organizations such as the European Union, International Monetary Fund, Organisation for Economic Co-Operation and Development, and WTO have also had a major impact on the diffusion of specific designs, policies, and strategies of organizations that aim to promote the academic capitalist knowledge/learning regime in different contexts. These processes thus provide an explanation of the partial isomorphism of education institutions in different contexts (e.g., in different European countries).

Mechanisms of the design and redesign of particular organizations are neither morally nor politically neutral (see Bunge 1998, part B). Design plans and policies for new organizations as well as for organizational reforms, instead of being mere technocratic matters, are always based on designers' (or redesigners') conceptions of the proper structure, goals, and social functions of the organization under design, which have their origins in the social and institutional environments of the designers. Individuals whose moral and political views differ from the designers often contest these conceptions. In addition, design policies and plans for new organizations typically define the norms and rules that the members of these organizations are expected to follow in their social actions and interactions. These norms and rules may also be enforced by designed incentives, sanctions, and social technologies (e.g., systems of quality control) that are supposed to guide and regulate the behaviors of the organization's members. Not all relevant parties have equal opportunities to affect the formulation of design (or reform) policies and plans (and the same applies, of course, to legislation).

Three types of designed organizations characterizing academic capitalism and their design mechanisms are particularly instructive. First, the design of "intermediating organizations external to universities that promote closer relations between universities and markets" (Slaughter and Cantwell 2012, 585) has contributed to the emergence of academic capitalism in various contexts. Organizations like the Business-Higher Education Forum (United States); Carnegie Commission on Science, Technology, and Government (United States); ERT (Europe); and Higher Education-Business Forum (European Union) were all designed (or redesigned) to promote and lobby neoliberal ideology as well as to reshape the political agenda with respect to higher education and its functions in society (Slaughter and Cantwell 2012).[4] Second, another important part of the restructuring of higher education has been the design of "interstitial organizations that emerge from within universities that intersect various market oriented projects" (Slaughter and Cantwell 2012, 585). For example, technology transfer offices were designed to establish patent policies for universities as well as to promote patenting of research discoveries and emergence of spin-off companies. Third, the redesign of higher education systems and universities by policymakers, university administrators, and managers has also paved the way for academic capitalism. The diffusion and implementation of management fads and ideologies—such as new public management, total quality management, and business process reengineering (e.g., Olssen and Peters 2005; Slaughter and Cantwell 2012)—are important for empirical studies on these processes because management theories do not function solely as (true or false) descriptions of educational organizations. They also include prescriptions as to how these organizations should be changed in order to achieve some more or less clearly defined goals. These theories are thus best termed as social technologies because they always contain moral and political elements regardless of whether their proponents are ready to admit it.

Conclusion

A mechanism-based approach to academic capitalism provides a fruitful framework for explanatory studies on the subject. Four generic social mechanisms that have contributed to the emergence of the academic capitalist knowledge/learning regime in the United States and elsewhere support our argument. Yet we do not claim that these mechanisms exhaust the list of all social mechanisms that have participated in the generation of academic capitalism. It is our opinion, however, that the generic mechanisms considered above are among the most important with respective to explanatory studies on academic capitalism in different contexts.

At this point it is not possible to focus systematically, owing to a lack of relevant empirical studies, on how transnationally or even globally operating social mechanisms have promoted academic capitalism. For this reason, we focused in this chapter on the United States but also provided some illustrative examples of regionally/globally operating social mechanisms. From this perspective, studies on the academic capitalism–globalization relationship are not only about finding empirical examples of transnational academic capitalism, but also exploring how academic capitalism has been enhanced at regional and global scales. The regional/global promotion of academic capitalism, as well as diffusion of such organizations that characterize it, does not necessarily lead to the strengthening of transnational academic capitalism, but rather (more or less) simultaneous adaptation of academic capitalism in different national contexts. Such adaptation occurs because transnationalization of those activities, flows, and networks that characterize academic capitalism does not automatically occur in different nation-states. Thus it is a fundamentally empirical question whether the globalization of academic capitalism is about the relative convergence of national higher education systems or the transnationalization of those elements that characterize academic capitalism. Of course, it can involve both of these trends.

In any case, even if a global trend toward the academic capitalist knowledge/learning regime did exist, this model nevertheless provides room for specialization and differentiation in different institutional contexts. Also, institutions and organizations in various national contexts do not have to be exact copies of each other in order to qualify as elements of the academic capitalist knowledge/learning regime. So, for instance, in Finland we find technology transfer offices, and they are not exactly like those in the United States, but they are similar enough to make it plausible to claim that academic capitalism has found its way into the Finnish higher education system (see Kauppinen 2013a). Further studies could determine what sorts of national and regional varieties of academic capitalism exist there, and to what extent these varieties also involve transnational aspects. Overall, we suggest there is a trend toward the model of academic capitalism in different national contexts owing to variety of reasons, but because of competition between universities, it is likely that this trend supports national and organizational specialization in order to achieve comparative advantage even if there seems to be also powerful templates, such as global research universities, for (re)designers to consider.

The methodological framework developed above is compatible with different types of research strategies on phenomena that characterize academic capitalism at different levels in higher education systems as well as at the transnational level. These research strategies may include case studies, comparative studies, and perhaps also survey studies. Different types of methods, including both qualitative and quantitative ones, may be utilized in explanatory studies that are based on a mechanistic approach. In these respects, the mechanism-based approach is compatible with a moderate methodological pluralism.

NOTES

1. A growing number of studies suggest that developments toward academic capitalism can be identified not only in the United States but also in many European (e.g., Kauppinen and Kaidesoja 2014; Slaughter and Cantwell 2012) and Latin American countries (Rhoades et al. 2004), as well as at the transnational scale (e.g., Kauppinen 2012, 2013b).

2. This finding is in line with the literature on academic capitalism because "the theory of academic capitalism sees groups of actors—faculty, students, administrators, and academic professionals—as using variety of state resources to create new circuits of

knowledge and link higher education institutions to the new economy" (Slaughter and Rhoades 2004, 1). Slaughter and Rhoades (2004) also emphasize that they "have come to see colleges and universities (and academic managers, professors, and other professionals within them) as actors initiating academic capitalism, not just as players being 'corporatized'" (12). The theory of academic capitalism thus explicitly recognizes role of various social actors in the emergence of the academic capitalist knowledge/learning regime, and these actors include both individuals and environmentally embedded organizations.

3. A similar type of categorization of social mechanisms recognizes three mechanisms that are active in cross-national policy transfer: imposition, harmonization, and diffusion (e.g., Dahan, Doe, and Guay 2006).

4. In the case of ERT, its aim was not to restructure higher education per se, but rather to increase the competitiveness of European-based transnational corporations in global capitalism. It was under this agenda that the ERT also identified the restructuring of European higher education as one of its key goals (e.g., Kauppinen 2014).

REFERENCES

Bastedo, Michael N., ed. 2012. *The Organization of Higher Education: Managing Colleges for a New Era*. Baltimore: Johns Hopkins University Press.

Beckert, Jens. 2010. "Institutional Isomorphism Revisited: Convergence and Divergence in Institutional Change." *Sociological Theory* 28, no. 2: 150–66. doi:10.1111/ j.1467 -9558.2010.01369.x.

Bradanini, Davide. 2009. "The Rise of the Competitiveness Discourse—A Neo-Gramscian Analysis." Bruges Political Research Paper 19. Bruges: College of Europe.

Braithwaite, John, and Peter Drahos. 2000. *Global Business Regulation*. Cambridge: Cambridge University Press.

Bunge, Mario. 1996. *Finding Philosophy in Social Science*. New Haven, CT: Yale University Press.

———. 1997. "Mechanisms and Explanation." *Philosophy of the Social Sciences* 27, no. 4: 410–65. doi:10.1177/004839319702700402.

———. 1998. *Social Science under Debate: A Philosophical Perspective*. Toronto: Toronto University Press.

———. 2003. *Emergence and Convergence: Qualitative Novelty and the Unity of Knowledge*. Toronto: University of Toronto Press.

———. 2004. "How Does It Work? The Search for Explanatory Mechanisms." *Philosophy of the Social Sciences* 34, no. 2: 182–210. doi:10.1177/0048393103262550.

Centeno, Miguel A., and Joseph N. Cohen. 2010. *Global Capitalism: A Sociological Perspective*. Cambridge: Polity Press.

Dahan, Nicholas, Jonathan Doe, and Terrence Guay. 2006. "The Role of Multinational Corporations in Transnational Institution Building: A Policy Network Perspective." *Human Relations* 59, no. 11: 1571–600. doi:10.1177/0018726706072854.

DiMaggio, Paul J., and Walter W. Powell. 1983. "The Iron Cage Revisited: Institutional Isomorphism and Collective Rationality in Organizational Fields." *American Sociological Review* 48, no. 4: 147–60.

Hedström, Peter. 2005. *Dissecting the Social: On the Principles of Analytical Sociology.* Cambridge: Cambridge University Press.

Hedström, Peter, and Petri Ylikoski. 2010. "Causal Mechanisms in the Social Sciences." *Annual Review of Sociology* 36: 49–67. doi:10.1146/annurev.soc.012809.102632.

Kaidesoja, Tuukka. 2012. "The DBO Theory of Action and Distributed Cognition." *Social Science Information* 51, no. 3: 311–37. doi:10.1177/0539018412441750.

———. 2013. *Naturalizing Critical Realist Social Ontology.* London: Routledge.

Kauppinen, Ilkka. 2012. "Towards Transnational Academic Capitalism." *Higher Education* 64, no. 4: 543–56. doi:10.1007/s10734-012-9511-x.

———. 2013a. "A Moral Economy of Patents: Case of Finnish Research Universities' Patent Policies." *Studies in Higher Education* doi:10.1080/03075079.2013.806457.

———. 2013b. "Academic Capitalism and the Informational Fraction of Transnational Capitalist Class." *Globalisation, Societies and Education* 11, no. 1: 1–22. doi:10.1080/147 67724.2012.678763.

———. 2014. "European Round Table of Industrialists and the Restructuring of European Higher Education." *Globalisation, Societies and Education.* doi:10.1080/14767724 .2013.876313.

Kauppinen, Ilkka, and Tuukka Kaidesoja. 2014. "A Shift towards Academic Capitalism in Finland." *Higher Education Policy* 27: 23–41. doi:10.1057/hep.2013.11.

Machamer, Peter, Lindley Darden, and Carl F. Craver. 2000. "Thinking about Mechanisms." *Philosophy of Science* 67, no. 1: 1–25.

Mayntz, Renate. 2004. "Mechanisms in the Analysis of Social Macro-Phenomena." *Philosophy of the Social Sciences* 34, no. 2: 237–59. doi:10.1177/0048393103262552.

Olssen, Mark, and Michael A. Peters. 2005. "Neoliberalism, Higher Education and the Knowledge Economy: From the Free Market to Knowledge Capitalism." *Journal of Education Policy* 20, no. 3: 313–45. doi:10.1080/02680930500108718.

Rhoades, Gary, Alma Maldonado-Maldonado, Imanol Ordorika, and Martín Velásquez. 2004. "Imagining Alternatives to Global, Corporate, New Economic Academic Capitalism." *Policy Futures in Education* 2, no. 2: 316–29.

Robinson, William I. 2004. *A Theory of Global Capitalism: Production, Class, and State in a Transnational World.* Baltimore: Johns Hopkins University Press.

Sell, Susan K. 2003. *Private Power, Public Law: The Globalization of Intellectual Property Rights.* Cambridge: Cambridge University Press.

Sell, Susan K., and Aseem Prakash. 2004. "Using Ideas Strategically: The Contest between Business and NGO Networks in Intellectual Property Rights." *International Studies Quarterly* 48, no. 1: 143–75. doi:10.1111/j.0020-8833.2004.00295.x.

Sklair, Leslie. 2002. *Globalization: Capitalism and Its Alternatives.* Oxford: Oxford University Press.

Slaughter, Sheila, and Brendan Cantwell. 2012. "Transatlantic Moves to the Market: The United States and the European Union." *Higher Education* 63, no. 5: 583–606. doi: 10.1007/s10734-011-9460-9.

Slaughter, Sheila, and Larry L. Leslie. 1997. *Academic Capitalism: Politics, Policies and the Entrepreneurial University.* Baltimore: Johns Hopkins University Press.

———. 2001. "Expanding and Elaborating the Concept of Academic Capitalism." *Organization* 8, no. 2: 154–61. doi:10.1177/1350508401082003.

Slaughter, Sheila, and Gary Rhoades. 1996. "The Emergence of a Competitiveness Research and Development Policy Coalition and the Commercialization of Academic

Science and Technology." *Science, Technology and Human Values* 21, no. 3: 303–39. doi:10.1177/016224399602100303.

———. 2004. *Academic Capitalism and the New Economy: Markets, State, and Higher Education.* Baltimore: Johns Hopkins University Press.

Tilly, Charles. 2001. "Mechanisms in Political Processes." *Annual Review of Political Science* 4, no. 1: 21–41. doi:10.1146/annurev.polisci.4.1.21.

van Apeldoorn, Bastiaan. 2000. "Transnational Class Agency and European Governance: The Case of the European Round Table of Industrialists." *New Political Economy* 5, no. 2: 157–81.

———. 2002. *Transnational Capitalism and the Struggle over European Integration.* London: Routledge.

Wan, Poe Yu-ze, 2011. *Reframing the Social: Emergentist Systemism and Social Theory.* Burlington, VT: Ashgate.

Ylijoki, Oili-Helena. 2003. "Entangled in Academic Capitalism? A Case-Study on Changing Ideals and Practices of University." *Higher Education* 45, no. 3: 307–35. doi:10.1023/A:1022667923715.

CHAPTER ELEVEN

Peripheral Knowledge-Driven Economies

What Does Academic Capitalism Have to Say?

ALMA MALDONADO-MALDONADO

> A book that does not contain its counter-book is considered
> incomplete.
>
> —*Jorge Luis Borges, 1940*

Seventeen years have passed since the publication of the first book on academic capitalism, *Academic Capitalism: Politics, Policies, and the Entrepreneurial University* by Slaughter and Leslie (1997), and ten since Slaughter and Rhoades (2004) published *Academic Capitalism and the New Economy: Markets, State, and Higher Education*. This chapter reflects on the influence of the two books and discusses the particular contributions of academic capitalism in understanding developing countries and emerging economies in particular. In his fictional account "Tlön, Uqbar, Orbis Tertius," Borges (2011) describes an invented world in which all works of "a philosophical nature invariably contain both the thesis and the antithesis, the rigorous pro and contra of every argument" (29). Although this chapter is far from becoming that with respect to academic capitalism, it at least attempts to establish a dialogue between the theory and the context of these countries, taking into consideration that neither book included direct references to developing countries. The first book deals with the cases of Australia, Canada, the United Kingdom, and the United States, while the second refers only to the United States. It therefore seems pertinent to include in this volume the debate on what the academic capitalism theory has to say about developing countries.

There have been important changes since the publication of the first book on academic capitalism and between the first and the second. One development has been a general expansion in higher education enrollments. In 1997 there was an impasse in the worldwide enrollment in higher education. But by 2004 there was increased enrollment in some countries, with high rates of participation including the United States and Russia, modest growth in the United Kingdom, and substantial growth in enrollments in large developing countries, including Brazil, China, India, and Mexico. With the exception of France and Japan, most other countries registered some increase in enrollment. Current data show that the increase in enrollment will probably continue, which is something to take into consideration given the demographic situation in most countries where the expansion of higher education enrollment will continue for at least a couple of decades (Lincoln 2013).

Another relevant situation has to do with the worldwide economic crisis from 2007, which has been an element shaping public policies in most countries, affecting the educational sector as a consequence. In fact, the way the crisis has affected educational policies has not been sufficiently explored. In addition to the way the crisis has affected national and local education policies, there have also been reductions in international aid provided to developing countries that may affect some education programs. This is one of the most pertinent aspects where academic capitalism maintains its relevance: a context with economic constraints along with the increasing social and economic relevance of higher education.

Theoretical Context

For over a decade the most popular "religion" in higher education might be referred to as the "Triple Helixists" (e.g., Etzkowitz and Leydesdorff 2000) or some derivative. One of the main ideas of the Triple Helix is that there is "a more prominent role for the University in innovation, on a par with Industry and Government in the Knowledge Society" (Triple Helix Research Group 2013). So many scholars, practitioners, and governments talk about the importance of higher education because it affects economic development and, more importantly, because it promotes innovation. A recent book published by Lane and Johnstone (2012) analyzes some of the most common assumptions and suggests the necessity of being more careful with them: "In light of this obstacle, the common practice used to capture outcome often takes the form of anecdotes and individual case studies that highlight the impact of a certain scientific discovery" (Mchenry, Sanderson, and Siegfried 2012, 115, cited in Lane and Johnstone 2012). In this sense, academic capitalism is relevant because it refers to economic constraints, while the situation has become worse in most counties. Among the different reasons why developing countries are not within the radar of the development of the theory of academic capitalism, one has to do with their diminished circuits and infrastructure of knowledge.

In 2011, Japan reported having 5,180 researchers per million inhabitants, the United States had 4,673, the United Kingdom had 3,947, and the European Union had on average 3,059. This was not the situation with the so-called BRICS (Brazil, Russia, India, China, and South Africa), except for Russia, which had numbers close to the countries named above (3,091). China reported 863, Brazil 668, South Africa 393, and India 136 (UNESCO Institute for Statistics 2011). The Organisation for Economic Co-operation and Development (OECD) found that countries like Brazil, China, India, or Mexico are mostly "users" of the knowledge that is produced in other countries (the producers; see OECD 2006). The rest of the countries are basically less equipped to participate in the global knowledge economy.

Countries defined as knowledge consumers are at a clear disadvantage with respect to countries such as the United States, with the largest percentage of gross domestic product (GDP) spent on higher education and research and development (R&D) and about 70% of Nobel Prize winners working there or having three-quarters of their universities sitting in the top ranks (United Kingdom / United States of America Study Group 2009). The United States also leads the world regarding other knowledge economy indicators, such as proportions of academic knowledge produced, publishers, citations, Internet penetration, and so on (Flick and Convoco Foundation 2011). Given this context, this chapter discusses the extent to which academic capitalism theory is useful in understanding and analyzing higher education in developing counties.

This chapter will not describe or summarize the main aspects of academic capitalism, which are included in chapter 1 in this volume. Here I stress that both books on academic capitalism explain similar transitions experienced by higher education institutions. According to academic capitalism, universities and their faculty increasingly struggle to secure resources. As a result, one of the main changes they are experiencing is to modify their behaviors with respect to what they do, and they must look for ways to obtain more revenue. That is the basic storyline. The differences have to do with the context: their pressures but also their margins to maneuver are different depending on whether we are discussing developing or developed countries, more prestigious or less prestigious institutions or fields of study. Slaughter and Rhodes (2004) also mention: "We track and explain how the change from one regime to another occurs . . . we point to the active, sometimes leading role that the academy plays in marketizing higher education, rather than portraying it as the victim of external, encroaching commercial interests" (305).

The economic constraints and the agency embodied by academics in changing attitudes and behaviors are two contributions made by academic capitalism that apply to most higher education reforms, but perhaps the blurred piece lies in the role of knowledge production. The reduction in public spending has produced and will continue to produce important changes in universities. Institutions that in the past refused to change may not have any alternative now. But to what extent are countries and institutions able to participate in the "new game" called the "knowledge-based economy," "brain race," "knowledge race," "knowledge society," or similar concepts?

Academic Capitalism and the Role of Knowledge Production: A Breakdown Point?

The link between education and industry in the United States registered its first antecedent at MIT in 1888, when the "Massachusetts Institute of Technology initiated the first four-year bachelor program in chemical engineering to meet the emerging demands of local industry" (Schultz 2012, 131). Since that time, the United States has been a key example in establishing relations between education and industry or, in other words, between knowledge and economic development. Slaughter and Leslie (1997) point out that "clear distinctions between basic and applied research emerged in the United States after World War II. The success of physicists and nuclear engineers with nuclear weaponry was presented to government and industry as a triumph of basic research" (180). According to Berman (2012), the most important element was a change that occurred in the public policies in the United States:

> Universities had already been experimenting with market–logic practices, but until the late 1970s those experiments remained limited in scope because the cultural, resource, and regulatory environment was unfavorable to them. In the late 1970s and early 1980s however, policy decisions—driven by the idea that innovation spurs economic growth—changed that environment in ways that removed regulatory barriers to such practices and provided new resources for them. In this new environment, market logic became stronger throughout the field. (12)

Naturally, many things have been written about the link between knowledge production, innovation, and development, and there are also many assumptions about this relationship. Among several possibilities, one can summarize in three main points a way to understand the economic impact of higher education:

> First, as already noted many studies have sought to define the effects of university economic activity as the rippling flow of university revenues and spending within a geographic region . . . A second approach views the economic consequence of

higher education in terms of the value of attaining a higher education credential . . . A third approach perceives university economic impact in terms of quantifiable indicators of commercialization activity—as a summing up of patents, licenses, and royalties earned through university research. (Gais and Wright 2012, 50)

If there are doubts about the hegemonic position of the United States, the clearest examples of the three aspects mentioned above belong to this country. Perhaps not because these situations do not occur in other nations, but most research published and circulated on knowledge and economic growth still comes from the United States, perhaps because, in part, more than institutions in other countries, US universities regularly have to describe their social impact in terms of economic return. Consider an example from Montana: "Based on 2008–09 figures, the $109.5 million in annual spending and the equivalent of approximately 730 high-paying jobs in [Montana State University] research would be lost to the state if the University did not exist." And a report from New York highlights the economic value of university credentials: "As of 2008–2009, 1.6 million alumni [from SUNY] still lived in New York and made up a large part of the state's highly educated workforce" (Gais and Wright 2012, 36). And, finally, on the relevance of patents and research capabilities: "About 3,000 U.S. patents are issued to universities each year—eight times the number in 1980 and more than thirty times that in the 1960s—and universities now bring in more than 2 billion in licensing revenue annually" (Berman 2012, 2).

Slaughter and Rhoades (2004) take the discussion further. They mention that there is a shift from what they call a "public good knowledge/learning regime" to an "academic capitalist knowledge/learning regime." As they explain, "The academic capitalism knowledge regime values knowledge privatization and profit taking in which institutions, inventor faculty, and corporations have claims that come before those of the public . . . Knowledge is construed as a private good, valued for creating streams of high-technology products that generate profit as they flow through global markets" (29).

There is a small contradiction here, or perhaps not. According to economists, knowledge is defined as a public good, but education is considered a service within economic discourse. Contrary to what some international organizations consider—such as UNESCO, some of whose members have looked to define higher education as a public service (Maldonado-Maldonado and Verger 2010)—the use of a piece of knowledge for one purpose does not preclude its use for others, say classic economists (Mas-Colell, Whinston, and Green 1995, 359). As time passes, however, there is a progressive development of advantage mechanisms to appropriate knowledge, which private publishers and patents have provoked. They enforce excludability with the purpose of generating revenues. For example, the *Economist* (2013) reports that Elsevier, a Dutch firm that is the world's biggest journal publisher, had a margin last year of 38% on revenues of £2.1 billion ($3.2 billion). Springer, a German firm that is the second-biggest journal publisher, made 36% on sales of €875 million ($1.1 billion) in 2011. According to Yanagisawa and Guellec (2009), the boom of receipts from international licensing in major OECD regions began in 1986, and by 1997, when *Academic Capitalism* was published, it was important, but by 2004, when *Academic Capitalism and the New Economy* was released, the increase was impressive. Meanwhile, part of the debate at universities surrounds the fact that most of these publishers do not pay for the contributions made by scholars in activities such as editing, reviewing, or authoring articles. However, universities pay high prices for publishers' publications and subscriptions. Even more, most of the published research results have been sponsored by public financing. The contradictions are evident, but the reality is how appropriation of knowledge has increased dramatically, at least in the context of developed countries, but remains concentrated in a few universities:

> More than 2,700 patents were issued to the United States' eighty-nine most research-intensive universities in 2000. The four more prolific patentors were granted more than 28 percent of those patents and the top ten accounted for nearly 45 percent . . . The top ten revenue earners garner more than 65 percent of the more than $1 billion intellectual property licenses returned to universities. The ten most successful institutions on several other measures (licenses that include equity in start-up firms, number of new start-ups, licenses executed, and licenses generating income) account for between 35 and 50 percent of all commercial action. (Association of University Technology Managers 2000, cited in Owen-Smith 2012, 243)

These data raise a few questions: What does it mean to privatize knowledge today? How does it contradict the traditional idea, in economics, that knowledge is a public good? Is it an anomaly within the classic economics model, or simply the result of capitalism advancing within higher education? The many geopolitical interests in knowledge production today might help to answer "yes" to all three questions. Are there limits in the privatization of knowledge? What is the situation of indigenous knowledge from developing countries?

The debate on indigenous knowledge is not pointless with respect to developing countries because there are many examples of the ways entities such as

Monsanto or the Millis Corporation have privatized indigenous knowledge and are taking advantage of it. Nixtamalization is a process developed in Mesoamerica that prepares corn by soaking the grain and cooling it with an alkaline mix. Today there are hundreds of patents associated with this process held not only by corporations from Latin America but also by important actors in the United States. The J. R. Short Milling Company (2000) patented a "Process for producing nixtamal and masa flour," and the Board of Trustees of the University of Illinois (2010) patented the "Nixtamalization process and products produced therefrom." Patenting an ancient invention seems to be a key symptom of the appropriation of knowledge; more people—particularly governments and international organizations—might need to give the matter more attention. One paradox in this case is that indigenous knowledge normally does not count in the knowledge economy except when this knowledge has been appropriated by a transnational or domestic industry. This type of phenomenon is something that academic capitalism does not discuss, although it does include the role and agency of academics in developing countries in such situations.

Another way to discuss where different nations stand in the global knowledge economy is to find out about their "knowledge stock" (a concept used by Schultz 2012). Several authors have attempted to offer some indicators, and some prestigious institutions have created their own indexes. Such is the case of Archibugi and Coco (2005), who made an important contribution when they compared three of the most important indexes to measure technological capabilities. They compared the World Economic Forum (WEF), the United Nations Development Programme (UNDP), the United Nations Industrial Development Organization, and the RAND Corporation's index. Archibugi and Coco (2005) also suggested their own index. In addition to analyzing each methodology and some of their assumptions, they presented a rank correlation among the four of them. Table 11.1 presents the four cases used in *Academic Capitalism*: Australia, Canada, the United Kingdom, and the United States. Also included are countries considered to have emerging economies, including the BRICS plus Chile, Mexico, South Korea, and Turkey (which are included because they are members of the OECD).

As table 11.1 indicates, the United States ranks number one in a group of forty-seven countries; Canada is second (ranked fourth overall), followed by Australia (fifth) and the United Kingdom (eighth). The case of South Korea, taken in this chapter as one of the countries defined as having an emerging economy, is distinct from the other developing nations in almost every category.

TABLE 11.1
A comparison between the four countries in Academic Capitalism *and nine emerging economies*

Country	Technological capabilities ranking (out of 47 countries)	Current population	Public expenditure on higher education (% of GDP)	Private expenditure on higher education (% of GDP)	Tertiary educational attainment (% of total population in that age group)	Youth aged 15–19 who are not in education or employment (%)	Youth aged 20–24 who are not in education nor employment (%)
Australia	5	23,091,091	0.7	0.9	38	8	11
Canada	4	35,141,542	1.5	0.9	51	8	15
United Kingdom	8	63,181,775	0.6	0.7	38	10	19
United States	1	316,285,000	1	1.6	41	8	19
Brazil	37	193,946,886	0.8			14	23
Chile	31	16,634,603	0.8	1.6	27		
China	39	1,354,040,000					
India	44	1,210,569,573	1.3				
Mexico	34	118,419,000	1	0.4	17	19	27
Russia		143,400,000	1.2	0.6			
South Africa	35	52,981,991	0.6				
South Korea	11	50,219,669	0.7	1.9	40	8	24
Turkey		75,627,384			13	26	44

Sources: Archibugi and Coco (2005) and OECD (2013a–2013h).
Note: The values have been calculated by the author and then adjusted to eliminate decimals in most cases. Empty spaces indicate that information was not available.

It is clear that South Korea is closer to being a developed nation than any other developing country. There are at least twenty rank spaces between South Korea and Chile (the highest-ranking country in the emerging economies group, followed by Mexico, South Africa, Brazil, China, and India). Unfortunately, Turkey and Russia do not appear in these rankings. Next to the column for technological capabilities is one for current population. Of course, it is important to consider a country's size when discussing each case. In table 11.1 it is clear that, except for the United States, the most populated countries struggle much more to have a better position in such indexes. That size matters makes sense, yet it is sometimes forgotten.

In order to define the stock of knowledge in these countries, I suggest combining several indicators, such as expenditure on higher education, R&D expediters, researchers per thousand employees, and triadic patents. The result of such an analysis confirms the hegemony of the United States in most aspects. In other words, the United States leads most measures of the knowledge economy, and most developing countries are far behind.

Gross domestic expenditure on R&D ($ million)	Gross domestic expenditure on R&D (% of GDP)	Researchers per thousand employees, full-time equivalent	Triadic patent families	Households with Internet access (%)	WEF	UNDP	Archibugi and Coco (2005)	RAND	Rank mean
	2.2		284	79	4	10	8	8	7.5
21,708	1.74	8.6	638	78	2	9	5	2	4.5
35,615	1.77	7.6	1,598	83	8	7	11	9	8.8
65,994	2.77		13,837	71	1	2	4	1	2
			60	38	37	37	38	35	36.8
	0.42		9		33	34	30	30	31.8
61,552		1.6	875	31	39	39	41	33	38
			201	6					
	0.44		12	23	29	30	35	36	32.5
23,394		6.3	73	46					
			26	10	34	35	32	32	33.3
49,394	3.74	11.1	2,184	97	7	5	15	16	10.8
7,664	0.84	2.9		42					

While it is clear that the first group in table 11.1, plus Korea, seems similar in many aspects and ranks in the top eleven countries, what is challenging is to define the second group of countries. In terms of volume, China and Russia seem distinct from the group in some indicators. China is the second country after the United States in terms of R&D expenditures, for example, but China lags in triadic patent registration, not to mention the percentage of researchers and households with access to the Internet, which is attributed to the country's massive population.

The percentage of youth who are neither educated nor employed is a worldwide preoccupation and may eventually affect the knowledge stock since it is also based on the number of educated people residing in a country. The countries with the highest numbers of youth who do not have jobs or participate in education are Turkey, Mexico, and Brazil, in that order. This number is closely related to higher education enrollment, as Australia, Canada, South Korea, the United Kingdom, and the United States report over 38% of their population achieving that level. Regarding the second group of countries, only Chile reports having 27% of the population with tertiary education, followed by Mexico and Turkey with 17% (the other countries did not have available data). The economic crisis seems to be affecting this particular area in most countries, and the perspectives do not look too promising, unfortunately. This indicator is especially important if one follows what Lane and Owens (2012) mention: "In the knowledge-based economy, human capital is the most critical resource. Companies require a skilled workforce to compete in national and global markets, while hospitals, schools and other institutions need skilled workers to provide high quality services" (212).

Some countries that are "knowledge consumers" are trying to reduce the gap that exists between them and producing countries. But such efforts prompt a dilemma. On the one hand is pressure to change patterns and higher education policies (this is where the adaptation of the academic capitalism theory might help), and on the other are the poor system, infrastructure, and human capital that complicate the fulfillment of this goal. "[Gibbons] contends that it is in knowledge production per se rather than in teaching that globalization has the most effects but observes that, whereas knowledge production can take place anywhere, the use of that knowledge in innovation tends to take place locally. Hence universities already in established networks can use those to exploit distributed knowledge systems, not necessarily globally but regionally" (Deem 2001, 18).

The Private Sector: The Missing Piece?

The most problematic aspect of emerging countries in the theory of academic capitalism might be the role of the private sector. Besides the role of government and universities, the third partner, according to the Triple Helix model, is industry, or the private sector. Slaughter and Rhoades (2004) say, "Corporations worked with universities to support Bayh-Dole (1980), which privatized federal research, but are unhappy with universities' aggressive claims to intellectual property and ligate regularly against them about ownership of broad patents that underlie a variety of pharmaceutical products. The 'firewall' that once separated public and private sectors has become increasingly permeable" (27). This is perhaps one of the most important differences between the situations of emerging economies versus developed countries. In fact, most developing countries assign up to 70% of governmental funding to R&D (OECD 2012). Even a country like the United Kingdom has struggled with this situation: "In Britain, which had scientific leadership but much less venture capital, the biotech sector remained stunted in comparison to the one that developed in the United States" (Berman 2012, 165). The biotechnology industry is one of the most important in terms of innovation development. Berman (2012) points out that "biotech entrepreneurship was first initiated by venture capitalists looking for faculty partners and then, once the practice had become more familiar, by faculty themselves" (162–63). In a list of 127 venture capital firms, ninety-eight are located in the United States even though some share locations in other countries, and only twenty-nine do not have any presence there (Wikipedia 2013).

When regarding some successful examples of spaces that combine academe, industry, and university, most eyes look to the United States, such as the "College of Nanoscale Science and Engineering (CNSE) in Albany, New York and Research Triangle Park (RTP) founded by North Carolina State and University of North Carolina at Chapel Hill" (Gais and Wright 2012). Also known as university-industry-government, these groups "come together to share the costs and risks associated with research and development" (Schultz 2012, 130). One of the key elements in these cases is the active role of the private sector. When considering other countries, however, particularly in developing countries, it is clear that the private sector plays a small role. The impulse of the private sector, particularly economically, has been decisive in building innovative spaces in developed nations, and it seems a necessary condition to develop these types of advances in research and development.

Despite what is believed—that the imperative role of the private sector lies in promoting innovation and so on—Berman's (2012) contribution is essential in emphasizing the role of government in the promotion of these tendencies. So perhaps this is a lesson these emerging economies must learn before indiscriminately repeating the homogenous speech on the Triple Helix. Without the intervention of the state, there would be no innovation platform. Are governments listening?

Berman argued that government decisions were the most important driver of this change, and that those decisions were made because a new way of thinking became politically important. In the late 1970s, the idea that technological innovation drives economic growth became increasingly influential among policymakers, giving a boost to policy proposals that could be framed as strengthening innovation. First, the policies that moved academic science toward the market were not uniformly free-market in orientation. Most of them—the capital gains tax cut, the strengthening of intellectual property rights, the relaxation of investment rules for pension funds—were. But state support for university research centers, as well as government subsidies for research parks, encouraged a market orientation but were clearly interventionist (Berman 2012, 158, 173).

Although some of the cases explored in the books on academic capitalism are more concerned with the ways academics adapt the ideology of market-like behaviors, other examples—because they belong to the US context or to Australia, Canada, and the United Kingdom—stress the role of the private sector. It must be taken into consideration how advanced some of these situations are in developing countries, mostly because their private sector is not strong enough or does not see the importance of investment in knowledge production and innovation, or both.

A Better Fit in the Understanding of Emerging Economies

One clear aspect is that *Academic Capitalism* fits perfectly with the emerging economy countries in terms of financing struggles. These countries are experiencing difficult economic situations and, in some cases, drastic reductions of their financing. The pressure to obtain alternative sources of financing cannot be harder than the one experienced in 1997, when the first book on academic capitalism was published. In many cases, along with the economic constraints, evaluation policies were implemented in order to compete for additional resources.

Regarding the second book, *Academic Capitalism and the New Economy*, some of the changes observed in 2004 are more present and perhaps more valid in emerging economies than when the book was released. When we talk about restructuring of higher education, we mean substantive organizational change associated with changes in internal resource allocations (reduction or closure of departments, expansion or creation of other departments, establishment of interdisciplinary units); substantive change in the division of academic labor with regard to research and teaching; the establishment of new organizational forms (such as arm's-length companies and research parks); and the organization of new administrative structures or streamlining or redesign of old ones (Slaughter and Leslie 1997, 11).

Most developed and developing countries have experienced, since the 1980s, several reforms in their higher education systems. Latin America has faced many economic difficulties and strict economic policies, even before the Washington Consensus. In short, over the last thirty years, seeking additional revenue in the face of fiscal constraint and increased demand has been a constant theme in higher education worldwide.

There are several important pieces written on the way academic capitalism has affected higher education systems in Australia, Canada, the United Kingdom, and the United States as well as in emerging countries. This chapter only lists a few examples. Three Canadian reforms are explained under the academic capitalism framework (Chan and Fisher 2009; Metcalfe 2010; Tudiver 1999). Work has also been done on the United Kingdom (Dickson 1999; Williams 2004) and on Australia (Marginson 2004; Marginson and Considine 2000). Some papers refer to changes related to academic capitalism in South Korea (Piller and Cho 2013; Seol 2012). There are additionally several examples about Latin America (Bernasconi 2008; Borón 2006; Brunner 2005), Mexico (Bensimon and Ordorika 2006; Rhoades, Maldonado-Maldonado, Ordorika, and Velásquez 2004), Brazil (Martins 2008), Turkey (Kurul Tural 2007), and South Africa (Mouton, Louw, and Strydom 2013; Stewart 2007; Subotzky 1999), or there are other revisions or general applications of academic capitalism as a framework (Lotter 2008; Mendoza 2007; Renault 2006). Even though this chapter does not attempt to discuss the content of each paper, it does acknowledge the debate that the theory of academic capitalism has generated among scholars around the world, particularly in the countries discussed here.

The amount of research that academic capitalism has inspired only reinforces the validation and pertinence this solid framework has. One basic aspect is that, despite the fact that the notion of knowledge stock must be improved, the positive externalities on that stock are more important. Economically and socially speaking, there are so many assumptions about the effect produced by knowledge that research is needed on this topic.

Still, when the pieces do not come together, knowledge must be discussed in emerging economies given their insufficient knowledge stock. Academic capitalism is embedded as a theory in the US context and can be applied comfortably in developed countries. So the challenge is how to continue working, theoretically and empirically, in the process in which emerging countries are living with respect to knowledge production and their worldwide position. The BRICS are closing some gaps here (the best example of a country with similar characteristics decades ago is South Korea), so between developing and developed countries gap there are bridges, which are being built and still many cracks to fix.

Conclusion

One might say that in the field of higher education there are few theoretical contributions. A number of observers have offered reasons why. Teichler (1996)

explained that "higher education as a field of research is certainly too small today to be characterized as a discipline" (433). Although most authors consider
that one of the main reasons this field seems small or weak is because it is
young, this cannot be the only explanation. Kaneko (2000), for example, points
out that "research in higher education is a body of knowledge and discourses
without clear boundary or logical connection with one another. It is not necessarily because the field is relatively young" (49). This author suggests a conceptual
model consisting of three layers: empirical studies, policy discourses, and paradigm in core.

Higher education has been defined as a "theme-focused area of research,
primarily characterized by themes investigated" (Teichler 2000, 15). An important aspect of this field is its multidisciplinary character. The combination of
the different disciplines and the diverse number of theme-focused areas of
research multiply the number of themes in the field. Some of the main disciplines are philosophy, sociology, economics, psychology, law, and history;
theme-focused areas could be on academics, students, financing, evaluation
and accountability, quality, government and management, diversification, gender, access, technology, religions, and the private sector, among many others. It
is possible to study the structure of higher education systems, but also their
different processes and relationships with actors in society. In addition, the field
is considered to have many theoretical inconsistencies. Higher education research "is not viewed as a very flourishing theme for scholarly investigation . . .
It is often described as being new, not greatly consolidated, lacking of a coherent
theoretical and methodological framework and fragmented in the knowledge
base thus laid down" (Teichler 2000, 3–4).

Some criticisms are more moderate. Altbach (2001) says that the study of
higher education "has been both strength and a weakness" (3). Szczepanski
(1997) suggests that it is mainly because the field is recent that it "has taken
quite a long time for the scholarly community to develop appropriate terminology and moderately precise methods of analysis for these problems" (351). Two
main reasons for this situation could be its recent development and its interdis-
ciplinarity; with no established methodologies, "it borrows from other fields"
(Altbach 2001, 3). The critiques are not only related to methods, but, as Teichler
has mentioned, they are related to the absence of theoretical developments. Kogan (1996) considers that the absence of sufficient hypotheses and theories in
this field is clear.

In this context, the contributions made by Slaughter, Leslie, and Rhoades
represent an important influence on the field. The authors built academic capi-

talism from thinkers such as Foucault to Marx, in addition to almost all of the most relevant higher education researchers. The effort made in the books on academic capitalism in putting together a group of theoretical assumptions to explain the transformations that higher education institutions have experienced is important, particularly because it breaks the simplistic idea that universities are changing because of external forces, and because most terms do not problematize internal contradictions. Examples of other concepts include the "McDonaldization of higher education" (Hartley 1995), as well as "neoliberal reforms" or "neo-managerialism" and the "entrepreneurial university." But these concepts are primarily descriptive.

Academic capitalism offers the possibility to link four elements: (1) the phenomenon of the economic constraints and crisis (experienced in every nation these days); (2) the relevance of knowledge production and innovation (understanding the tremendous disparities among countries and also the reproduction of dynamics and players); (3) the agency of the State, governments, private sector, and universities; and (4) the complexity of positions of academic departments, units, scholars, university managers, and even students. Therefore the main contribution of academic capitalism is having a framework that speaks to the developed and developing world on these issues. Or, if it is preferred, it speaks to nations that are dealing with definitions such as "knowledge producers," "knowledge consumers," "knowledge disconnected," or "consolidated economies" versus "emerging economies." No matter what terms or classification are used, academic capitalism seems to be a valid contribution, pertinent and necessary in the same way it was seventeen years ago, with the caveat that more still needs to be developed precisely for the so-called developing countries.

There are a number of questions that should be answered in order to better the theory of academic capitalism in the context of developing countries. For example, how different is agency in these contexts? This is important because faculty in developing countries may play different roles than in developed countries. How does power work in institutions with an entirely different structure and governance than those in developed countries? For example, there are important differences in terms of the concept of autonomy or accountability. Even more complex is to think that one main challenge for the first book on academic capitalism was to organize the discussion among the cases of Australia, Canada, the United Kingdom, and the United States. It was clear then that Canada was the most different case among the four. Now, when discussing emerging economies, the differences among them are by far deeper and more complex. Finding similarities between Brazil, Chile, China, India, Mexico, and South Africa—or, even worse, Russia and South Korea—seems to be an incredibly challenging task. Perhaps the lesson from *Academic Capitalism* has to do with how to start building "localized theories" and then moving toward more general ones. Finally, two other aspects that should be explored in emerging economies involve the role of academics in these countries—how different or similar their situations are—and also the appropriation of knowledge as mentioned above.

The influence of the market in higher education is now ubiquitous, so it seems improbable that knowledge production will remain isolated. Given the market exposure experienced by many domains, including contemporary art, one cannot help but wonder whether education and science will face the same issues. The British artist Damien Hirst attempted to modify the market of contemporary art simply by creating a piece of skeleton made of diamonds—a work titled *For the Love of God*—and it is believed that at the end he had to buy it for himself given its high price. Villoro (2013), one of the most famous Mexican writers alive, wonders whether it is possible that high prices of contemporary art are able to paralyze its own market. It seems likely that the market economy will continue to be the dominant social force for the foreseeable future, so what should we expect regarding knowledge production and commercialization in higher education? How will new ways of knowledge production and education consumption modify current markets, and how sustainable will this be? Just by looking at the hype and fog produced by MOOCs (McClure 2013), it is hard not to question the instability of the market of knowledge and education as well as how expensive it can become. One must also wonder whether it will be possible for higher education to reach the same ridiculous situation of Damien Hisrt when he had to consume his own piece of art because it was simply inaccessible for the rest of the people. Two examples show that this idea may not be too extreme. First, increasing tuition costs in the United States, as well as in other countries such as the United Kingdom. In the American case, "College costs [have surged] 500% in the U.S. since 1985" (Jamrisko and Kolet 2013). How much higher can tuition prices go? Second, consider new strategies employed by major academic publishers such as Elsevier to charge publication fees ranging from $500 to $5,000 to publish articles in their so-called "open journals" (Elsevier 2014). What will happen to the authors unable to cover that fee? Such examples demonstrate that academic capitalism will likely prove to be theoretical device useful for explaining the relationship between higher education and the knowledge economy in Mexico and other emerging economy contexts. Certainly, the dialogue with academic capitalism will continue for at least another seventeen years.

REFERENCES

Altbach, Philip G. 2001. "Research and Training in Higher Education: The State of Art." In *Higher Education: A Worldwide Inventory of Centers and Programs,*" edited by Philip G. Altbach and David Endberg, 1–24. Phoenix: Oryx Press.

Archibugi, Daniele, and Alberto Coco. 2005. "Measuring Technological Capabilities at the Country Level: A Survey and a Menu for Choice." *Research Policy* 34, no. 2: 175–94. doi:10.1016/j.respol.2004.12.002.

Bensimon, Estella M., and Imanol Ordorika. 2006. "Mexico's Estímulos: Faculty Compensation Based on Piecework." In *The University, State, and Market: The Political Economy of Globalization in the Americas,* edited by Robert A. Rhoads and Carlos Alberto Torres, 250–74. Stanford, CA: Stanford University Press.

Berman, Elizabeth Popp. 2012. *Creating the Market University: How Academic Science Became an Economic Engine.* Princeton, NJ: Princeton University Press.

Bernasconi, Andrés. 2008. "Is There a Latin American Model of the University?" *Comparative Education Review* 52, no. 1: 27–52.

Board of Trustees of the University of Illinois. 2010. "Nixtamalization Process and Products Produced Therefrom." US patent 7,740,895, filed February 28, 2005, and issued June 22, 2010.

Borges, Jorge Luis. 2011. *Ficciones.* Buenos Aires: Random House Mondadori.

Borón, Atilio. 2006. "Reforming the Reforms: Transformation and Crisis in Latin American and Caribbean Universities." In *The University, State, and Market: The Political Economy of Globalization in the Americas,* edited by Robert A. Rhoads and Carols Alberto Torres, 141–63. Stanford, CA: Stanford University Press.

Brunner, José Joaquín. 2005. "Transformaciones de la Universidad Pública." *Revista de Sociología* 19: 31–49.

C. H. 2013. "The Supreme Court Rules That Genes May Not Be Patented. Patently False." *Economist,* June 13. www.economist.com/blogs/babbage/2013/06/supreme-court-rules -genes-may-not-be-patented.

Chan, Adrienne S., and Donald Fisher, eds. 2009. *The Exchange University: Corporatization of Academic Culture.* Vancouver: University of British Columbia Press.

Deem, Rosemary. 2001. "Globalisation, New Managerialism, Academic Capitalism and Entrepreneurialism in Universities: Is the Local Dimension Still Important?" *Comparative Education* 37, no. 1: 7–20. doi:10.1080/03050060020020408.

Dickson, David. 1999. "Britain Excels in Academic Capitalism." *Nature Medicine* 5, no. 2: 131–32. doi:10.1038/5484.

Economist. 2013. "Academic Publishing: Free-for-All." *Economist,* May 4.

Elsevier. 2014. "Open-Access Journals." www.elsevier.com/about/open-access/open-access -journals.

Etzkowitz, Henry, and Loet Leydesdorff. 2000. "The Dynamics of Innovation: From National Systems and 'Mode 2' to a Triple Helix of University-Industry-Government Relations." *Research Policy* 29, no. 2: 109–23. doi:10.1016/S0048-7333(99)00055-4.

Flick, Corrine M., and Convoco Foundation. 2011. *Geographies of the World's Knowledge.* Oxford: Oxford Internet Institute, University of Oxford.

Gais, Thomas, and David Wright. 2012. "The Diversity of University Economic Development Activities and Issues of Impact Measurement." In *Universities and Colleges as Economic Drivers: Measuring Higher Education's Role in Economic Development,* edited by Jason E. Lane and D. Bruce Johnstone, 31–60. Albany: State University of New York.

Hartley, D. 1995. "The 'McDonaldization' of Higher Education: Food for Thought?" *Oxford Review of Education* 21, no. 4: 409–23. doi:10.1080/0305498950210403.

Jamrisko, Michelle, and Ilan Kolet. 2013. "College Costs Surge 500% in U.S. Since 1985: Chart of the Day." *Bloomberg News,* August 26. www.bloomberg.com/news/2013-08-26/college-costs-surge-500-in-u-s-since-1985-chart-of-the-day.html.

Johnston, Ane Turner, and Joan B. Hirt. 2011. "Reshaping Academic Capitalism to Meet Development Priorities: The Case of Public Universities in Kenya." *Higher Education* 61, no. 4: 483–99. doi:10.1007/s10734-010-9342-6.

J. R. Short Milling Company. 2000. "Process for Producing Nixtamal and Masa Flour." US Patent 6,025,011, filed June 9, 1997, and issued February 15, 2000.

Kaneko, Motohisa. 2000. "Higher Education Research Policy and Practice: Contexts, Conflicts and the New Horizon." In *Higher Education Research: Its Relationship to Policy and Practice,* edited by Ulrich Teichler and Jan Sadlak, 47–58. Oxford: IAU Press.

Kogan, Maurice. 1996. "Comparing Higher Education Systems." *Higher Education* 32, no. 4: 395–402. doi:10.1007/BF00133254.

Kurul Tural, Nejla. 2007. "Universities and Academic Life in Turkey: Changes and Challenges." *International Journal of Educational Policies* 1, no. 1: 63–78.

Lane, Jason E., and D. Bruce Johnstone, eds. 2012. *Universities and Colleges as Economic Drivers: Measuring Higher Education's Role in Economic Development.* Albany: State University of New York.

Lane, Jason E., and Taya L. Owens. 2012. "International Dimensions of Higher Education's Contributions to Economic Development." In *Universities and Colleges as Economic Drivers: Measuring Higher Education's Role in Economic Development,* edited by Jason E. Lane and D. Bruce Johnstone, 205–38. Albany: State University of New York.

Lincoln, Daniel. 2013. "Research Universities: Networking the Knowledge Economy." Paper presented at the IHERD-OECD Expert Meeting, Marseille, France, July 1–2.

Lotter, Don. 2008. "The Genetic Engineering of Food and the Failure of Science, Part 2: Academic Capitalism and the Loss of Scientific Integrity." *International Journal of Sociology of Agriculture and Food* 16, no. 1: 50–68.

Maldonado-Maldonado, Alma, and Antoni Verger. 2010. "Politics, UNESCO and Higher Education." *International Higher Education* 58: 8–9.

Marginson, Simon. 2004. "Australian Higher Education: National and Global Markets." In *Markets in Higher Education: Rhetoric or Reality?,* edited by Pedro Teixeira, Ben Jongbloed, David Dill, and Alberto Amaral, 207–40. Dordrecht: Kluwer Academic.

Marginson, Simon, and Mark Considine. 2000. *The Enterprise University: Power, Governance and Reinvention in Australia.* Cambridge: Cambridge University Press.

Martins, André Luiz de Miranda. 2008. "The March of 'Academic Capitalism' in Brazil during the 1990s." *Avaliação (Campinas)* 13, no. 3: 733–43. http://dx.doi.org/10.1590 /S1414-40772008000300006.

Mas-Colell, Andreu, Michael D. Whinston, and Jerry R. Green. 1995. *Microeconomic Theory*. New York: Oxford University Press.

McClure, M. W. 2013. "Hope and Hype in Viral Technologies and Policies." *Excellence in Higher Education* 4, no. 1: 7–18.

Mendoza, P. 2007. "Academic Capitalism and Doctoral Student Socialization: A Case Study." *Journal of Higher Education* 78, no. 1: 71–96.

Metcalfe, Amy Scott. 2010. "Revisiting Academic Capitalism in Canada: No Longer the Exception." *Journal of Higher Education* 81, no. 4: 489–514. doi:10.1353/jhe.0.0098.

Mouton, N., G. P. Louw, and G. L. Strydom. 2013. "Present-Day Dilemmas and Challenges of the South African Tertiary System." *International Business and Economics Research Journal* 12, no. 3: 285–300.

OECD (Organisation for Economic Co-operation and Development). 2006. "The Knowledge-Based Economy." OECD/GD(96)102. Paris: OECD.

———. 2012. "Modes of Public Funding of R&D: Towards Internationally Comparable Indicators." Science, Technology and Industry Working Paper 2012/4. Paris: OECD.

———. 2013a. "Education Expenditure." In *OECD Factbook 2013: Economic, Environmental and Social Statistics*. Paris: OECD. doi:10.1787/factbook-2013-80-en.

———. 2013b. "Educational Attainment." In *OECD Factbook 2013: Economic, Environmental and Social Statistics*. Paris: OECD. doi:10.1787/factbook-2013-77-en.

———. 2013c. "Youth Inactivity." In *OECD Factbook 2013: Economic, Environmental and Social Statistics*. Paris: OECD. doi:10.1787/factbook-2013-75-en.

———. 2013d. "Expenditure on R&D." In *OECD Factbook 2013: Economic, Environmental and Social Statistics*. Paris: OECD. doi:10.1787/factbook-2013-60-en.

———. 2013e. "Gross Domestic Expenditure on R&D as Percentage of GDP." In *Main Science and Technology Indicators, OECD, Science, Technology and R&D Statistics*. Paris: OECD. doi:10.1787/rdxp-table-2013-1-en.

———. 2013f. "Researchers." In *OECD Factbook 2013: Economic, Environmental and Social Statistics*. Paris: OECD. doi:10.1787/factbook-2013-1-en.

———. 2013g. "Patents." In *OECD Factbook 2013: Economic, Environmental and Social Statistics*. Paris: OECD. doi:10.1787/factbook-2013-62-en.

———. 2013h. "Computer, Internet and Telecommunication." In *OECD Factbook 2013: Economic, Environmental and Social Statistics*. Paris: OECD. doi:10.1787/factbook-2013-67-en.

Owen-Smith, Jason. 2012. "Unanticipated Consequences of University Intellectual Property Policies." In *Universities and Colleges as Economic Drivers: Measuring Higher Education's Role in Economic Development*, edited by Jason E. Lane and D. Bruce Johnstone, 239–78. Albany: State University of New York.

Piller, Ingrid, and Jinhyun Cho. 2013. "Neoliberalism as Language Policy." *Language in Society* 42, no. 1: 23–44. doi:10.1017/S0047404512000887.

Renault, Catherine Searle. 2006. "Academic Capitalism and University Incentives for Faculty Entrepreneurship." *Journal of Technology Transfer* 31, no. 2: 227–39. doi:10.1007/ s10961-005-6108-x.

Rhoades, Gary, Alma Maldonado-Maldonado, Imanol Ordorika, and Martín Velásquez. 2004. "Imagining Alternatives to Global, Corporate, New Economic Academic Capitalism." *Policy Futures in Education* 2, no. 2: 316–29.

Schultz, Laura I. 2012. "University Industry Government Collaboration for Economic Growth." In *Universities and Colleges as Economic Drivers: Measuring Higher Education's Role in Economic Development*, edited by Jason E. Lane and D. Bruce Johnstone, 129–62. Albany: State University of New York.

Seol, Sung-Soo. 2012. "A Model of University Reform in a Developing Country: The Brain Korea 21 Program." *Asian Journal of Innovation and Policy* 1, no. 2: 31–49. doi:10.7545/ajip.2012.1.1.031.

Slaughter, Shelia, and Larry L. Leslie. 1997. *Academic Capitalism: Politics, Policies, and the Entrepreneurial University*. Baltimore: Johns Hopkins University Press.

Slaughter, Shelia, and Gary Rhoades. 2004. *Academic Capitalism and the New Economy: Markets, State, and Higher Education*. Baltimore: Johns Hopkins University Press.

Stewart, Peter. 2007. "Re-Envisioning the Academic Profession in the Shadow of Corporate Managerialism." *Journal of Higher Education in Africa* 5, no. 1: 131–47.

Subotzky, George. 1999. "Beyond the Entrepreneurial University: The Potential Role of South Africa's Historically Disadvantaged Institutions in Reconstruction and Development." *International Review of Education* 45, no. 5–6, 507–27. doi:10.1007/978-94-011-4076-8_9.

Szczepanski, Jan. 1997. "Higher Education as an Object of Research: A Reflection." In *Higher Education Research at the Turn of the New Century: Structures, Issues and Trends*, edited by Jan Sadlak and Philip G. Altbach, 349–57. Paris: UNESCO.

Teichler, Ulrich. 1996. "Comparative Higher Education: Potentials and Limits." *Higher Education* 32, no. 4: 431–65. doi:10.1007/BF00133257.

———. 2000. "The Relationships between Higher Education Research and Higher Education Policy and Practice: The Researchers' Perspective." In *Higher Education Research: Its Relationship to Policy and Practice*, edited by Ulrich Teichler and Jan Sadlak, 3–36. Oxford: IAU Press.

Triple Helix Research Group. 2013. "Official Website, University of Stanford." http://triplehelix.stanford.edu/node/63.

Tudiver, Neil. 1999. *Universities for Sale: Resisting Corporate Control over Canadian Higher Education*. Toronto: Canadian Association of University Teachers and James Lorimer.

UNESCO Institute for Statistics. 2012. "Human Resources in R&D." *UIS Fact Sheet* December, no. 21. www.uis.unesco.org/ScienceTechnology/Documents/sti-hr-rd-en.pdf.

United Kingdom / United States of America Study Group. 2009. *Higher Education and Collaboration in Global Context: Building a Global Civil Society. A Private Report to Prime Minister Gordon Brown*. London: United Kingdom / United States of America Study Group. http://globalhighered.files.wordpress.com/2009/07/final-report_28_7_09.pdf.

Villoro, Juan. 2013. "Damián Ortega: Cómo desarmar el mundo." *Gatopardo*. www.gatopardo.com/ReportajesGP.php?R=201.

Wikipedia. 2013. "List of Venture Capital Firms." http://en.wikipedia.org/wiki/List_of_venture_capital_firms.

Williams, Gareth. 2004. "The Higher Education Market in the United Kingdom." In *Markets in Higher Education: Rhetoric or Reality?*, edited by Pedro Teixeira, Ben

Jongbloed, David Dill, and Alberto Amaral, 241–69. Dordrecht: Kluwer. doi:10.1007/1-4020-835-0_11.

Wyness, Gill. 2013. "Higher Education in 2013: The Year of Marketisation—But to What Extent?" *Guardian*, December 23. www.theguardian.com/higher-education-network/blog/2013/dec/23/higher-education-policy-2013-marketisation.

Yanagisawa, Tomoyo, and Dominique Guellec. 2009. "The Emerging Patent Marketplace." Science, Technology and Industry Working Paper 2009/9. Paris: OECD.

CHAPTER TWELVE

Academic Capitalism in Greater China

Theme and Variations

HEI-HANG HAYES TANG

Education in Greater China—which constitutes mainland China, Hong Kong, Macao, and Taiwan—is phenomenal with regard to shared traditional culture, yet its diverse educational systems emerged from different modernization projects in contemporary history. Educational activities and exchanges are institutionalized by diverse academic structures and systems of credentials. Against the backdrop of globalization, the landscape of Chinese higher education has undergone remarkable transformation. The complex processes of transformation can be uncovered by examining the varied responses to knowledge entrepreneurialism by the national systems in Greater China.

This chapter examines the theme and varied manifestations associated with the phenomenon of academic capitalism in Greater China. It borrows the ideas of Burton Clark (1983) on power coordination among the state, market, and academic profession in higher education systems with a view toward understanding the political configurations of academic capitalism. I identify and describe three "ideal types" that locate the centrality of authority in different national higher education sectors: the state system, the market system, and the academic/professional system. The following sections chronicle the developmental pathways of Greater China's four higher education systems, in particular scrutinizing the collaborations and tensions among the state, economy, and academia during the capitalizing processes of knowledge and educational credentials in the Chinese setting. This chapter purposes to add to the substantial body of literature on academic capitalism and to enhance an understanding of contemporary Chinese higher education in constant transformation.[1]

Academic Capitalism and Political Configurations of Higher Education

In preference to engaging in theoretical discussions about academic capitalism,[2] this chapter offers new insights into the way in which academic capitalism manifests itself in the internal logics of Chinese higher education systems. But internal logics are increasingly affected by the transnationalization of social relations that span across economic, political, and cultural spheres between mainland China, Hong Kong, Macao, and Taiwan. To the end of providing an enhanced understanding of the varied response to the common theme of academic capitalism in Greater China, this chapter suggests an operational definition of academic capitalism in the first place. The definition will be employed in making sense of the historical accounts addressing the issues of increasing marketization of academic programs, prevalence of private institutions of higher education, as well as capitalization of knowledge- and profit-driven academic activities in Greater China.

The operational definition of academic capitalism is formulated as three dimensions of this multifaceted notion. More importantly, I borrow ideas from Clark (1983) on power coordination among state, market, and academic profession in higher education systems with the aim of shedding light on an understanding about the political configurations of academic capitalism in this Chinese region.

First, academic capitalism refers to the phenomenon that higher education institutions and academic units increasingly operate as economic organizations. Within a higher education system, resources are allocated on the basis of performance rather than on the membership of academic units and individual intellectuals. Competition is the "lifeblood" of academia, as in capitalist economy. A market framework is developed to regulate the activities of knowledge production. Like a typical market framework, in academic capitalism on one side reside the supply of educational services, research and knowledge products, consultancy and knowledge-based services, and demands from knowledge consumers and knowledge users reside on the other side. The market is differentiated into the market for students (consumer market) and the market for academics (labor market), both of which are highly influenced by the institutional market. The institutional market refers to the quests by higher education institutions for performance, prestige, and reputation—and hence for good students and scholars. More often than not, the mobility of both pupils and teachers is from a less attractive place to a more attractive one. The wide-reaching quest for talent and brains becomes a global phenomenon through highly competitive academic salaries and remuneration packages for scholars, as well as attractive scholarships and stipends for students. Knowledge and education are becoming less a public good but increasingly "capitalized" (Etzkowitz, Webster, and Healey 1998). Through globalization, the market framework is more open, competitions are intensified, and cross-border capitalist academic activities are more commonplace.

Second, an ideology of academic capitalism legitimates the domination of university managerialism and inequalities between the privileged groups and their disadvantaged counterparts in academia (Slaughter and Rhoades 2004). The ideology constitutes the "superstructure" of an academic enterprise and indoctrinates a new understanding of academic excellence, which is redefined as excelling in the academic game by accumulating prestige and profits. Different institutional support (funding and manpower) for academic units and individual academics represents the social returns of the contributions they make. Narratives and discourses surrounding "value for money," economic productivities, city/national competitiveness, as well as capitalization of human talents and knowledge facilitate indoctrination of the ideology. Since the rise of neoliberalism in the 1980s, competitiveness discourses gained currency—through wide circulation—among policymakers, elite circles of business leaders, university administrators, the mass media, and general public. According to Slaughter and Cantwell (2012), human capital and competitiveness discourses justify and normalize neoliberal changes in higher education, which utilize education as an investment for economic returns rather than for social good and social justice. The concerned narratives and discourses further elaborate and articulate the ideology of academic capitalism through "social technologies" of various ranking methods of "world-class universities," citation indices of journal publications, and audit exercises for quality assurance. The circuits of production and reproduction of such narratives and discourses reveal that the prevalent economic culture forms, transpires, and reinforces the rudiments of academic capitalist ideology, in line with the existing political agenda and ideology. Corporate leaders, in capitalist economies in particular, are the key players in the initiation, articulation, and advocacy in the abovementioned competitiveness narratives. The corporate elites, despite being external to the academic profession, are commonly on the board of trustees or regents, and they phase in corporate-like governance of higher education to universities' "executive management" (Slaughter and Cantwell 2012).

The ideology of academic capitalism induces profound changes in the meanings and ideals of academic autonomy and freedom. Academic freedom has more to do with the freedom to perform and excel in a liberal academic system than with the high calling of intellectuals to speak truth to the powerful. The ideology of academic capitalism blinds the members of academia to the contradictions in capitalist society, and to their mission to pursue social justice for the people.

Third, academic capitalism further empowers the bureaucracies of academic enterprises. Higher education administrators and their managerial capacity increasingly oversee the professional activities of academics (Slaughter and Rhoades 2004). In the name of efficiency and cost-effectiveness, administrators tighten the control and coordination of resource allocation, curriculum, and research agenda (strategic research planning). There is likewise an increasing lack of academic staffs' involvement in the decision-making process. The phenomenon of having more appointed academic deans and top-down management is prevalent. "Accountability"—whether to the government, private sponsors, general public, or students—justifies such managerialism. University administration imposes laissez-faire principles and formulates pro-competition policies in their institutions so as to provide the conditions conducive to capital accumulation in the economy. Market forces are allowed to enter academe to shape the future of higher learning, to determine the career prospects of individual scholars, and to achieve the goal of advancing growth and competitiveness in a capitalist economy.

Examining the political configurations of academic capitalism can enable an enhanced understanding of the concept. These configurations can be understood by borrowing the ideas of Burton Clark (1983) on power coordination among state, market, and academic profession in higher education systems. Clark (1983, 136) formulates three "ideal types" of systems that locate the centrality of authority in different national higher education sectors: the state system, the market system, and the academic/professional system. Putting the three systems at each corner of a triangular conceptual space (as shown in fig. 12.1), with the corners resembling the extreme, the framework illustrates the forms of authority that pull in different directions. The resultant position in the triangle locates the centrality of authority of a particular higher education system. In actuality, power relations in every higher education system are a result of combinations of three forms of authority in varying degrees.

At the top corner of the triangle, we have an extreme form of state authority over affairs of higher education. With unitary state coordination, policy goals are uniformly set and planned, problems are commonly defined, and all solutions are centrally decided. The formal higher education structure is tightly regulated and inclusive. The totality of power originates in the state, but at the discretion of state policy, power can pass on to select capitalists and some prominent scholars who are more than often pro-regime. In Greater China, mainland China demonstrates the characteristics of a state-led model. In line with the spirit of its planned economy, the mainland Chinese higher education system holds the strongest form of state coordination.

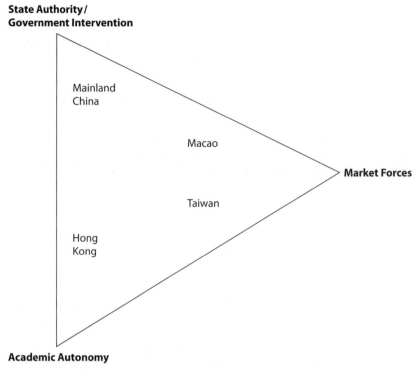

Figure 12.1. Academic capitalism in Greater China: Locating the centrality of authority of various higher education systems. Modified from Clark (1983, 143)

At the other end of the conceptual triangle is the sole coordination by the "invisible hand" of the market. Unlike the state-led model, there are no inclusive goals in the pure academic marketplace. Academic higher education initiatives are taken on the basis of "social choice," which refers to "a resultant of actions and competitive interactions of autonomous organizations, rather than a solution to common problems" (Banfield 1961, 326–27, as cited in Clark 1983, 137). Taiwan's higher education system shares the attributes of this market model. In view of the massification of higher education in Taiwan since the late 1990s, the number of tertiary education institutions proliferated, and more than 70% were privately run. Taiwan's democratic development provides checks and balances against possible state-capitalist cooptation from intervening in higher education affairs. This is contrasted with the marketization of Macao's higher education, which is more shaped by the government-capitalist collaborative power, the personalization of politics, and the lack of checks and balances against the nondemocratic government.

Lastly, at the bottom corner is the academic/professional system. In the professional model where academic autonomy is valued and protected to the fullest extent, the government mainly funds higher education institutions. Decision making is based on the professional expertise of academics, whereas the distribution of power and resources is based on academics' representation and their membership in academia. One example is the United Kingdom before state power increased in the 1960s. Academics were protected from the influence of the market and the state by a buffer body, namely, the university grant committee, which upheld its mission to defend the intact value of both university autonomy and individual academic freedom. Peer review by experts in the academic profession maintained academic quality. Therefore the main authority in the professional higher education model was regarded as a form of academic power, in a way "taking the government's money without taking orders from the government's officials" (Clark 1983, 141).

If the state coordination of higher education is weak, the academic profession can modulate state-initiated rules. Take the case of Hong Kong. Its government does not have concrete long-term higher education policies. The influential mass media offers checks and balances against the government from time to time, safeguarding the rule of law, which is one of Hong Kong's core values even though it is not a democracy. Along with the buffer body of the University Grant Council, in existence since colonial times,[3] the mostly publicly funded Hong Kong academic profession is less affected by market forces and direct intervention by the government. In a comparative but not a normative sense, Hong Kong can perhaps be located at the bottom of the conceptual triangle, a position closer to the corner of "academic autonomy." Unlike Hong Kong, Macao does not have a buffer body to protect the autonomy of its academic profession. The centrality of authority in Macao's higher education system lies close to the market model. Concerted efforts by state officials and business leaders contribute to the dynamics of academic capitalism in Macao. Applying my conceptual framework, the following sections will provide historical accounts of the varied developmental pathways of higher education in Greater China.

"Managed" Marketization of Higher Education in Mainland China

Private education had been commonplace before the establishment of the People's Republic of China (PRC) by the Chinese Communist Party in 1949. Private schools constituted around two-fifths of all schools in operation before 1949. Nonetheless, for ideological reasons, a nationalization project from the 1950s until the early 1980s transformed all private schools into public institutions.

Market forces had been incorporated in China's higher education system since the 1980s (Law 1995), particularly in line with the 1978 open-door policy of China's leader Deng Xiaoping. Demands for education increased along with rising economic development across the nation (Law and Pan 2009). Education was strategically regarded as a component essential to the tertiary industries in mainland China, as explicitly stated in the 1992 state document "Decision on Facilitating Tertiary Industries" (Zhu and Li 2012). In the same year, the National People's Congress stated in Education Law, Article 25, a preference for private education, though noting that it should be regulated and not focused on profit making. With this law, the congress allowed private education for the first time. Further, in enacting the law, the "Outline of the Reform and Development of China's Education" (released in 1993) put forward a new negotiated dynamic among government, tertiary education, and market forces. Thereafter the PRC state government published the 1998 policy "A Plan for Promoting Education in the 21st Century," which stated a goal of orienting its higher education toward massification.

The state government steers the "managed" marketization of higher education in mainland China through legislation, control of information, and funding appropriation. A significant piece of legislation, the Law of Private Education Promotion, was enacted in 2002 for the purpose of regulating private education institutions from expanding their enterprise beyond earning "reasonable profits." Allowing public universities to set up and operate affiliated "independent colleges," which could generate profit, the Ministry of Education issued a set of policies known as "Regulating and Facilitating Independent Colleges Managed by Public Higher Education Institutions" in 2003 and "Implementation Rules of the Law of Private Education Promotion" in 2004.

Chinese higher education experienced rapid growth during the 2000s, especially through the establishment of private—or *minban*, meaning operated by the people—institutions. In 2000, there were 1,041 institutions with a total enrollment of 5.57 million students. By 2009, there were 1,983 institutions, of which 334 were privately owned (accommodating 4.36 million students, or 20.3% of the total student enrollment). Lately, more than 2,500 senior vocational and technical institutes and nearly 300 higher education institutes are run as private institutions. In 2011, 309 independent colleges were in operation (Ministry of Education of the People's Republic of China 2011).

To explain the state-controlled marketizing processes in China's higher education, Zhu and Li (2012) argue that there was not sufficient government budgetary support in response to the accelerating expansion of student enrollment

(183). Following the "user-charge principle," higher education institutions were to explore alternative measures to fund operational costs, including increased student tuition fees and bank loans. Across the nation, bank loans to higher learning institutions were recorded at more than $32.4 billion in 2009 (Zhu and Li 2012, 186).

In the course of expanding the higher education sector in mainland China, power began to decentralize among higher education institutions. They had greater autonomy in administering university affairs, student admissions, and the deployment of academic staff (including managing their salaries) and, more importantly, in transforming orientation of knowledge creation and knowledge dissemination. Through the education reforms of 1985, the "president-responsibility system" was initiated with the goal of insulating institutional operation of Chinese universities from the power of the local Communist Party, with private institutions free to appoint their own presidents. But the changes were minimal owing to strong state control (e.g., non-mainlander organizations or institutes did not receive total ownership of private colleges or universities but instead had to cooperate with local partners). Soon after the June 4 student democratic movement in 1989, the policy initiative was put on hold, and in the 1993 education reform the government resumed its control of the system.

Law (1995) argues that knowledge structure is the area in which the state has the least control in transformations owing to marketization (335). University research is increasingly oriented toward creating (or applying) knowledge for economic development. Higher education institutions introduced academic subjects that are instrumental to the workplace and hence preferred by students, including business, engineering science, foreign language, and international trade. Self-financed academic programs became increasingly common. They widen access to higher education and increase the number of students, who are admitted to universities with lower entrance scores, on average, than their peers who are admitted through the state-controlled enrollment quota. On the basis of financial circumstance and budgeting, China's institutions can devise their own performance-based salary scale for academic staff. Academics can increase or supplement their income on top of the institutional pay scale by taking up assignments from external sources. Zhu and Li (2012) observe that engagement in entrepreneurial activities, including applied research, constitutes part of the academic life of some university researchers (188).

In all, academic capitalism reshapes the landscape of institutional autonomy of China's universities. But the transformation processes are conditioned through subtle negotiation on the government's terms (Law 1995, 355). Specifically, Law and Pan (2007) make the case that the legislative processes of private education law are a "game of negotiation" among China's State Council, the National People's Congress Standing Committee, and investors of private education institutes. In the midst of "managed" marketization of higher education in mainland China, bureaucratization is another impediment to market forces that may have affected higher education activities (Zhu and Li 2012, 187). Time will tell whether private higher education in mainland China will continue to play a minimal role.

Entrepreneurial Higher Education Governance and the Performance-Driven Academic Profession in Hong Kong

Hong Kong is known as an economic success. From a "barren rock" to one of Asia's "four little dragons," the economic development of Hong Kong spurred many to seek explanations for this "economic miracle." Market forces have always been an almost sacred part of the Hong Kong culture (Postiglione 2006). The value system of Hong Kong is arguably dominated by the operational logic of capitalism (Lung 2006). Profit, free-market competitiveness, pervasive efficiency, capital accumulation, global trade, consumerism, and land development constitute the "central value" that flourishes in both business and politics (Lee 2008, 5). All the same, within the operational logic of Hong Kong capitalism, its higher education sector was never central to the economy during the colonial era. It was treated as a social service rather than a commodity. Provided that Hong Kong's colonial government controlled a limited expansion of higher education, many students needed to look for higher education overseas. Research provisions and productivity from Hong Kong universities were all the while minimal. When the government or industry was in need of knowledge for policy design or technological innovation, they purchased research from foreign countries, especially Britain. The research tradition in Hong Kong universities only started in the 1990s.

By and large, the Hong Kong government plays a dominant role in the provision of higher education and hence the sector's development. Except for a private liberal arts college (which became a university in 2006) and an open university (which runs programs on a self-financed basis), all Hong Kong universities are publicly funded. The government also funds an institute of education (which is currently in preparation for pursuing the status of university) and an academy for performing arts. Higher education policies are implemented neither directly nor top-down by the government but through a buffer organization, namely, the University Grants Committee of Hong Kong (UGC). Legally speaking, Hong Kong higher education institutions are autonomous bodies that are run and ruled by institutional ordinances and governing bodies. The Basic Law's Article 137 of the Hong Kong Special Administrative Region protects academic freedom (Postiglione 2006). The practice that to the institutions possesses the capacity to spend recurrent grants at will is based upon philosophies of academic freedom; it is also concerned with efficiency and effectiveness. The issues of excellence, cost-effectiveness, and public accountability are keys to the policy agenda (UGC 1996). The entrepreneurial governance (Slaughter and Cantwell 2012) of Hong Kong higher education is evident in this regard, especially within an environment where a culture of consensus exists (Postiglione 2002) and managerialism is embraced.

The government's promotion of entrepreneurial governance in universities was reinforced by the austerity affected by the Asian financial crisis of 1997. Amid a massive expansion of opportunities for undergraduate education in early 1990s, the local community, to which publicly funded institutions are accountable, raised questions regarding efficiency, cost-effectiveness, and economy of service (Postiglione and Mak 1997). The government announced that government-funded institutions should consolidate their competitive strengths in order to attain international excellence (Tung 1997). Managing research for the knowledge economy, six interdisciplinary "centers of excellence" for research were strategically formulated. Accordingly, strategic plans of local universities during that period mirrored the government's strategic research themes by akin categorization.

In the educational reforms of 2000, an initial funding cut of 4% for the higher education sector took place. The government directed a higher target of massification, for 60% of secondary school graduates to purse tertiary education by 2010, with private initiatives creating the expansion. The American system of associate's degree programs was then introduced on a self-financed model and has become part of Hong Kong's higher education structure. According to the government report "Higher Education in Hong Kong in 2002," only selected institutions should strategically receive focused public and private support for the sake of enabling them to be competitive at the highest international levels (Sutherland 2002, 6–7). Within the performance-driven academic profession, research productivities, which are competitive at an international level, would be favorably rewarded. The report produced the narrative of "value for money" (Slaughter and Cantwell 2012) and indoctrinated the respective ideology into the funding mechanism of academic programs in Hong Kong universities. In March 2003, the government suddenly announced a 10% cut in funding for UGC-funded institutions for the following academic year (with forthcoming further cuts). More significantly, the government induced the marketization of higher education by requiring that all taught postgraduate and subdegree programs operate on a self-financed basis. To open the market for mainland and international students, the government removed the quota for nonlocal research postgraduate students, and relaxed the quota for nonlocal students in publicly funded undergraduate and taught postgraduate programs to 4%. Universities may, for the sake of cost recovery, prefer exploring the markets of mainland Chinese and international students to retaining a focused commitment of educating the local students. Delinking the salary scale of UGC-funded institutions with that of civil service was one policy that also helped the Hong Kong academic profession to be more adaptive to the academic labor market.

The tightening of the government's purse for higher education was unquestionably not favorable for universities. Yet, after voicing their discontent about the issue (e.g., through the news media), universities were ready to cope with the new reality. Economizing academic life (Bok 2003) became core thinking to the strategic adaptation of Hong Kong academic professionals, particularly leaders and achievers. To increase accountability, the president of the Chinese University of Hong Kong advocated that universities continuously improve their curricula so as to guarantee the standard of graduates and to meet the changing needs of society. He furthermore encouraged universities to conduct more applied research and to develop more links with the business and industrial sectors, particularly to attract external funding (Mok 2001).

Amid prevailing pro-competition policies and the academic culture in a quest for world-class research and institutional prestige through various global rankings, the government's role has changed from a sponsor of educational services to a regulator (Mok 1999, 2003). That said, managerialism in Hong Kong academia can accommodate dynamic negotiations, which are conditioned in the pro-competition and performance-driven academic culture of its higher education system. One counterexample of top-down managerialism is the institutional merger plan of the mid-2000s. The UGC set up the ad hoc working group Institutional Integration Working Party and published a report in 2004 to propose the possible merger of the Chinese University of Hong Kong, Hong Kong University of Science and Technology, and Hong Kong Institute of Education. Yet the institutional merger proposal could not win the general support of academics from these institutions, and the plan was not actualized. Comparatively but not normatively speaking, Hong Kong higher education resembles the "ideal type" professional model.

Macao's Casino Economy and Academic Capitalism

The history of Macao's higher education is short. A small population is one of the factors unfavorable for government investment on higher education. Macao's Portuguese colonial government had only lukewarm concern for higher education and tended to encourage sending students across the border for university education. The diversity of high school systems (e.g., in Hong Kong, Portugal, Taiwan, and the United States) complicated any possible initiatives to establish the first university. Therefore the establishment of the first university in 1981—the University of East Asia (UEA)—was neither a venture by the Portuguese Macao government nor an initiative from the private sector of Macao. Instead, UEA was established by a group of Hong Kong business leaders who wanted to expand the study opportunities of Hong Kong's young people at that time. As the private provision of education disagreed with the prevailing educational philosophy of Hong Kong's colonial government, UEA's founders approached the Macao government, which agreed to support the UEA proposal with a land grant. That venture was realized despite the fact that the university's mission was to serve external students from mainland China, Hong Kong, and Malaysia, and that its language of instruction was English. The founding of the first modern university in Macao as a private entity reflected the education philosophy of Portuguese administration, a philosophy that would shape the future marketization of higher education in Macao.

Regarding the provisions of educational service, Macao is adopting a strategy of diversified provision by various types of higher education institutions. Privatization has become the trend for the expansion of Macao's higher education since the 1990s. There are four public higher education institutions and six privately run institutions in Macao. Instead of merging the smaller institutions with their larger counterparts, the diversification of institutional types is sustained and so are their provisions. The existing ten institutions are of different sizes and shapes, ranging from a small nursing college with 270 students to universities with more than 8,000 students. Recently, most of the institutions have substantially expanded their bachelor's programs, including Asia International Open University, the Institute for Tourism Studies, Millennium College, University of Saint Joseph, and University of Science and Technology. Four out of these five institutions are private institutions (Gabinete de Apoio ao Ensino Superior 2008) that are as active as their public counterparts in Macao's development of its higher education. The proportion of students registered at private institutions accelerated from 39.5% (of the total student population) in 1999–2000 to

67.4% in 2008–9. In a decade's time, actual student registrations experienced more than a sixfold expansion, from 3,385 students to 21,059 students.

Amid the globalization of knowledge-based economies, education services offer a promising source of entrepreneurial opportunities and economic revenue. Privatization serves also as a form of strategic development for higher education's expansion across the region of Asia (Shin and Harman 2009). Macao's universities take an active role in this regard. In March 2011, the Macau University of Science and Technology cohosted the University Presidents Forum with private universities in Japan, South Korea, and Taiwan for collaborations and strategic planning for cross-border higher education development in the Asia-Pacific region. The forum was well received by presidents from more than twenty Asian private universities and was well supported by the Macao government (*Macao Daily News* 2011).

Nationally, Macao is a destination of study opportunities for students from mainland China. As shown in educational statistics for the 2008 and 2009 school years, more than half (52%) of student enrollments were from places outside Macao, while local citizens constituted the remaining 48%. More specifically, nonlocal students outnumber the locals in doctorate programs, master's programs, and postgraduate diploma programs. Macao's postgraduate programs are attractive to mainland graduates who wish to work and reside in Macao after graduation as well as to those who might later use Macao as a springboard for overseas education. Among the ten institutions, four are providing postgraduate programs. The Macau University of Science and Technology has been the most responsive to the continual increase of doctorate students by accommodating about 70% of students at that level.

Taking advantage of most of the entrepreneurial opportunities for the sake of increased revenue and hence expansion of higher education, Macao needs to be strategic in its student recruitment. During the 2006–7 academic year, 57.4% of students enrolled in the studies of business or gaming management, 10.3% in tourism and entertainment (being the second largest), but only 0.2% of students enrolled in the humanities, which remains perhaps the least popular subject in Macao. In a 2008 country report to UNESCO, the Macao Tertiary Education Services Office addressed questions of revising higher education regulations for more flexible systems (e.g., credit unit and double-degree system) and establishing a tertiary education fund for students' financial aid (Gabinete de Apoio ao Ensino Superior 2008, 15) in the hopes of attracting more students to study in Macao. Professor Sou Chio Fai, the newly appointed director of the Tertiary Education Services Office in March 2011, supported scholarships to assist Guangdong students pursuing higher education in Macao (*Hou Kong Daily* 2011). The Macao government also endeavors to solve the problem of drop-outs (which is rather unusual in other Chinese higher education systems) and to increase the attractiveness of its higher education institutions as the first choice for high school graduates, especially male students.

Increasing philanthropic donations to higher education by capitalists also reflect the closer link between the university sector and the business world. From 2007 to 2008, the Venetian, a luxury hotel and casino owned by the Las Vegas Sands Corporation, twice gave the University of Macau a donation of 650,000 patacas for setting up a new scholarship and fellowship program at the university. It was the largest donation the university ever received from a single sponsor. In May 2008, this university-capitalist partnership signed an agreement to establish the 1,435-square-meter Adelson Advanced Education Centre of the University of Macau at the company's casino-hotel complex in Cotai. Under the patron-client relationship, the University of Macau is responsible for running professional training programs in the areas of hospitality, entertainment, and retail (*Macao Post Daily* 2008). It is anticipated that, to better finance additional higher education activities, more university-business cooperation will be forged in the future. Academic capitalism is intensifying in Macao.

Academic Capitalism in Democratic Taiwan

Taiwan is the only democratic regime in Greater China. Accommodating more than 160 universities, Taiwan higher education embraces diversities of the public/private divide, size, and academic orientation. But in terms of Taiwan higher education history, it did not have a "democratic start." Since independence from Japanese colonial rule in 1945, the Ministry of Education in Taiwan held tight control of higher education institutions, be they public institutes or private institutes. One of the functions of the ministry is to protect the ideology of the government in power at that time, namely, the National Party (known as Kuomintang). At the same time that opinions and commentary on political affairs were restricted, the number of higher education institutions was also limited. There were only two universities and twelve colleges with fewer than 1,500 academics in 1954.

With an intention to supply manpower for the skilled labor force, the number of higher education institutes proliferated in late 1950s and 1960s, particularly industrial junior colleges, the dominant majority of which were private institutes. During that period, the number of university students also increased by more than tenfold. Given such profound growth, the Taiwanese government started to intervene in the 1970s through early 1980s by limiting the growth rate of higher education institutions and disallowing the status upgrading of industrial junior colleges to colleges. The only exception is the establishment of graduate schools that the government encouraged.

Through offering subsidies, the Ministry of Education intervened in the governance of Taiwan's private higher education institutions. There had been tight scrutiny on how private universities managed their financial resources. Notwithstanding being wholly responsible for their financial management, private higher education institutions in Taiwan needed to charge the amount of tuition fees standardized by the Ministry of Education.

The Taiwanese government had control in all aspects of university affairs through strict legislation in the name of "national security" (Chiang 2004), which Mok (2002) understands as a top-down nationalizaton project in line with the prevailing political authoritarianism. Decisions about the allocation of higher education funding from the state were not made with academic but rather political consideration. A norm of high conformity was observed among Taiwanese universities until the late 1980s. In terms of the pattern of scholarship, the humanities and social sciences were less emphasized than natural sciences, lest democratic ideas emerge from engagement in the soft disciplines of political science, sociology, or the like (Chan 2010).

Democratization emerged in the late 1980s in Taiwan. Democratic ideas spread wide following the abolition of the Order of Martial Law on July 15, 1987, in particular. Taiwan started to have opposition institutionalized into its political system. In the sector of intelligentsia and higher education, Taiwanese scholars became involved in various attempts to establish academic democratization, especially in search of intellectual freedom and institutional autonomy. Yuen Tseh Lee, the first Taiwanese Nobel Prize laureate, chaired a review organization in 1994 and designed the democratic slogan "professor rules the campus," which gained popularity at that time (Chan 2010, 148). In the same year, the Council of Education Reform embraced the theme of liberalization (or, in Mandarin Chinese, *song-bang*, meaning "liberation from tight control"). University law was revised to allow democratic governance in Taiwanese universities. University members could elect their own presidents, whereas a higher-level council for institutional affairs would democratically make institutional policies. In confirming the scope of institutional autonomy of Taiwanese universities, interpretation number 380 of the Council of Grand Justice was set up in 1995. As a result, Taiwanese public universities were officially allowed to accumulate the financial resources they raised, beginning with the establishment of the University Development Foundation Fund.

Two years after the initiative of liberalization by the Council of Education Reform, in 1996, some selected public universities received financial autonomy in fundraising and managing money from nongovernment sources. The idea of decentralization was subsequently incorporated in the White Paper on Higher Education in 2001 (Chan 2010). It was proposed that Taiwanese universities should enjoy autonomy in institutional finance, human resources management, and curriculum design. Private corporations were allowed to open new universities and colleges during this period of "academic democratization." The number of higher education institutes had been growing, from 105 in 1996 to 165 in 2006.

After the massification processes of more than a decade, the issue of quality assurance became part of the agenda. Globalization quickens the development of knowledge economies, which treat universities as part of the engine in producing knowledge for the economy. Top-down policies have been implemented to enable effective production and application of knowledge for top research institutes, world-class universities, and the advanced knowledge economy. A 2001 initiative that merged smaller public higher education institutes with sizable established universities, for example, was introduced for the sake of economies of scale and effective deployment of resources.

Despite their status as public institutions, Taiwanese national universities and colleges have less than 80% of their institutional budgets funded by the Ministry of Education (Mok 2002). Given the amendment to the University Law in 2005, public universities are endowed with the legal status to own assets and property. Not unlike other higher education institutions in Taiwan or Greater China, they are to be entrepreneurial in pursuing multiple sources of funding. The democratic values do not significantly affect the way in which academic capitalism is manifest in Taiwan through national education policies.

Conclusion

This chapter examined the political configurations of higher education systems in mainland China, Hong Kong, Macao, and Taiwan, with a particular focus on how academic capitalism manifests itself variedly in Greater China. I borrowed Clark's (1983) ideas about the coordination of power among the state, market, and academic profession to investigate the developmental pathways of these four higher education systems. Results of the study demonstrate that in a comparative but not normative sense, mainland China resembles the "ideal type" of state system, Hong Kong resembles a professional system, and Macao and Taiwan resemble a market system. Specifically, the findings are obtained in terms of the centrality of authority located in the respective higher education sectors from a comparative perspective. Collaborations and tensions arise in various patterns among the state, economy, and academia during the capitalizing processes of knowledge and educational credentials in the Chinese setting.

The model setting suggested by this study is by no means static. Under the context of globalization coinciding with the rise of mainland China the twenty-first century, the internal logics of Greater China's higher education system started to be affected by the transnationalization of social relations that span across economic, political, and cultural spheres in the Chinese region. Inflows of students from mainland China to Hong Kong and Macao reconstitute student demography and reshape the campus cultures. On account of a considerably high concentration of world-class universities in Hong Kong, some Chinese students consider Hong Kong to be a springboard for entering a more prestigious university in the West. The mobility of academics, including the return of those who studied in the West, facilitates the change of academic cultures to some extent. Demands of knowledge from China's growing innovative industries incentivize cross-border knowledge transfer from Hong Kong, for example, through the adjacent city of Shenzhen (Sharif and Tang forthcoming). Given the rising power of mainland China's political economy, however, the distribution of influences tends to be more dominated by the mainland; hence Greater China's subtle transformations are understood to be the process of "Mainlandization." That said, globalization does not necessarily quicken the rate of transformation in the Chinese academic capitalism. At the base of the four systems in Greater China we find different academic/institutional structures, systems of credentials, academic cultures, ideological foundations, and local cultures. They add up to and act as impediments to changes generated by the transnational spread of academic capitalism. On account of academic capitalism and globalization, changing higher education is the new reality. But the transformations are the result of complex processes involving tensions and collaboration between the state, market, and academy in response to the global trend of academic capitalism. In Greater China, time will tell whether the variety of responses may arrive at some sort of convergence under a vision called "One China." But thus far, it is quite unlikely.

NOTES

1. Substance in the sections of "Political Configurations of Higher Education and Academic Capitalism" and "Macao's Casino Economy and Academic Capitalism" is borrowed from Tang (forthcoming).

2. For in-depth theoretical discussions about the concept, see chapters 2 and 7 in this volume.

3. The University Grants Committee of Hong Kong was set up according to suggestions made by the Hong Kong Legislative Council during the 1964 budget debate. It was recommended that a committee similar to the British University Grants Committee should be set up in Hong Kong to advise the Hong Kong government on the facilities, development, and financial needs of universities in the territory. The committee was formally appointed in October 1965. In light of the needs of the Hong Kong community, these principles and practices have been adapted over the years with reference to the situation of Hong Kong (information retrieved from www.ugc.edu.hk). For example, Postiglione and Tang (2008) find that more than half (53.8%) of Hong Kong academics agree that the administration of their institution supports academic freedom (241).

REFERENCES

Banfield, Edward C. 1961. *Political Influence*. Glencoe: Free Press.

Bok, Derek. 2003. *Universities in the Marketplace: The Commercialization of Higher Education*. Princeton, NJ: Princeton University Press.

Chan, Sheng-Ju. 2010. "Shifting Governance Patterns in Taiwanese Higher Education." In *The Search for New Governance of Higher Education in Asia*, edited by Ka-Ho Mok, 139–52. New York: Palgrave Macmillan.

Chiang, Li-Chuan. 2004. "The Relationship between University Autonomy and Funding in England and Taiwan." *Higher Education* 48, no. 2: 189–212. doi:10.1023/B:HIGH .0000034314.77435.bf.

Clark, Burton R. 1983. *The Higher Education System: Academic Organization in Cross-National Perspective*. Berkeley: University of California Press.

Etzkowitz, Henry, Andrew Webster, and Peter Healey, eds. 1998. *Capitalizing Knowledge: New Intersections of Industry and Academia*. Albany: State University of New York Press.

Gabinete de Apoio ao Ensino Superior. 2008. "Documentation Provided for the Country Report to the UNESCO Asia-Pacific Sub-Regional Preparatory Conference." Paper presented at the 2009 World Conference on Higher Education, Macao, Bangkok, September 25–26.

Hou Kong Daily. 2011. "Gradual Implementation of the Framework in Socio-Cultural Aspects." March 10, B01.

Law, Wing-Wah. 1995. "The Role of the State in Higher Education Reform: Mainland China and Taiwan." *Comparative Education Review* 39, no. 3: 322–55.

Law, Wing-Wah, and Su-Yan Pan. 2009. "Game Theory and Educational Policy: Private Education Legislation in China." *International Journal of Educational Development* 29, no. 3: 227–40. doi:10.1016/j.ijedudev.2008.04.003.

Lee, Leo Ou-fan. 2008. *The City between Worlds: My Hong Kong*. Cambridge, MA: Harvard University Press.

Lung, Y. T. 2006. *Lung Ying-tai's Hong Kong Notebook*. Hong Kong: Cosmo.

Macao Daily News. 2011. "Asia-Pacific Private University Presidents Forum Was Launched Yesterday." March 29, B06.

Macao Post Daily. 2008. "University of Macau, Venetian Sign Deal on Education Centre." May 13, P05.

Ministry of Education of the People's Republic of China. 2011. "Education Statistics in 2011." Beijing: Ministry of Education of the People's Republic of China. www.moe.edu.cn/publicfiles/business/htmlfiles/moe/s7308/index.html.

Mok, Ka-Ho. 1999. "The Cost of Managerialism: The Implications for the 'McDonaldisation' of Higher Education in Hong Kong." *Journal of Higher Education Policy and Management* 21, no. 1: 117–27. doi:10.1080/1360080990210109.

———. 2001. "Academic Capitalisation in the New Millennium: The Marketisation and Corporatisation of Higher Education in HONG Kong." *Policy and Politics* 29, no. 3: 299–315.

———. 2002. "From Nationalization to Marketization: Changing Governance in Taiwan's Higher-Education System." *Governance* 15, no. 2: 137–59. doi:10.1111/1468-0491.00183.

———. 2003. "Globalisation and Higher Education Restructuring in Hong Kong, Taiwan and Mainland China." *Higher Education Research and Development* 22, no. 2: 117–29. doi:10.1080/0729436030411.

Postiglione, Gerard A. 2002. "The Transformation of Academic Autonomy in Hong Kong." In *Crisis and Transformation in China's Hong Kong*, edited by Ming Kou Chan and Alvin Y. So, 307–21. Hong Kong: Hong Kong University Press.

———. 2006. "The Hong Kong Special Administrative Region of the People's Republic of China: Context, Higher Education, and a Changing Academia." In *Reports of Changing Academic Profession Project Workshop on Quality, Relevance, and Governance in the Changing Academia: International Perspectives*, 97–114. Hiroshima: Research Institute for Higher Education, Hiroshima University.

Postiglione, Gerard A., and Grace C. L. Mak, eds. 1997. *Asian Higher Education: An International Handbook and Reference Guide*. Westport, CT: Greenwood Press.

Postiglione, Gerard A., and Hei-hang Hayes Tang. 2008. "A Preliminary Review of the Hong Kong CAP data." In *The Changing Academic Profession in International, Comparative and Quantitative Perspectives: Report of the International Conference on the Changing Academic Profession Project, 2008*, 227–49. Hiroshima: Research Institute for Higher Education, Hiroshima University.

Sharif, N., and Hei-hang Hayes Tang. Forthcoming. "Hong Kong and Shenzhen: New Trends in Innovation Strategy at Chinese Universities." *International Journal of Technology Management*.

Shin, Jung Cheol, and Grant Harman. 2009. "New Challenges for Higher Education: Global and Asia-Pacific Perspectives." *Asia Pacific Education Review* 10, no. 1: 1–13. doi:10.1007/s12564-009-9011-6.

Slaughter, Sheila, and Brendan Cantwell. 2012. "Transatlantic Moves to the Market: Academic Capitalism in the United States and European Union." *Higher Education* 63, no. 5: 583–603. doi:10.1007/s10734-011-9460-9.

Slaughter, Shelia, and Gary Rhoades. 2004. *Academic Capitalism and the New Economy: Markets, State, and Higher Education.* Baltimore: Johns Hopkins University Press.

Sutherland, Stewart R. 2002. "Higher Education in Hong Kong: Report of the University Grants Committee." Hong Kong: University Grants Committee of Hong Kong.

Tang, H. H. Forthcoming. "Academic Capitalism and Higher Education in Macao." In *China's Macao Transformed: Challenge and Development in the 21st Century,* edited by Eilo W. Y. Yu and Ming K. Chan. Hong Kong: City University of Hong Kong Press.

Tung, C. H. 1997. *Building Hong Kong for a New Era: Policy Address for 1997.* Hong Kong: Hong Kong Special Administrative Region Government.

UGC. University Grants Committee of Hong Kong. 1996. *Higher Education in Hong Kong: A Report.* Hong Kong: UGC.

Zhu, Fengliang, and Sumin Li. 2012. "Marketization in Chinese Higher Education." In *State and Market in Higher Education Reforms: Trends, Policies and Experiences in Comparative Perspective,* edited by Hans Georg Schütze, Germán Álvarez Mendiola, and Diane Helen Conrad, 181–99. Rotterdam: Sense.

CHAPTER THIRTEEN

Risky Business

Academic Capitalism, Globalization, and the Risk University

ROGER P. KING

This chapter examines the development of the "risk university" and its potential global diffusion as an organizational and policy template. Risk has long been associated with capitalist entrepreneurial activity as a source of potential value and creative innovation, although in everyday discourse, risk is more generally regarded as indicating possible hazard and danger. Alongside the suggestion of quirky and individualistic and speculative behavior, risk also suggests a rather modernist belief in human ability to manage the probabilities of the future through rational planning and administrative controls. Such instruments are needed in order to productively structure and organize innovative activity (to realize full value), and also to ameliorate unwanted outcomes, either for an organization (regarding reputation especially) or the wider public (e.g., environmental pollution from industrial plants). As with capitalism more generally, therefore, risk reflects both the creativity of enterprise and the constant tendency to realize its fruits through organizational planning. Although studies of risk often examine its implications for individuals and whole societies (Beck 1999; Giddens 2002), here I examine risk as an organizational and policy characteristic. With corporatized academic capitalism, one expects to find increased risk and attempts to both encourage and to minimize it. Marketization incentivizes risk taking by universities in search of value and competitive edge (such as overseas ventures), but these organizations also possess, through increased internal control systems, the organizational means for coordinated forms of risk mitigation.

The use of risk as a key organizing principle in higher education reflects the increased competitiveness and accountability of most contemporary universities as well as the spread of neoliberal public management models of governance. Essentially, the growth of risk models in universities and their sectors further exemplifies the increased transfer to public organizations of practices and standards found in explicitly commercial parts of economies, sometimes occurring through forms of public-private partnerships that are found worldwide. Nonetheless, although there are clear diffusion dynamics to risk university models as they are picked up globally, significant barriers and obstacles to their universalization exist as well. Here I examine both aspects.

Isomorphism

Higher education systems tend to be isomorphic in their worldwide convergence on curricula, operations, and governance models. Institutional homogeneity may reflect the organizational searches for legitimacy found in many sectors, but broader economic and cultural change in societies also plays a part, including moves in some emerging markets toward more innovative, knowledge-based, and entrepreneurial economies, with consequences for university systems. In the countries of East Asia, for example, such economic developments are associated with increased policy interest in risk, as the risk-absorbing characteristics of long-standing institutions, such as the family, appear to be losing some of their potency in the face of social and demographic change.

Although risk concepts have tended not to loom large in the countries of East Asia, there is evidence that more formalized risk management and regulatory policies are now emerging, which not only influence the management of universities but also what is taught. Business schools' curricula in China, Hong Kong, Malaysia, and Singapore, for example, increasingly contain units on risk, entrepreneurialism, and innovation, particularly executive MBA programs taught jointly with prestigious schools in Europe and the United States (*Financial Times* 2012). Such changes reflect wider shifts in society as much as curricula isomorphism, as government policymakers seek to move from low-cost manufacturing and dependence on inward foreign investment in their economies to more innovative, enterprising, and creative local systems. They expect higher education programs to support such changes. As they do, universities also begin to assimilate notions of risk in their organizational practices. Like elsewhere in the world, such developments offer the prospect of a diffusing risk university model in global academic capitalism.

The idea of the risk university is particularly associated with the growth of risk governance, notably the emergence of strategic risk management in institutions, and the beginnings of more explicit and formal risk-based regulation in external quality assurance. Risk governance involves the management of risk through stronger forms of internal administrative controls and also regulation by risk, in which institutions viewed as possessing less risk to regulatory objectives than others (e.g., recent private for-profit entrants being considered especially risky) are "freed" from many of the burdens of standard cyclical review, in part to allow them the time and resources to become more entrepreneurial. Relatedly, the notion of external bureaucratic interventions by state-backed agencies for the assurance of quality tends to be regarded as inferior in driving up quality compared to more consumerist notions of "satisfaction" and the exercise of choice by students and others. Competitive market behavior by institutions, based on better-informed student choice, is regarded as improving the quality of student learning, which tends to be lost in the face of the incentives for research standing otherwise found in university systems.

At the same time, however, the more circumscribed and focused role of external agency scrutiny found in risk-based regulation is also meant to improve regulatory performance as monitoring methods become more proportionate, targeted, and explicit. Moreover, the Higher Education Funding Council for England (HEFCE) found that such risk-based approaches offer incentives for regulatory compliance and control by promising future "deregulation" for institutions in return for compliance and good behavior (for developing a good quality assurance "track record"), thus building in a trajectory of increased autonomy and self-regulation for maturing systems and institutions (HEFCE 2012).

Risk-based regulation increasingly becomes a form of "meta-regulation" as it regulates regulation. That is, agencies and accreditors regulate the internal (self-regulatory) controls and processes of institutions using internal institutional data turned "inside-out" for external inspection. Consequently, in that organizational risk management is a form of self-regulatory activity, which risk-based regulation largely encourages, both forms of risk governance (risk management and risk-based external regulation) tend to be closely linked in practice. Regulators and quality assurers also need to manage their own risks as organizations, as they often operate in quite volatile political contexts.

The Risk University

The risk university exhibits four key characteristics:

1. It corporately regards entrepreneurial risk taking as a potential source of value as well as a hazard in its status and economic competition with other similarly located universities.
2. It is increasingly subject to risk, not only as a result of increased marketization and often declining per-capita public funding, but also because of

its organizational reputation through external—often media amplified—evaluations by standards setters, such as those found in national and global university rankings, professional accreditation processes, and the activities of quality assurance agencies and other regulators.

3. It is increasingly required to introduce risk management models as a key issue of corporate governance, in part as a response to a rise in external threats, and also as a result of encouragement by regulators.

4. In some countries, it is increasingly subject to the introduction of risk-based regulatory approaches by government-supported quality assurance and funding regulators. Operating with broadly deregulatory objectives in mind, these regulators focus selectively on those institutions judged to offer the most risk to themselves and to the system overall. They thus exercise diminishing regulatory attention on the majority of perceived low-risk providers.

The notion of the risk university indicates that, with academic capitalism, the idea of risk is increasingly pervading the field of higher education, informing organizational strategy and actions, and also notions of appropriate external assurance. Increasing marketization, competition, and commercialism place universities "at risk." But so do the media, research assessments, and other accounts of rankings and performance, as does the associated strengthening of universities as corporate actors with self-responsibility for their own futures.

The notion of formalized risk management by universities, and risk-based external regulation of universities, is now found in various countries, including Australia, the United Kingdom, and the United States. For example, HEFCE requires institutions to introduce risk management controls and associated risk registers as a condition of funding. It also periodically issues various risk management templates and standards, generally derived from the private sector, to facilitate good practice in establishing robust internal controls based around risk amelioration. Moreover, as found increasingly in other sectors, HEFCE regards enterprise risk management by universities as a matter of high-level governance and accountability, not a specialist, rather technical, activity.

Risk

Although the notion of risk has quite a long history—the idea of probability theory, which is often regarded as a key mathematical tool for risk assessments, goes back many centuries—only in recent years have more systematic and scientific attempts to identify risks and respond rationally to them appeared in organizations. In the financial world particularly, this development has been reinforced by a succession of large and publicized corporate failures in the last decade or so (e.g., Enron, Lehman Brothers, and Northern Rock) and a consequently greater appreciation of the wider scope of the risks confronting organizations. As a result, risk management has become a central focus for business and government and is beginning to characterize the strategic and reputational concerns of universities, as one example of the steady adoption of capitalist instruments within the "new public management."

Risk reflects a belief in having the capacity to manage uncertainties in an age of increased complexity, contingency, and interdependency. It expresses the confidence that uncertainties can be controllable (Aven and Renn 2010, v–vi). For some, this understanding of risk expresses an Enlightenment-era belief in the power of reason to control nature and society. While in medieval times the future was largely determined (religiously) and was relatively immune to human intervention, this hierarchical system eroded in favor of "controlling the future" with the expansion of two distinct processes: global merchant capitalism and scientific reasoning. The future became amenable to transformation and planning in this view, thus opening up the opportunity for notions of risk as a means of calculating and controlling the uncertainties of this future. Events came to be seen as part of patterns that were susceptible to statistical probabilities, not as individually disconnected, and these notions were underpinned by scientific beliefs in fixed laws and causations of the universe that could be discovered (Reith 2009).

Modern revolutions in science—notably, quantum physics—and the development of complexity and chaos theory have undermined older notions of fixed causal laws in the universe and replaced them with the idea that risk has a more probabilistic dimension. Risk management itself may create risks in this view and is best regarded as one element in a range of contingencies. Nonetheless, risk has come to be regarded as a justifiable way of making decisions: the future may be uncertain, but risk creates the means for acting as though it was capable of being directed (Luhmann 1993, 13).

Sociologists have also become interested in risk ideas in recent decades. "Risk society" theorists (Beck 1999; Giddens 2002), for example, argue that modern society is characterized by the rise of reflexive individuals as the result of the spread of knowledge through education and media technology. There is consequently a greater awareness of potential risks, lower capacity to tolerate them, and a growing confidence in our knowledge to assess and manage risk. In policy and organizational terms, ideas of risk have been reinforced by the diffusion of neoliberal and academic capitalist agendas. As collective forms of state-based risk management for individuals, historically provided by national and governmental welfare systems, start to defray, people (including "public" organizations)—in the West at least—now must assume greater individual responsibility for managing more of their own risks.

Risk and Society

Social scientists generally have adopted a socially constructivist approach to risk. Rather than seeing risk as existing objectively in the world, risk is regarded as requiring mental imaginaries in order to be real. That is, perceptions of risk are socially variable, as are the risk appetites that different groups may possess. Even within countries, considerable variation exists between sectors as to which risks are chosen for regulatory action and how punitive and sanctioning the regulatory approaches are (Hood, Rothstein, and Baldwin 2001). This cultural variability between and within countries over risk may raise doubts as to how globalizable risk governance models in higher education and other sectors are likely to be.

Nonetheless, the advance of risk management and risk regulatory models in higher education governance reflects the increased role of private actors within academic capitalism, not least as commercial allies for institutions in public-private partnerships. Robertson, Mundy, Verger, and Menashy (2012) note that while the putative aim of such arrangements is to transfer much of a venture's risk to the private partner and away from the higher education institution, often "sharp differences in expectations about lead actors, basic mechanisms, and motivations often emerge" (6). Rather than transferring risk, inadequate capacity for managing such partnerships and for calculating optimal levels of risk sharing may actually increase risk for the university (and also raise levels of profitability for the private actor).

The notion of risk as a socially constructed concept has implications for the ways in which universities and other organizations manage risk and establish risk strategies. Bradbury (2009), for example, has noted that different concepts of risk have policy consequences. One approach (the "technical") views risks as objective facts that can be scientifically understood, forecasted, and managed. A second approach (she calls this the "psychometric" but it may be regarded as the social constructivist) sees risk as value laden and interpretative. Risk communication in the first method tends to consist of persuading others to the objective correctness of a view forged by experts and corporate leaders. These risk strategies need to be "sold" to those who are either subject to such risks or have the professional job of operationalizing top-down organizational risk strategies. The second approach, however, recognizes the social variability and social construction of risk perceptions and seeks resolution and compromise through negotiations between all stakeholders based on a view that "all are experts."

In organizations generally (including universities), recent notions of holistic enterprise and strategic risk management tend to result in hierarchical forms of persuasion and interpretation that are often neglectful of the importance of employees' views of risk ventures and methods of risk mitigation. Risk decisions are "rolled out" to incorporate others necessary for their implementation, but largely after the strategic decision has been made (which could have been different had other views been taken into account). Yet risk, as a socially constructed idea, is dependent on the cultural and other milieus of individuals and groups. Simply seeking to persuade others (academics, students, external stakeholders) of the objective rightness of a risk-based decision is unlikely to work effectively.

Risk Governance

Risk is usually defined as the combination of the probabilities of an event with estimations of its impact (positive and negative). Risk essentially refers to events, or changes in circumstances, in which potential dangers or opportunities crystallize. In corporatized universities and colleges, control and relative predictability (not certainty) are intended consequences of risk management systems. As a result, university governors and other leaders are unwilling to accept unanticipated adversities for loss, either of reputation or finance. If loss occurs, increasingly they want immediate remedial action. As a result, risk management processes also serve as a further form of accountability and transparency, as well as an intended enhancement of organizational resilience.

Three categories of risk usually confront universities and other organizations: "hazard" risks, such as minor transgressions of health and safety regulations that are managed according to levels of tolerance within the entity; "control" risks, or the kind that tend to occur in project management (such as setting up an overseas branch campus), when not every event can be exactly planned for; and "opportunity" risks, which involve the possibility of achieving high-value outcomes from investments that may be quite speculative in the expectation of increased markets, profits, or status.

Some opportunities are inherently risky (e.g., university franchising or brand licensing to relatively unknown third parties), and residual risks remain even after being subject to internal control systems. In such cases, among available options are to accept the risk, to transfer it (by taking out insurance, dealing in derivatives, or partnering with a private sector provider), or to turn down the opportunity. But this last move may not work if failing to seize opportunities in dynamic environments containing fast-growing and increasingly entrepreneurial competitors runs the risk of relative failure through loss of reputation and markets to others. Doing nothing can also be risky.

Although organizations, including some universities, increasingly exercise what is called "enterprise risk management"—a holistic or comprehensive model that originates in the strategic concerns of the boardroom—generally it is less easy for risk universities to follow suit. The purpose of enterprise risk management is to avoid the chance of risk incubating in organizational silos (departments) and not being picked up more centrally, yet universities are not as fully corporatized and hierarchical as large private-sector businesses. If universities and colleges are less "loosely coupled" than before, notions of academic freedom and departmental autonomy remain sufficiently strong to resist full-blooded top-down management. As a result, higher education institutions have difficulty controlling the core functions of teaching and research through the typical and diverse risk management strategies available to other organizations. They tend to use "proxies," particularly the idea of reputation risk, as "an all-purpose tool for risk management, allowing universities to capture all possible challenges and problems in terms of risk" (Huber 2011, 18).

Moreover, councils and boards of governors traditionally have been reluctant to enter too forcibly into the domain of "academic matters," even if academic risk poses a major source of reputation risk. Usually, as occurred in the case of the London School of Economics in 2011, after revelations about financial support from Colonel Gaddafi of Libya and the doctoral performance of his son came to light, ex post facto investigations into academic or related matters may be instigated by governors.

In risk universities, risk control and compliance mechanisms are not only regarded as costs to be incurred to maintain strategic and operational control as well as external regulatory legitimacy, but also as an entrepreneurial source of value generation and protection. Enterprise requires both opportunism and systematic planning. Risk controls are coming to be viewed as adding business value—as a "product" in its own right—and not simply as the exercise of prudent transactional scrutiny. Overseas collaborations with commercial partners abroad, for example, are viewed as especially risky for higher education institutions and as requiring strategic risk advice to enable calculated risks in order to maximize expected returns (economic and noneconomic).

There is increased recognition in some universities and colleges that institutional risk appetites are important to calculate, to ensure that increased risk for the organization does not result from forfeiting opportunities as a result of high-risk averseness. In other sectors, senior risk advisors have become strategic partners in businesses rather than cautious controllers of proposed activities (Power 2005). Positions such as chief risk officers may come to mark the modern university as much as they do in a number of business sectors (especially financial services), professionalizing and managerializing risk management away from its current "collegiate" approach in higher education (particularly such as found in the predominant risk management role of audit committees) toward more senior executive responsibilities.

Accreditors, quality assurers, and funding agencies in higher education, like the universities and colleges they monitor, are also subject to heightened risk management processes, even if they are charged formally with operating risk-based forms of regulation. Risk-based regulators, like the organizations they regulate, must also manage risk related to their own reputations, funding, and longevity in the face of competing and changing regulatory demands from external stakeholders, such as government, the media, and the wider public. In such cases, there is always the danger of organizational goals becoming displaced, away from the major purpose of protecting consumers and the wider public, to that of primarily defending the regulatory organization itself. This could include the reintroduction by the regulator of more bureaucratic and protocolized internal processes for "blame avoidance" reasons, replacing those procedures based on selective risk analyses of institutions despite the public mandate to operate a risk-based regulatory system (Hood 2011).

Having a recognizable internal risk management system is likely to become a basic university requirement for both entrepreneurial and accountability reasons. Once such a system is in place, the regulator is in a position to rank (perhaps informally at first) different universities on their risk controls, which becomes a basis for developing the regulator's own risk-based approaches to the field. As regulators gain experience, the status of a university's risk management system becomes more than a legitimizing necessity; it becomes a reputation resource that helps to constitute the relationship with the regulator (Power, Scheytt, Soin, and Sahlin 2009, 306).

Capitalism and Democracy

A range of risk management standards are increasingly becoming globally available, such as the International Organization for Standardization's ISO

31000, which suggests increasing diffusion of risk governance frameworks across sectors and countries. International bodies such as the European Commission, Organisation for Economic Co-operation and Development (OECD), and World Bank encourage the use of such standards. In 2010, for example, the OECD issued case studies and guidance "to assist OECD governments to develop coherent frameworks for the governance of risk in regulatory policy," including encouragement for the "better regulation" agenda associated with risk-based regulation.

As we are seeing in higher education, particularly in Australia and the United Kingdom (predominantly England), the selective aim of risk-based quality assurance is to introduce the discriminatory methods of capitalism rather than the egalitarian approaches of juridical statism. Not everyone is to be treated the same. As with insurance policies, the cost of coverage and premiums depends on the track record and the risk crystallization probabilities of the entity concerned. They do not depend on treating everyone equally. Risk-based regulation requires agencies to be similarly selective in their focus and resources, which contrasts with a traditional statist or public administration approach, as the aim is not a proceduralized, standardized, judge-all-equally process to ensure universal compliance with a set of rules (OECD 2010).

What we may term new public risk management, or NPRM, utilizes capitalist economics to address issues of democratic politics. Discriminatory treatment of individuals and organizations on the basis of the different risks they pose (as in insurance), not notions of formal equality, characterizes the approach. But it creates powerful tensions, originating in the way democracy and capitalism rest on different principles of social organization.

At the heart of modern democratic politics is the presumption of equality in citizenship. Behind the workings of the judicial system is the assumption that all are equal in the eyes of the law. By contrast, the principles of a capitalist economy presume inequality in the distribution of productive resources and in the outcomes of market forces (its defenders argue that inequality is necessary to encourage enterprise and risk taking). With the introduction of risk-based regulation into higher education, the divisions and inequalities created by marketized and status-reproducing systems permeate the regulatory system and inhibit its ability to realize the egalitarian principles of democratic citizenship. Risk-based regulation may also inhibit the protective or social sheltering aspects of regulation associated with democratic perspectives by subordinating regulation primarily to the overriding purpose of market enhancement.

Economic risk-based regulators (including governments seeking to mar-
ketize their higher education sectors) reinterpret risk according to the principles of economic neoliberalism—regulation is justified principally in terms of
its role in correcting market failures, such as in controlling monopolies, barriers to entry, externalities, information asymmetries, or principle/agent problems. In part, such moves reflect an absence of a transnational consensus as to
what constitutes risk: it is a highly culturally contestable concept. A high substi-
tutability between risk categories and economics, in part at least, reflects difficulties in providing the notion of risk with a theoretically sound and globalizable
basis. Thus there is a temptation to translate risk regulatory objectives into the
discourse of economics so that, for example, environmental pollution is regarded as a classical example of negative externalities, information asymmetries, and principal-agent problems; that is, risks to markets rather than public
risks that must be regulated for citizens' protection (Black 2010).

The principles of economic neoliberalism are consequently seen in some
regulatory circles as providing a more acceptable, clear, and stable basis than
risk notions in deciding when and how to regulate, and "risk" becomes translated into "market risk" as a consequence. Economics provides a theoretical and
universal model of markets, a basis that gives it globalizability. Competition
rather than monopolies, information disclosure to consumers and the public,
and internalization of negative costs and minimization of impacts become the
universal objectives for risk governance in the absence of an adequately theorized and universal model for risk. It is the very social construction of the risk
concept that places limits on its globalizability.

In contrast, markets are broadly regarded as the same everywhere, as consisting of common features and processes, which ensures that economic neoliberal
models readily cross boundaries. It is much less contestable than risk. Recent
UK government reforms for English higher education, for example, despite in-
sistence on risk as a key governance principle, are arguably not so much about
risk as neoliberalism. Competition, market access, consumer satisfaction, and
increased public information are the building blocks for regulatory proposals.
Risk targeting comes to be interpreted as a form of deregulation; essentially it is
determined economically.

Nonetheless, although there is no similar theorized model of risk as found
with economic neoliberalism and theories of markets, which helps to provide
the object and justification for organizational and regulatory intervention, the
possibilities for the globalization of risk models and risk universities may be less
hopeless than such a picture suggests, as described below.

Diffusion across Cultures

Some national institutions and cultures and their higher education systems may be more resistant to NPRM than others. Risk is a concept that is highly contextualized and socially interpreted; consequently, it may not diffuse well across states. What might appear only moderately risky to a financier in London may be the height of cavalier behavior to a Japanese industrialist, for example. Undoubtedly, risk management remains less widespread in organizational and policy discourse throughout East Asia than, say, in the West.

There are only a few signs to date of Asian universities adopting formal risk models. Some attribute such a comparative absence to strong Confucian notions of fatalism, the strength and risk absorption of extended family support networks, and traditions of strong bureaucratic centralism. Elite-dominated technocracies with top-down styles of management have largely seemed resistant to any pressure for formalized and widely available risk systems, in both organizational practice and policy discourse (Chan, Takashaki, and Wang 2010). Nonetheless, these attitudes may be changing as a result of global economic and other pressures. Many Asian countries are facing changes and conflicts similar to those in the West, including the erosion of traditional family structures, the rise of divorce, and the inability of extended family networks to cope with illness, unstable employment, and aging. The result is a demand for more collective forms of risk management, including by the state.

Elsewhere, despite the apparent universality of the scientific modernism and rationalism characteristic of risk governance approaches (and as encouraged by influential international organizations), risk-based approaches have spread unevenly across countries, with more limited application in France and Germany than in the United Kingdom or the United States, for example (Rothstein, Borraz, and Huber 2012). Strong statist and bureaucratic institutions with highly influential legal traditions of equality before the law found in some continental European countries find difficulty in adopting more market-like notions of risk and their essentially discriminatory and selective principles. It is likely that such national traditions find reflection in their higher education organizations, and we might expect in some European countries a consequential lack of risk models. But empirical evidence to date is still minimal.

Ignoring variations in cultural approaches to risk holds dangers for university leaders. As universities globalize their activities and become like transnational corporations, there is a danger that their senior executives and governors may believe that what suffices for risk-oriented and risk-managed behavior domestically will also work abroad. Moreover, the assessment of risks—their perception, interpretation, and operationalization in different jurisdictions— becomes vital for organizations spreading their activities internationally. Globalization heightens the perceived function of reputation risk management within universities and underlines the corporate need to protect organizational brand assets across all locations as a unifying endeavor.

Regulatory and partnering risks loom particularly large for globally aspirant universities as they enter complex overseas environments, and where (e.g., as in China) choosing a foreign partner (university, property developer, or government) is obligatory and necessary. Yet a poor relationship, not least around cultural and institutional differences regarding issues of quality control and prudent financial management, may lead to severe reputation risk.

Limited evidence from UK studies suggests that high-status, research-strong universities seeking predominantly to extend global scientific and reputation reach through niche partnerships abroad may exercise quite strong and partici- pative, if not fully formalized, forms of risk management before embarking on such endeavors, and a high number of stakeholders, including councils, appear to be involved (Fielden 2011). Status protection is highly valued by such entities, and considerable care is taken of both the excellence of the institution's disci- plines chosen for international expansion and the research advantages that are likely to accrue from selective partnering.

It would appear, however, that broader commercial ventures abroad by lower- ranking universities, partnering with private entrepreneurs such as property developers or private non-degree-granting colleges, have lacked similar strategic corporate decision making around risk (Fielden 2011). This is perhaps unex- pected, as risk models are generally perceived as a major instrument drawn from the commercial private sector and would seem even more appropriate as a gov- erning tool for what are essentially income-raising ventures. Yet formalized risk planning is perhaps a second-stage development in capitalist venturing. It may occur in both university and non-university organizations after an initial stage of high entrepreneurialism. There are signs that various adverse media and regula- tory commentary in the United Kingdom (and also Australia) on international commercial joint ventures by universities is encouraging both a more targeted approach to global ventures (including staged withdrawals) by such institutions and awareness by governing bodies of the need to establish more systematic and accountable risk strategies for overseas activities (Fielden 2011).

For relatively high-status and research-intensive universities, offering only one or few programs abroad in subjects where the university is particularly strong may be an effective risk-minimizing strategy, especially where critical partners tend to be governments or similar public agencies (although unexpected budget cuts to governmental expenditures can be a source of unexpected risk). In such cases, such as University College London's niche campuses in a number of countries, the strategy is research focused rather than set on large undergraduate student recruitment. Risk crystallization or disasters in such circumstances tend to be confined to a particular discipline rather than contaminate the institution overall. Yet the relatively small size of such operations may also make the underlying funding model more challenging, especially once initial pump-priming investment from an international (usually governmental) partner ceases.

International collaborative partnerships are for the most part a high-risk activity, with the potential for significant financial and reputational loss in the case of failure. Generally, however, there is little research available on institutional decisions both to start an overseas partnership (such as a branch campus) and to decide against doing so (Wilkins and Huisman 2012). We particularly lack evidence for risk management processes in such deliberations and the type of risk frameworks that may be used. Moreover, we lack studies of whether universities in, say, East Asia that are increasingly collaborating with universities from around the world utilize formal risk models in their decision making. Is the risk management and regulatory model—NPRM—potentially globalizable?

Global Risk

Universities remain, for the most part, status-enhancing organizations, despite the growth of both for-profit private conglomerates and enhanced capitalist and corporate behavior within more publicly maintained institutions. This focus on prestige, rather than increasing profits or market share, is a strong feature of high-status, research-intensive universities and is reflected in their often risk-averse approaches to international ventures and commercial partnering. The increased elevation of risk management to a preoccupation at board level is reinforced by a growing concern with reputational risk. Apart from external factors, such as university league tables and similar rankings, as well as increased media interest in the commercial and particularly global activities of universities and colleges, the imperatives of increased marketization require enhanced risk identification and due diligence processes, monitored at the highest levels of the organization.

We have noted above the constraints on senior university leaders of introducing the full-throated and formalized risk management processes of non-university corporations, such as notions of academic freedom and autonomy. As such, risks may be generated under the radar within institutions as academic faculty, often inexperienced in the world of practical business, may undertake commercial and international activities that lack adequate risk assessment and controls. Moreover, top-down enterprise risk management can result in inadequate strategic thinking prior to decisions by not taking account of key stakeholders. In some cases, academics have forced universities to retract key global plans, such as those at Warwick University in the United Kingdom. Well-advanced blueprints for an overseas branch campus in Singapore were abandoned on the grounds that faculty expressed severe doubts about the diversion of resources away from the UK campus, and also because of fears about barriers to the functioning of academic freedom in Singapore. Even when such plans do go ahead, academics may feel that their research and promotion prospects are hurt by moving to overseas branch campuses, reinforced by the perceived difficulty in securing research funds in the new foreign environment.

Yet, in seeking to cater to the rising demand for higher education in emerging markets, leading universities in Australia, the United Kingdom, the United States, and other advanced systems have undertaken forms of international collaboration that seek to minimize rising risks in domestic markets but also raise new risks. To some extent, international partnerships for delivery abroad are a form of risk insurance against declining student numbers, constraining new visa systems for incoming international students and lowering levels of public funding at home. Exhortations to be entrepreneurial and internationalist from politicians with responsibility for highly marketized higher education systems (such as in Australia, the United Kingdom, and the United States), help to legitimate such developments and overcome risk averseness. The UK government encourages its universities in England to undertake further ventures abroad with borrowed private capital and offers cross-government advisory services to assist. Yet privately financed transnational operations offer considerably enhanced hazard as well as opportunity. Such activities should undoubtedly be subject to highly professional risk management, but it is not clear that this is always the case.

While universities may not always practice more formalized risk identification, there is evidence that risk thinking is taking place. International branch campuses established by Western universities, for example, tend to be concentrated in locations where either institutional similarity, or the prospect of realistic adaptation, help to reduce risk (they are predominantly found in China, Qatar, Singapore, and the United Arab Emirates). Moreover, elite universities especially have seemed inclined to turn down such opportunities in favor of maintaining or enhancing their domestic investments, reputations, and priority to home students, which they may perceive as threatened by risky overseas ventures (Wilkins and Huisman 2012).

Conclusion

The notion of risk in higher education and its inclusion in institutional and regulatory policy and governance may not be found in some parts of the world where cultural and other institutional configurations may militate against the universalistic possibilities of the new public risk management model. Yet economic and isomorphic pressures appear to be at work in such locations that may be undermining traditional cultural assumptions about risk. As ambitious, competitive, and autonomous higher education corporations begin to look remarkably like global corporations in other sectors, forms of the risk university are likely to diffuse.

Global higher education is a social system that has become "thicker" in its social relationships in recent years, reflecting increased interaction and policy isomorphism. That is, certain models and standards (particularly of governance) have become widely diffused and quite dominant. Although global networks operate as coordinating devices for people and organizations, they also act as processes of power. Power is expressed through the standards and models that come to define networks and characterize the particular way in which a network is a network. Will NPRM gather the global power of models such as new public management and the global research university?

Models like NPRM are the means by which we access networks for the process of social cooperation. They are similar to the protocols and codes that enable computer networks to function. Accepting such models may indicate a desire to avoid marginalization and exclusion in global policy circles as much as the conviction that a model has powerful instrumental payoffs. Policy networks can function to ensure that, through such processes, some ideas and models become powerful, particularly if they appear to gel with new requirements from changing economic and sociopolitical contexts. Once a certain level of adoption or diffusion of a model has been reached—a tipping point—then it becomes hard to counteract. As with telecommunication networks, the more subscribers (access) a particular network has, the increased chance it has of attracting even more (Grewal 2008).

The diffusion of NPRM would be further indication of the increased universalization of regulatory and governance models in higher education (and other domains). We are witnessing the introduction and diffusion—across social worlds and across time and space—of new technologies of control and account-ability, and NPRM is an example. Hard, strongly linear procedures of risk man-agement are slowly becoming buttressed by softer technologies based around communication, negotiation, and compromise, reflecting the influence of a more social constructivist approach to ideas of risk governance. Yet cultural bar-riers, adoptions, and adaptions are bound to ensure that any diffusion of a risk university model will also reflect wider social interpretations across territories. Only an economizing of risk as a noncultural, profoundly economic, and capi-talist notion—another way of describing neoliberalism—would produce a more homogenizing process based on capitalist theories of markets. But such an ap-proach lacks the fuller explanatory richness of a more specifically risk-based model.

REFERENCES

Aven, Terje, and Ortwin Renn. 2010. *Risk Management and Governance: Concepts, Guide-lines and Applications*. Dordrecht: Springer.

Beck, Ulrich. 1999. *World Risk Society*. Malden, MA.

Black, Julia. 2010. "The Role of Risk in Regulatory Processes." In *The Oxford Handbook of Regulation*, edited by Robert Baldwin, Martin Cave, and Martin Lodge, 302–48. Oxford: Oxford University Press.

Bradbury, Judith A. 2009. "The Policy Implications of Differing Concepts of Risk." In *The Earthscan Reader on Risk*, edited by Ragnar Löfstedt and Åsa Boholm, 27–42. London: Routledge.

Chan, Raymond K. H., Mutsuko Takahashi, and Lillian Lih-rong Wang, eds. 2010. *Risk and Public Policy in East Asia*. Farnham: Ashgate.

Fielden, John. 2011. *Leadership and Management of International Partnerships*. Research and Development Series 2. London: Leadership Foundation for Higher Education.

Financial Times. 2012. "The Top 100 EMBA Programs." *Financial Times*, October 15, 26–27.

Giddens, Anthony. 2002. *Runaway World: How Globalization Is Reshaping Our Lives*. 2nd ed. London: Profile Books.

Grewal, David S. 2008. *Network Power: The Social Dynamics of Globalization*. New Haven, CT: Yale University Press.

HEFCE. Higher Education Funding Council for England. 2012. *A Risk-Based Approach to Quality Assurance: Outcomes of Consultation and Next Steps*. Bristol: HEFCE.

Hood, Christopher. 2011. *The Blame Game: Spin, Bureaucracy and Self-Preservation in Government*. Princeton, NJ: Princeton University Press.

Hood, Christopher, Henry Rothstein, and Robert Baldwin. 2001. *Government of Risk: Understanding Risk Regulation Regimes*. Oxford: Oxford University Press.

Huber, Michael. 2011. *The Risk University: Risk Identification at Higher Education Institutions in England*. CARR Discussion Paper 69. London: London School of Economics and Political Science and Centre for the Analysis of Risk and Regulation.

Luhmann, Niklas. 1993. *Risk: A Sociological Theory*. Berlin: Walter de Gruyter.

OECD. Organisation for Economic Co-operation and Development. 2010. *Risk and Regulatory Policy: Improving the Governance of Risk*. Paris: OECD.

Power, Michael. 2005. "Organizational Responses to Risk: The Rise of the Chief Risk Officer." In *Organizational Encounters with Risk*, edited by Bridget Hutter and Michael Power, 132–48. Cambridge: Cambridge University Press.

Power, Michael, Tobias Scheytt, Kim Soin, and Kerstin Sahlin. 2009. "Reputational Risk as a Logic of Organizing in Late Modernity." *Organization Studies* 30, no. 2–3: 301–24. doi:10.1177/0961463X04045672.

Reith, Gerda. 2009. "Uncertain Times: The Notion of 'Risk' and the Development of Modernity." In *The Earthscan Reader on Risk*, edited by Ragnar Löfstedt and Åsa Boholm, 53–68. London: Routledge.

Robertson, Susan, Karen Mundy, Antoni Verger, and Francine Menashy. 2012. "An Introduction to Public-Private Partnerships and Education Governance." In *Public-Private Partnerships in a Globalizing World*, edited by Susan Robertson, Karen Mundy, Antoni Verger, and Francine Menashy, 1–17. Cheltenham: Edward Elgar.

Rothstein, Henry, Olivier Borraz, and Michael Huber. 2012. "Risk and the Limits of Governance: Exploring Varied Patterns of Risk-Based Governance across Europe." *Regulation and Governance* 7, no. 2: 215–35. doi:10.1111/j.1748-5991.2012.01153.x.

Wilkins, Stephen, and Jeroen Huisman. 2012. "The International Branch Campus as Transitional Strategy in Higher Education." *Higher Education* 64, no. 5: 627–45. doi:10.1007/s10734-012-9516-5.

CHAPTER FOURTEEN

Developing a Conceptual Model to Study the International Student Market

ILKKA KAUPPINEN, CHARLES MATHIES, AND LEASA WEIMER

The rise of the new economy—marked by a shift from industry to knowledge-based pursuits—has transformed the way different groups use, or at least perceive, knowledge and its supposed economic importance as well as how societies value knowledge (Castells 1996; Jessop 2008; Slaughter and Leslie 1997; Slaughter and Rhoades 2004). Thus the productivity and competitiveness of contemporary nation-states commonly rely on knowledge as a raw material and means for how people and organizations are organized around the creation and dissemination of knowledge (Castells 1996). In this context, the globally oriented commercial export of education is one strategic activity that governments and higher education institutions use to increase their competitiveness (Marginson 2011). In this chapter we see the international student market as one such empirical example of academic capitalism, revealing quite clearly how the latter is not only a product of different globalization-related subprocesses but also a part of multicentric globalization.

Our strategy of approaching the constitution and internal dynamics of the international student market is based on the idea of "knowledge as commodity" (Kauppinen 2013). Karl Polanyi (1944) pointed out in his seminal work *The Great Transformation* that the commodification of land, labor, and money in the nineteenth century led to a transformation toward market society ideals; that is, the type of society where markets operate in a more autonomous and self-regulating environment. In this respect it can be said that one of the distinctive features of the current globalizing knowledge economy is a systematic and intensified commodification of knowledge. Similar to the transformation of land, labor, and money, various forms of knowledge have been actively translated into commodities and drawn to markets so that it can be exchanged (i.e., bought and sold). When developing ideas regarding knowledge as a commodity, it is important to notice that knowledge has material preconditions—it must be stored in one form or another, whether it be books, journals, computers, or human brains. Also, the usage of knowledge implies the existence of "user(s)"; that is, individual human beings, research teams, and so forth. Moreover, individual "containers" or "vessels" of knowledge are positioned in some particular structural context that enables and restricts their possibilities to use their knowledge or acquire new knowledge.

The recognition that higher education institutions (as one of the key sources of alienable knowledge) play an increasingly important role in the advancement of economic competitiveness has led to an increase in the promotion of commodification of knowledge. This promotion has been facilitated, for instance, through the development of the knowledge-based economy as a "hegemonic economic imaginary" (Jessop 2008, 18). In this economic imaginary, knowledge and higher education are valued as preconditions of economic competitiveness, economic growth, wealth, and jobs. The most obvious illustration of this concept is technology/knowledge transfer (i.e., follow-up activities of research). For example, in knowledge transfer, research results are protected by intellectual property rights such as patents and then sold (i.e., licensed to market actors). Commodification of knowledge in the field of higher education is not only related to follow-up activities of research (Kauppinen 2013). In this chapter we are interested in the commodification of knowledge from the perspective of the international student market.

We argue that the conceptualization of knowledge as a commodity increases understanding of the complexities of the international student market, which is achieved through analysis and synthesis of existing theoretical and empirical research conducted in the fields of higher education studies and sociology. We develop a model conceptualizing the international student market as a multidimensional and temporal object of study. While we do not analyze any specific case, we discuss and give examples of four market behaviors of two actors, international students and university and governments, and how they interact with one another. We conclude by discussing implications of the international student market.

Commodification of Knowledge

The concepts of commodity and commodification as social processes are vastly discussed topics in the field of social sciences. Commodification refers to a process in which an object becomes an entity that can be sold and bought in markets—i.e., raw material such as corn, copper, or coffee—that has financial value, and that can be bought and sold. Commodification of new objects thus expands the boundaries of markets.

Reflecting a shift toward a knowledge-based economy, or at least its emergence as hegemonic economic imaginary (Jessop 2008, 18), there is an ever-increasing amount of literature that directly or indirectly discusses commodification of knowledge (Jessop 2007). The same is true with a growth in the literature focused on the commodification of higher education (Radder 2010). Here we do not provide an overview regarding the concepts of commodity and commodification, or even commodification of knowledge and higher education (see Kauppinen 2013 for overview of literature). Instead, we aim to clarify different meanings of commodification of knowledge and knowledge as a commodity in the context of the international student market.

With respect to commodification, "labour power cannot be separated from the laboring body" because "the capacity to do useful work is not materially distinct from the body that exercises such capacity" (Paton 2010, 82). Moreover, "labour power cannot be left on a shelf awaiting demand for it to surge. Without an income, its 'vessel' (the labouring body) has no means of survival or reproduction" (82). More specifically, students' labor power (i.e., capacity to do knowledge work) may not be separated from their laboring body. In this way, students can be seen as vessels of knowledge, and because governments, corporations, and higher education institutions are eager to gain economically valuable knowledge, they are interested in securing the labor power of students; that is, vessels of the supposedly economically important knowledge.

The previous argument can be used as a heuristic starting point to explore the commodification of knowledge. Similar to labor power, it can be claimed that knowledge, or human capital, cannot be separated from the laboring body. But knowledge can of course be stored "on a shelf," for instance, and knowledge can be sold at least in some cases (e.g., in the form of books or articles) without selling the vessel (i.e., the human body or brains), which has produced or stored knowledge. Commodification of knowledge is often enhanced and, more strongly, made possible through intellectual property rights, because property rights regulate who can and who cannot own something, what can and cannot be owned, and what an owner can do with her property. In other words, property structures social relations by establishing unequal positions: we have owners and nonowners (Carruthers and Ariovich 2004; May and Sell 2006).

Commodification of Higher Education

In the context of higher education, there are at least two modes of the commodification of knowledge. First, there is the "commodification of academic research"

(Radder 2010, 4), a category that in turn refers to "commercialization, that is, the pursuit of profit by academic institutions through selling expertise of their researchers and the results of their inquiries" (4). Second is the commoditized educational process as delivered by higher education institutions "for the purpose of commercial transaction" (Noble 2002). Commodification of educational processes implies that students are increasingly seen as customers whose "needs and wants . . . [are placed] at the centre of organizational focus and strategy" (Sappey 2005, 496). This chapter focuses on the various transactions of buying and selling within the international student market, for instance, with students as buyers of knowledge and universities as sellers of knowledge.

In the context of a knowledge-based economy, governments and private corporations view students as actual or at least potential owners of one particular kind of property—intellectual property. Moreover, students are seen by a variety of actors as one form of commodity that can be bought and sold; that is, they are seen as actual or potential commodities that carry, or will carry, within themselves another form of commodity, namely, knowledge. In short, students can be seen as vessels that carry economically valuable cargo.

But students themselves orientate toward other forms of commodity. For instance, Marginson (2004) claims that in different layers of competition (status, economic, and capitalist competition) within universities, "higher education is understood as a commodity that can be secured by individuals to their private advantage" (196). Moreover, "Current thinking sees international higher education as a commodity to be freely traded and sees higher education as a private good, not a public responsibility" (Altbach and Knight 2007, 291). Finally, knowledge may have many faces within higher education: it can be used to increase one's economic, cultural, social, intellectual, and academic capital.

International Student Market

Universities produce educational products for markets such as degrees, and international students can buy these products by paying tuition fees unless host universities or governments are willing to pay for their studies. The crucial point here is that a price can be attached to higher education services so that they can be bought and sold in markets. In order to clarify how the international student market is conceptualized, we turn our attention to the concept of markets.

Conceptualizing markets is a complicated endeavor, as numerous examples in the sociological literature show (Manicas 2006; Sayer 1995). We refer to the term "market" not only as commodity exchanges between individual and institutional buyers and sellers as well as exchanges of property rights, but also as the rules, norms, practices, and settings that enable and enhance market exchanges (Sayer 1995). On the basis of this definition, one can refer to many kinds of actual markets. Some markets have a specific location (e.g., a farmers market in some particular town), while other markets operate globally (e.g., financial markets). In this respect the international student market is somewhere in between. Moreover, in sociological terms, the international student market is always socially embedded. It operates within culturally, economically, and politically heterogeneous social settings as well as presupposes trust and intersubjective understanding regarding regulative rules.

But is it plausible to claim that the international student market operates like any other market? In the literature on higher education, some scholars define higher education as a quasi-market (Dill 1997). For de Wit and Verhoeven (2009), the higher education market "is at most a quasi-market" because "most customers do not 'pay' for the product themselves; most 'producers' obtain their basic funding from the government; and the 'market' is not free but regulated" (275). Indeed, "markets in all sectors, especially state-regulated higher education, are partly formed by government action and always conditioned by social interests" (Marginson 2004, 177). Higher education simulates market behaviors as government interventions (subsidies and regulation) introduce market-based mechanisms. In this sense, higher education can be conceptualized as a quasi-market, and the international student market is one of many submarkets within it (Teixeira, Jongbloed, Dill, and Amaral 2004).

The international student market may not be a spontaneous achievement of exchange activities between buyers and sellers, but it is socially constructed by skilled actors and regulated in various degrees by state agencies, international organizations (e.g., the World Trade Organization), supranational entities (e.g., European Union), or other (in)formal agencies. Moreover, actual existing markets often involve some "information channels" (Sayer 1995, 83) bringing buyers and sellers together. In the case of international student markets, higher education fairs operate as information channels bringing together buyers and sellers from different countries. But in no way does it suggest that international student markets operate under perfect competition in the sense that there is "universal availability of the necessary information" (Sayer 1995, 85), implying that the concrete understanding of the international student market requires us to take into consideration actors other than just students and universities.

Within the limits of this chapter, however, we focus only on these actors and governments.

Overview of the Conceptual Model

While the international student market is complex, multidimensional, and has many actors, we develop a conceptual model explaining the various behaviors of market actors. Perhaps the most common way to think about knowledge as commodity in the case of international students is to consider students as buyers of educational products and higher education institutions as sellers of their services/knowledge. But our point in this chapter is not merely to demonstrate that markets exist for the buying and selling of educational products. We also argue that internationally mobile students are increasingly seen in contemporary knowledge economies as commodities or, more precisely, as vessels of economically valuable knowledge. Lyotard (1984) claims "it is conceivable that the nation-states will one day fight for control of information, just as they battled in the past for control over territory, and afterwards for control of access to and exploitation of raw materials and cheap labor" (5). With the increasing numbers of international students, global university rankings, national innovation systems, and nation-state-specific strategies and visions of the knowledge economy, Lyotard's claim seems relevant. From this perspective, instead of seeing international students only as buyers, we expand the concept of educational products and also define them as sellers of their knowledge and skills, their human capital, or their potential knowledge and skill acquisition. The push (factors in the home country that drive students to consider international education) and pull (factors in the host country that attract international students) dynamics (Becker and Kolster 2012; Weimer 2012) are inherent in the conceptual model.

Our conceptual model views international students as the vessels or raw material of knowledge, which can be filled with knowledge (provided by universities) or valued by its contents (academic ability, skills, etc.) and potential. We posit that two market behaviors (buying and selling) exist in the international student market, and we highlight two groups of actors: international students and universities and governments. We argue that universities and governments should be grouped together as they are, in this particular market, collectively working to attract international students. Both universities and governments have differing reasons and motives for their actions, but in large part they work together. We envision each actor taking on the role of buyer or seller, their roles switching throughout the process; that is, the roles of the actors are not rigid

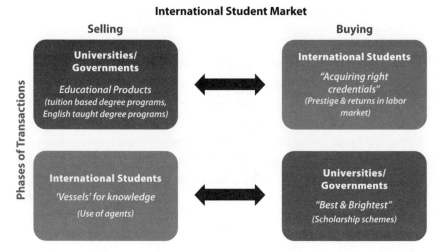

Figure 14.1. International student market transactions.

and in many cases switch back and forth (from buying and selling) over the life of a student (resulting in many transactions). Figure 14.1 is a visualization of the transactions between the two actors and their market behaviors. The roles between actors are binary in the sense that when one is selling, the other is buying. When one actor's role switches, the other switches in response.

Our model is based on the concept of transactions in a market, which in turn is based on the conceptions of capital. However, a full discussion of the various forms of capital (cultural, economic, human, informational, social, etc.) and its relation to the international student market is beyond the scope of this chapter (Weimer, Mathies, and Kauppinen 2012). While "market forces play an increasing role in matching demand and supply," students often use their own social and cultural capital (i.e., personal networks) to choose countries and programs "rather than through government or institutional sponsorship" (Li and Bray 2007, 792). Various forms of capital—and in particular access to capital—are relevant to understanding the international student market.

Universities and Governments Selling Education

Many governments and universities invest in the development, promotion, and marketing of educational products to be sold in the international student marketplace. Educational products in the form of distance learning, English language degree programs, and study abroad programs can be viewed as commodities. Educational degrees and experiences are packaged, labeled, branded, marketed, and sold (often in the form of tuition fees) to eager students seeking, in subjective terms, a valuable international educational experience that will set them up for future success in the global labor market.

There is an assumption that international students can be a new source of economic capital. "Nation-states have an increased interest in the role international students can play in economic development and competitive advantage" (Weimer 2012, 84). The neoliberal agenda aimed at opening up cross-border trade perpetuates the idea that international students are consumers (Britez and Peters 2010). Universities meet this demand, both for new sources of income and international students vying for study rights, by supplying the market with myriad educational products. Yet questions remain about whether international students are truly new revenue streams or if the revenue generated is simply cost recovery for the additional marketing, branding, and administrative capacity incurred when engaging in the market (Knight 2004).

One trend that demonstrates the move to generating revenue from international students is the introduction of tuition fees. Denmark and Sweden made significant moves toward the marketization of higher education through various reforms, including the introduction of tuition fees for non–European Union / European Economic Area (EU/EEA) students. As part of a larger university reform in 2006, Denmark was the first Nordic country to implement international student tuition fees. In June 2010, Sweden passed legislation, Competing on the Basis of Quality—Tuition Fees for Foreign Students, leading to the collection of tuition from non–EU/EEA students for enrollment in bachelor's and master's programs in the fall of 2011 (*The Local* 2010). In addition to a new mandatory application fee of SEK 900 ($140), non-European students pay tuition fees ranging from SEK 80,000 ($12,400) to SEK 245,000 ($35,700) per year depending on the university and field of study (Myklebust 2011).

Another Nordic country, Finland, has also shifted toward the idea of "selling" higher education. The export of higher education has become a common narrative in Finnish higher education reform policy over the past five years. In 2007, amendments to both the Universities and the Polytechnics Acts allow institutions to collect fees from a third-party organization, not individual students, for "made-to-order" educational programs (Cai and Kivistö 2010). The Finnish Education Export Strategy states, "Education commerce is a growing business and it provides many opportunities for Finland" and implicates universities in the business of selling education: "Higher education institutions will be encouraged to be active and assume a major role as education export operators" (Ministry of Education and Culture 2010, 13). In addition, Finland launched a tuition pilot program in 2010 for international students, changing tuition from a taboo topic to a policy instrument (Weimer 2013).

Another general trend is the growth of English language educational products, specifically bachelor's and master's degrees, designed to attract international students. In 2008, the Academic Cooperation Association conducted a study exploring the growth of English-taught degrees and surveyed 2,200 higher education institutions in twenty-seven non-English-speaking European countries (Wächter and Maiworm 2008). The findings revealed that English-taught degrees tripled in five years to 2,400 programs; the main motivation for initiating these programs was to attract international students (84%). In countries where English is the native language, however, efforts are also being made to commodify knowledge in the international student market. Every year the British Council, a nonprofit organization representing UK higher education, tours the world selling the "Education UK" brand to international students earning millions of pounds for selling education products such as English language courses and examinations abroad (Brooks and Waters 2011).

Universities and Governments Buying Students

Competition for global talent is one way to secure labor market prospects and to invest in the future economic capital of the nation or, in some cases, the region. When a country or region does not have local talent to produce the knowledge needed for the knowledge economy, the other option is to buy global talent, also known as "brain gain." This "battle for minds" (Robertson and Keeling 2008) continues to evolve as primarily developed countries invest in programs and marketing campaigns to recruit the "best and brightest" international students. Enticing scholarship programs and guaranteed residency programs are used to recruit global talent.

In 2000, the Lisbon Strategy called for more regional efforts aimed at making the EU a leading knowledge economy in the world, which served as the political backdrop for the creation of the Erasmus Mundus (EM) program in 2004. EM is a regional scholarship program aimed at recruiting the best and brightest non-European talent to pursue graduate-level study (masters and doctorates) in the European region. One distinct characteristic of the EM program includes joint degree programs, wherein at least three partner universities (in the European region) coordinate curriculum, a student mobility plan, and joint recognition of credits leading to a joint degree. These unique joint degree programs, coupled with a lucrative scholarship scheme, attract many international students seeking master's and doctoral degrees. The EM program does not have regulations requiring participating international students to return to their home country, providing students the opportunity to stay within the region after graduation.

In addition, individual countries compete for the "best brains" as more national scholarship schemes are created to attract international students. In France, the Eiffel Excellence Scholarship Program began in 1999 "in a context of mounting competition among developed countries, to attract elite overseas students on master's, engineering and PhD courses" (Égide 2012). In the United Kingdom, the Chevening Scholarship Program began in 1983 to recruit international "students with demonstrable potential to become future leaders, decision-makers and opinion formers" (UK Foreign Commonwealth Office 2012). Since introducing tuition fees in 2012, Sweden has also introduced the Swedish Institute Study Scholarship, which covers living expenses and tuition for highly qualified students coming from select developing countries (Study in Sweden 2012).

In addition, fast-track visa and residency programs attract global talent. In 2010, Canada implemented a fast-track residency program available to any foreign-born individual who has a Canadian doctorate; the aim of this program is to retain global talent, who moved to study in Canada, for the Canadian labor market. In Europe, regional human resources development was facilitated by the creation of a "blue card" in 2008. This new skilled migration visa card aims to bring twenty million globally talented individuals to Europe (EurActiv Network 2012). The labor projection in Europe over the next ten years declares an overwhelming shortage of highly skilled workers. CEDEFOP (2010) projects that from 2010 to 2020 the percentage of highly skilled workers will increase from 29% to 35%; therefore the need to "recruit, train, and retain" highly skilled workers, as Canada is doing, is a high priority in European policy making.

Students Selling Themselves

While students are not literally "selling" themselves to universities, they are positioning themselves as a desired educational product. In this scenario, students embody the very essence of raw material or educational vessels where information (knowledge) can enter or be extracted. International students enter the market selling their skills and abilities or their potential for acquiring such skills and abilities. As such, they market themselves as raw material in the commodification process and attempt to position themselves in the best possible way.

Choudaha, Orosz, and Chang (2012) categorize international students into four groups on the basis of academic preparation (high/low) and financial resources (high/low). A sliding scale can be conceived where "highly desired" students are able to negotiate admissions with elite programs (high/high) to students who "struggle to be noticed" and are left being less selective in their program choice (low/low). Which group a student is in also determines how they market themselves to universities. Those with high academic preparation emphasize their abilities or potential, while those with high financial resources are more likely to highlight their capacity to pay the full cost of the program.

While not new, there is a growing trend of international students hiring third-party recruiters and agents to assist them in securing enrollment abroad (Altbach 2011; Dessoff 2009). Students (and families) are often heavily dependent on agents to help them decipher the overabundance of available information about universities abroad and to guide them in their selection process (Dessoff 2009). Agents, sometimes also called counselors, are hired by students to assist in preparing application materials, writing cover letters and essays, and providing practice exams and mock interviews to promote the student's abilities and potential. Parts of Asia—particularly China, India, and South Korea—have extensive networks of agents (Dessoff 2009) and are prime recruiting markets for universities worldwide.

There has been significant criticism of the use of agents in the international student market, however. The main criticism is that agents steer students into particular programs and universities with which they have financial ties, thus providing academically and socially unprepared students (typically language proficiency) to universities and delivering/steering students just for the money (Altbach 2011; Dessoff 2009). A notable example of concern over the use of paid agents was when the US Department of State prohibited EducationUSA, the main portal the US government promotes American higher education abroad (EducationUSA 2009), to form partnerships and relationships with paid agents because "such recruiters lack objectivity and may restrict foreign student's college options" (Fischer 2009, 1).

While students aim to present themselves in the best way, there have been cases where students falsify their documents. The three main types of international fraud among students are doctoring or fabricating documents from legitimate institutions, using or purchasing fraudulent credentials (diploma mills), and inflating the educational significance of exchange programs (Tobenkin 2011). While fraud in academia is not new, international fraud (particularly by students) is difficult to monitor and evaluate owing to the ease of electronic communication crossing borders and the various interacting cultures and agencies (academe, society, government, etc.). In short, it can be difficult for universities to determine which student credentials are legitimate and which are not.

Students Buying an Education

In a globalized marketplace, students increasingly feel a need for an "international degree" and have a willingness to leave their home country for it. International students are "deeply concerned with acquiring the 'right' credentials and other embodied traits, which ultimately will be converted into social status and economic capital" (Waters and Brooks 2010, 218). When a student considers studying abroad, they face many choices. Considerations of degree program, cost, quality, institutional type, and location are just a few of the choices international students make. Altbach and Knight (2007) refer to this as the "consumption abroad model," where the consumer (student) moves to another country for the specific purpose of receiving an education. When a student "purchases" an education, in plain economic and human capital terms, it is seen as an investment with the benefits accruing to the individual over time (Throsby 1998). In the context of an international student, the same principles apply as the international student identifies the clear costs (including travel and differential costs on accommodation and board) and the benefits (likely higher income and improved language skills and cultural awareness) they anticipate as a result of their decision (Throsby 1998).

Framing international students' choice of educational provider is their knowledge of higher education abroad and their perceived value of it. In short, social class differentiates educational opportunities for international students, as they do for domestic students (Waters and Brooks 2010). Labor market returns are often a key aspect in the enrollment decision. The choice of degree program by international students is often closely aligned to specific career and employment goals (Waters and Brooks 2010). As such, concerns over the quality and prestige of the degree program, institution, and (national) system of higher education are key dynamics in the international student's decision-making process of not only what, but also where, to study. For example, in a study of UK students going abroad for bachelor's degrees, Ivy League (high-level status) universities in the United States were the most common destinations (Waters and Brooks 2010).

But economic rationales are not the only framework used by international students to choose where and what to study. In Turkey, international students from Western and economically developed countries used private reasons (climate preference, urban/rural context, language skills, etc.), while students from Eastern and economically developing countries used economic and academic (prestige of the program and institution) rationales (Kondakci 2011). In a study of Chinese students, students used (in order) academic, social, cultural, and economic reasons to study in Hong Kong but used (in order) economic, social, cultural, and academic reasons to study in Macao (Li and Bray 2007). In summary, while international students use a variety of rationales to choose where and what to study, the level of capital they possess (economic, social, human, etc.) has the most influence over their decision.

Conclusion

The conceptual model described in this chapter illustrates how the primary actors interact in the international student market. Overall, we argue that the international student market serves both the students' desire for an international education and the nation-states' rationale for entering the market; students increase their human capital while nation-states invest in economic competiveness strategies. Moreover, students comprise the future workforce, and labor is treated in capitalist market economies as if it was a real capitalist commodity produced for market exchange. In the case of international students, knowledge, skills, production, and the application of knowledge makes them attractive fictitious commodities (Polanyi 1944) because they (as human beings) are not originally produced for markets. Market actors take interest in higher education, as it is supposed to produce high-quality knowledge workers for labor markets. Private corporations want to buy students' human capital, and state agencies aim to increase the attractiveness of their national innovation system for direct foreign investments by recruiting new brains from international student markets. States see a skilled work force (Carey 2011; European Commission 2010, 2011; World Bank 2012) as a key ingredient in economic development strategies. The European Commission's (2011) Modernisation Agenda is a clear example, stating that the EU needs an additional million "skilled workers" (researchers) by 2020 to meet economic development targets. It supports strengthening international student mobility programs and networks (researchers and students) as a way to meet the economic development goals of the EU.

Participation in the international student market is asymmetrical, and this model in no way assumes a normative position, but the model is designed to offer a descriptive perspective. Wealthy and English-speaking countries dominate global flows (Marginson 2007). The Organisation for Economic Cooperation and Development (OECD) found that in 2010, more than 4.1 million students enrolled outside their country of citizenship, representing an increase of more than 10% over the previous year (OECD 2011). But the distribution of international students globally indicates that 77% are enrolled in OECD countries. In absolute terms, the largest numbers of international students are from China, India, and Korea; Asians account for 52% of all students studying abroad globally. Six countries (Australia, Canada, France, Germany, the United Kingdom, and the United States) host more than half of the world's students in a given year. This stratification points to academic capitalism and suggests that there are a number of students, academic disciplines (not in science, technology, engineering, and mathematics), universities, and countries being left behind. For example, Slaughter and Cantwell (2012) suggest that smaller countries have a more difficult time competing for international students than larger countries.

It is no surprise that wealthy and developed countries prosper in the new economy and have more resources to invest in internationalization efforts. Huang (2007) claims that developed countries have the luxury of being more entrepreneurial in their internationalization strategies, whereas developing countries are more dependent on the wealthy countries. National modes of capitalism also affect the type of internationalization strategy that national governments choose to implement (Graf 2009). Because the United Kingdom is based on a market-entrenched mode of capitalism, for example, it was one of the "first movers" to participate and compete in the international student market. For countries such as China and Japan, their national mode of capitalism is different, leading to strategies to "catch up" with the first movers (Graf 2009; Huang 2007). Then there are those countries that simply do not have the capacity (resources, infrastructure, etc.) to compete and attract students in the international student market, which leads to brain drain and brain gain as global externalities occur when one country's higher education system has an impact on the people of another country (Marginson 2007). Good externalities include the flow of research and knowledge across borders, leading to a more connected world, as well as the benefits to receiving countries that gain global talent for their labor market. But with the good comes the bad. Bad externalities include brain drain, wherein the sending country loses global talent to the receiving country.

Higher education institutions are often seen as some of the central actors in the production and allocation of social status (e.g., Marginson 2004, 178), which is one reason why the idea of commodification of higher education can be an attractive option for many. That is, it suggests that higher education institutions are capable of producing such products and services that have not only use values and exchange values, but also sign values for potential buyers. Studies of domestic students' educational choice, enrollment, and attainment commonly use the concepts of capital, and the same conceptions can be applied to international students (Waters 2006). In our analysis of the international student market, the importance of capital to participate in the market is apparent. Students must have knowledge of educational products (social), understand the worth of educational products (economic and cultural), and hold the academic qualifications (informational) to participate. For universities and governments, the prestige/branding (cultural) and finances (economic) dictate who can participate successfully. In short, the more capital one possesses (student, university, or government), the better one can participate in the market.

But acting in a market is not costless (Sayer 1995). In other words, universities have to invest their resources in information gathering, advertising, marketing, and other activities to attract potential students, which is one reason why universities' active involvement in international student markets tends to increase the need to hire nonacademic staff. On the other hand, the international student market has transformed students into consumers. The consumer mentality in students has resulted in a loss of responsibility for their learning and unwillingness to be judged (Naidoo, Shankar, and Veer 2011). It has transformed learning into a process of picking up, digesting, and reproducing series of unconnected, short, packaged segments of information (Naidoo and Jamieson 2005; Naidoo et al. 2011).

In this chapter we argue that the international student market constitutes a socially constructed field of power struggle and competition, and also of collaboration between higher education institutions, nation-states, international organizations, supranational entities, and corporations. Higher education institutions compete with each other, and use different strategies depending at least partially on their position in these stratified markets, to attract the best and brightest. Nation-states and supranational political organizations are similarly competing to attract international students by providing incentives and subsidizing the higher education industry, retaining the best brains or recruiting them back to their home countries. Corporations are also competing for the best brains by hiring them during or after a student's mobility period. International students compete for scholarships and enrollment in prestigious universities and programs, which is often facilitated by the capital they possess (i.e., social, cultural, and economic).

The international student market is fundamentally about cross-border flows of people, capital, and knowledge. The international student market integrates, for instance, different nation-state agencies, universities, and students into the same uneven system, and at the same time it is possible to speak of both national and transnational academic capitalism. This chapter suggests that this market can be seen as an empirical marker of the emergence of phenomena that allow us to move beyond methodological nationalism when studying academic capitalism in the context of globalization and the knowledge-based economy.

REFERENCES

Altbach, Philip. 2011. "Agents and Third-Party Recruiters in International Higher Education." *International Higher Education* 62: 11–14.

Altbach, Philip, and Jane Knight. 2007. "The Internationalization of Higher Education: Motivations and Realities." *Journal of Studies in International Education* 11, no. 3–4: 290–305. doi:10.1177/1028315307303542.

Becker, Rosa, and Renze Kolster. 2012. *International Student Recruitment: Policies and Developments in Selected Countries.* The Hague: Nuffic.

Britez, Rodrigo, and Michael A. Peters. 2010. "Internationalization and the Cosmopolitical University." *Policy Futures in Education* 8, no. 2: 201–16. doi:10.2304/pfie.2010.8.2.201.

Brooks, Rachel, and Johanna Waters. 2011. *Student Mobilities, Migration and the Internationalization of Higher Education.* New York: Palgrave Macmillan.

Cai, Yuzhuo, and Jussi Kivistö, J. 2010. "Towards a Fee-Based Education in Finland: Where to Go?" Paper presented at the Organisation for Economic Co-operation and Development Institutional Management Higher Education General Conference, Paris.

Carey, Kevin. 2011. "Breaking the Mold: New Approaches for Higher Education in Tough Economic Times." Briefing paper. Washington, DC: National Governors Association.

Carruthers, Bruce G., and Laura Ariovich. 2004. "The Sociology of Property Rights." *Annual Review of Sociology* 30: 23–46. doi:10.1146/annurev.soc.30.012703.110538.

Castells, Manuel. 1996. *The Information Age: Economy, Society and Culture.* Vol. 1, *The Rise of the Network Society.* Oxford: Blackwell.

CEDEFOP. 2010. "Skills Supply and Demand in Europe: Medium-Term Forecast up to 2020." Luxembourg: Publications Office of the European Union. www.cedefop.europa.eu/EN/Files/3052_en.pdf.

Choudaha, Rahul, Kata Orosz, and Li Chang. 2012. "Not All International Students Are the Same: Understanding Segments, Mapping Behavior." New York: World Education Services. www.wes.org/ras/downloads/NotAllInternationalStudentsAreTheSame.pdf.

Dessoff, Alan. 2009. "Recruiting's Brave New World." *International Educator* 18, no. 6: 16–26.

De Wit, Kurt, and Jef C. Verhoeven. 2009. "Features and Future of the Network Society: The Demographic, Technological and Social Context of Higher Education." In *The*

European Higher Education Area: Perspectives on a Moving Target, edited by Barbara M. Kehm, Jeroen Huisman, and Björn Stensaker, 263–80. Rotterdam: Sense.

Dill, David D. 1997. "Higher Education Markets and Public Policy." *Higher Education Policy* 10, no. 3–4: 167–85. doi:10.1057/palgrave.hep.8380082.

EducationUSA. 2009. "Policy Guidance for EducationUSA Centers on Commercial Recruitment Agents." Washington, DC: EducationUSA. www.educationusa.info/pdf/Policy_Guidance_for_EducationUSA_Centers.pdf.

Égide. 2012. "Eiffel Scholarships, Call for Applications." Paris: Égide. www.egide.asso.fr/jahia/Jahia/lang/en/accueil/appels/eiffel.

EurActiv Network. 2012. "An EU Blue Card for High-Skilled Immigrants?" www.euractiv.com/en/socialeurope/eu-blue-card-high-skilled-immigrants/article-170986.

European Commission. 2010. *Europe 2010: A Strategy for Smart, Sustainable, and Inclusive Growth*. Brussels: European Commission.

———. 2011. *Supporting Growth and Jobs: An Agenda for the Modernisation of Europe*. Brussels: European Commission.

Fischer, Karin. 2009. "State Department Issues Guidance on Student-Recruitment Agents." *Chronicle of Higher Education*, September 2. http://chronicle.com/article/State-Department-Issues/48276/.

Graf, Lukas. 2009. "Applying the Varieties of Capitalism Approach to Higher Education: Comparing the Internationalization of German and British Universities." *European Journal of Education* 44, no. 4: 569–85. doi:10.1111/j.1465-3435.2009.01401.x.

Huang, Futao. 2007. "Internationalisation of Higher Education in the Era of Globalisation: What Have Been Its Implications in China and Japan?" *Higher Education Management and Policy* 19, no. 1: 1–16. doi:10.1787/hemp-v19-art3-en.

Jessop, Bob. 2007. "Knowledge as a Fictitious Commodity: Insights and Limits of a Polanyian Perspective." In *Reading Karl Polanyi for the Twenty-First Century: Market Economy as a Political Project*, edited by Ayse Bugra and Kaan Agartan, 115–33. New York: Palgrave Macmillan.

———. 2008. "A Cultural Political Economy of Competitiveness and Its Implications for Higher Education." In *Education and the Knowledge-Based Economy in Europe*, edited by Bob Jessop, Norman Fairclough, and Ruth Wodak, 13–39. Rotterdam: Sense.

Kauppinen, Ilkka. 2013. "Different Meanings of 'Knowledge as Commodity' in the Context of Higher Education." *Critical Sociology* doi:10.1177/0896920512471218.

Kauppinen, Ilkka, and T. Kaidesoja. 2013. "A Shift towards Academic Capitalism in Finland." *Higher Education Policy* 27: 23–41. doi:10.1057/hep.2013.11.

Knight, Jane. 2004. "Internationalization Remodeled: Definition, Approaches, and Rationales." *Journal of Studies in International Education* 8, no. 1: 5–31. doi:10.1177/1028315303260832.

Kondacki, Yasar. 2011. "Student Mobility Reviewed: Attraction and Satisfaction of International Students in Turkey." *Higher Education* 62, no. 5: 573–92. doi:10.1007/s10734-011-9406-2.

Li, Mei, and Mark Bray. 2007. "Cross-Border Flows of Students for Higher Education: Push-Pull Factors and Motivations of Mainland Chinese Students in Hong Kong and Macau." *Higher Education* 53, no. 6: 791–818. doi:10.1007/s10734-005-5423-3.

Local. 2010. "Swedish Universities Prep for Tuition Fee Fallout." *Local*, December 1. www.thelocal.se/30544/20101201/.

Lyotard, Jean Francois. 1984. *The Postmodern Condition: A Report on Knowledge*. Manchester: Manchester University Press.

Manicas, Peter T. 2006. *A Realist Philosophy of Social Science: Explanation and Understanding*. Cambridge: Cambridge University Press.

Marginson, Simon. 2004. "Competition and Markets in Higher Education: A 'Glonacal' Analysis." *Policy Futures in Education* 2, no. 2: 175–244.

———. 2007. "Global Position and Position Taking: The Case of Australia." *Journal of Studies in International Education* 11, no. 1: 5–32. doi:10.1177/1028315306287530.

———. 2011. "Imagining the Global." In *Handbook on Globalization and Higher Education*, edited by Roger King, Simon Marginson, and Rajani Naidoo, 10–39. Cheltenham: Edward Elgar.

May, Christopher, and Susan K. Sell. 2006. *Intellectual Property Rights: A Critical History*. Boulder, CO: Lynne Rienner.

Ministry of Education and Culture. 2010. *Finnish Education Export Strategy: Summary of the Strategic Lines and Measures*. Helsinki: Ministry of Education and Culture.

Myklebust, Jan Petter. 2011. "Sweden: Fees Deter Foreign Applicants." *University World News*, January 30. www.universityworldnews.com/article.php?story=20110 128224609573.

Naidoo, Rajani, and Ian Jamieson. 2005 "Empowering Participants or Corroding Learning? Towards a Research Agenda on the Impact of Student Consumerism in Higher Education." *Journal of Education Policy* 20, no. 3: 267–81. doi:10.1080/02680930500108585.

Naidoo, Rajani, Avi Shankar, and Ekant Veer. 2011. "The Consumerist Turn in Higher Education: Policy Aspirations and Outcomes." *Journal of Marketing Management* 17, no. 11–12: 1142–62. doi:10.1080/0267257X.2011.609135.

Noble, David F. 2002. "Technology and Commodification of Higher Education." *Monthly Review* 53, no. 10. http://monthlyreview.org/2002/03/01/technology-and-the-commodification-of-higher-education.

OECD. Organisation for Economic Co-operation and Development. 2011. *Education at a Glance 2011: OECD Indicators*. Paris: OECD. doi:10.1787/eag-2011-en.

Paton, Joy. 2010. "Labour as a (Fictitious) Commodity: Polanyi and the Capitalist 'Market Economy.'" *Economic and Labour Relations Review* 21, no. 1: 77–88. doi:10.1177/103 53046100210010 7.

Polanyi, Karl. 1944. *The Great Transformation*. New York: Beacon.

Radder, Hans. 2010. "The Commodification of Academic Research." In *The Commodification of Academic Research: Science and the Modern University*, edited by Hans Radder, 1–23. Pittsburgh: University of Pittsburgh Press.

Robertson, Susan L., and Ruth Keeling. 2008. "Stirring the Lions: Strategy and Tactics in Global Higher Education." *Globalisation, Societies and Education* 63, no. 3: 221–40. doi:10.1080/14767720802343316.

Sappey, Jennifer. 2005. "The Commodification of Higher Education: Flexible Delivery and Its Implications for the Academic Labour Process." Paper presented at the Reworking Work conference, Sydney, Australia, February 9–11.

Sayer, Andrew. 1995. *Radical Political Economy: A Critique*. London: SAGE.

Slaughter, Sheila, and Brendan Cantwell. 2012. "Transatlantic Moves to the Market: Academic Capitalism in the United States and European Union." *Higher Education* 63, no. 5: 583–603. doi:10.1007/s10734-011-9460-9.

Slaughter, Sheila, and Larry L. Leslie. 1997. *Academic Capitalism: Politics, Policies, and the Entrepreneurial University.* Baltimore: Johns Hopkins University Press.

Slaughter, Sheila, and Gary Rhoades. 2004. *Academic Capitalism and the New Economy: Markets, State, and Higher Education.* Baltimore: Johns Hopkins University Press.

Study in Sweden. 2012. "Swedish Institute Study Scholarships." www.studyinsweden.se /Scholarships/SI-scholarships/The-Swedish-Institute-Study-Scholarships/.

Teixeira, Pedro, Ben B. Jongbloed, David D. Dill, and Alberto Amaral, eds. 2004. *Markets in Higher Education: Rhetoric or Reality?* Dordrecht: Kluwer Academic.

Throsby, Charles David. 1998. *Financing and Effects of Internationalisation in Higher Education: The Economic Costs and Benefits of International Student Flows.* Paris: OECD Centre for Educational Research and Innovation.

Tobenkin, David. 2011. "Keeping It Honest." *International Educator* 20, no. 1: 32–42.

UK Foreign Commonwealth Office. 2012. "Chevening Scholarships." www.fco.gov.uk/en /about-us/what-we-do/scholarships/chevening/.

Wächter, Bernd, and Friedhelm Maiworm. 2008. *English-Taught Programmes in European Higher Education: The Picture in 2007.* ACA Papers on International Cooperation in Education. Bonn: Lemmens.

Waters, Johanna. 2006. "Geographies of Cultural Capital: Education, International Migration and Family Strategies between Hong Kong and Canada." *Transactions of the Institute of British Geographers* 31, no. 2: 179–92. doi:10.1111/j.1475-5661.2006.00202.x.

Waters, Johanna, and Rachel Brooks. 2010. "Accidental Achievers? International Higher Education, Class Reproduction, and Privilege in the Experience of UK Students Overseas." *British Journal of Sociology of Education* 31, no. 2: 217–28. doi:10.1080/014 25690903539164.

Weimer, Leasa. 2012. "Economics of the International Student Market." *Journal of the European Higher Education Area* 3: 84–98.

———. 2013. "Tuition Fees for International Students in Finland: A Case Study Analysis of Collective Action and Social Change." PhD diss., University of Georgia.

Weimer, Leasa, Charles Mathies, and Ilkka Kauppinen. 2012. "Knowledge as a Commodity? The Case of International Students Markets." Paper presented at the Conference on Higher Education and Innovation Research: University in Transition, Helsinki, Finland, April 12–13.

World Bank. 2012. *China 2030: Building a Modern, Harmonious, and Creative High-Income Society.* Washington, DC: International Bank for Reconstruction and Development, World Bank, and Development Research Center of the State Council, P. R. China.

BRENDAN CANTWELL is an assistant professor of higher, adult, and lifelong education at Michigan State University. His research addresses the political economy of higher education, including questions related to policy, finance, and organization.

TUUKKA KAIDESOJA is a postdoctoral researcher in the philosophy of the social sciences at the Finnish Centre of Excellence in the Department of Political and Economic Studies at the University of Helsinki. His research interests include social ontology, social theory, and science policy.

ILKKA KAUPPINEN is a university lecturer in the Department of Social Sciences and Philosophy at the University of Jyväskylä. He also is an Institute of Higher Education fellow at the University of Georgia. His main research interests are social theory, globalization, and transnational higher education.

ROGER P. KING is a visiting professor at the Universities of Bath and Queensland as well as a member of the UK Parliamentary Higher Education Commission. Formerly he was vice chancellor and president of Lincoln University.

ALMA MALDONADO-MALDONADO is a researcher at the Departamento de Investigaciones Educativas-CINVESTAV in Mexico City. Her research interests are comparative higher education, internationalization, globalization, academic mobility, and highly skilled migrants. Follow Alma on Twitter at @almaldo2.

CHARLES MATHIES is the senior expert in the Division of Strategic Planning and Development at the University of Jyväskylä. His research interests focus on higher education policy, science policy, and evidence-based university governance and management.

BRIAN PUSSER is an associate professor of higher education in the Curry School of Education at the University of Virginia. His research focuses on politics and policy in higher education, understanding the university as a public sphere, and the organization and governance of postsecondary institutions. He is a coeditor of *Universities and the Public Sphere: Knowledge Creation and State Building in the Era of Globalization.*

KEIJO RÄSÄNEN is a professor of organization and management at the Aalto University Business School in Helsinki. He is doing participatory and theoretically practice-oriented research in academic work.

GARY RHOADES is a professor and director of the University of Arizona's Center for the Study of Higher Education. His research focuses on the restructuring of academic professions and institutions, as in his books *Managed Professionals: Unionized Faculty and Restructuring Academic Labor; Academic Capitalism and the New Economy* (with Sheila Slaughter); as well as the forthcoming *Organizing Professionals: Negotiating a New Academy.*

JACOB H. ROOKSBY is an assistant professor of law at Duquesne University School of Law in Pittsburgh, where he teaches courses in intellectual property, torts, and law and higher education. His ongoing research interests concern intellectual property law and policy issues in higher education. He holds MEd, JD, and PhD degrees from the University of Virginia.

SHEILA SLAUGHTER spent many years at the Center for the Study of Higher Education at the University of Arizona before moving to the University of Georgia to be the first occupant of the McBee Professorship of Higher Education in the Institute of Higher Education. The author of many books and articles, she is probably best known for *Academic Capitalism: Politics, Policies and the Entrepreneurial University* (with Larry Leslie) and *Academic Capitalism and the New Economy: Markets, State, and Higher Education* (with Gary Rhoades). Slaughter's scholarship concentrates on the relationship between knowledge and power as it plays out in higher education policy at the state, federal, and global levels.

HEI-HANG HAYES TANG is a college lecturer in Asian studies at the University of Hong Kong's School of Professional and Continuing Education. A sociologist, Hayes specializes in the fields of academic profession, internationalization, and scholarship of application. He is working on a book titled *Scholarship Reconsidered in an Era of Entrepreneurialism: Academic Professions in Hong Kong and South Korea.* Living in Hong Kong, he serves a campus evangelical ministry amidst his intellectual pursuits.

JUSSI VÄLIMAA is a professor of higher education at the University of Jyväskylä. His research addresses higher education as a social phenomenon.

JUDITH WALKER is a postdoctoral fellow in adult and health professions education in the Faculties of Education and Dentistry at the University of British Columbia. She is interested in understanding how to create teaching and learning environments that stretch us cognitively, nourish us emotionally, and give us a greater appreciation for our interconnectedness.

LEASA WEIMER is a postdoctoral researcher at the University of Jyväskylä. Her research interest focuses on the international student market and the implications of tuition, policy, student flows, and university services for international students.

Abbot, Andrew, 104–5
academic capitalism, 209–11; and academic
autonomy, 49, 210, 215–16; and academic
freedom, 122–23, 210; actors in, 28, 152,
183–84n2, 210; alternatives to, 103, 123, 126,
128, 141; designed organizations characterizing, 181–82; faculty's changed role under,
48–49, 66; and globalization, 59, 137,
142–44, 166, 182, 224; in Greater China,
208–25; ideology of, 198, 210, 217; and
international student market, 246–61; and
knowledge, 119, 121, 124, 129, 148–49, 180–81,
183, 188, 190–96, 209; labor/management
relations under, 123–28; and legislation,
177–78; and managerial professionals, 114–18,
128; multiple types of, 179–80, 183; patent
enforcement as frontier of, 83–84; pedagogical practices under, 48; power relations in,
47, 113–14, 211–13; and practical activity,
94–109; research about, 167, 199; and risk,
228–44; social mechanisms' contribution to
emergence of, 173; social relations changes
under, 48–49, 116; social stratification in,
120, 121, 125, 156, 259; and state-university
relationship, 49–50; time regime of, 56–70;
transnationalization of, 143, 147–62
*Academic Capitalism and the New Economy:
Markets, State, and Higher Education*
(Slaughter and Rhoades), 49, 74, 94, 115, 122,
123, 137, 152, 184n2, 187, 191, 192, 196, 198; on
commercialization activities, 4, 189; on
competitiveness coalition, 176, 177, 178;
domestic focus of, vii, 46, 129; higher
education changes explained in, 166, 167, 168

"Academic Capitalism and the New Economy:
Privatization as Shifting the Target of Public
Subsidy in Higher Education" (Rhoades and
Slaughter), 74, 86–87
*Academic Capitalism: Politics, Policies and the
Entrepreneurial University* (Slaughter and
Leslie), vii, 4, 5, 47, 56, 76, 116, 129, 137, 187,
190, 192, 198; on market forces, 46, 48; on
mechanisms, 166, 168–69
academic capitalism theory, vii–viii, 5–7, 12–13,
178–79, 201; academic reputation of, 50–51;
on academics' agency and constraints,
189–90; ambiguity of, 167; application of,
to practice of, 51, 94, 95; on circuits of
knowledge, 20, 152, 188; conceptual strands
in, 6, 10–11, 74; controversies generated by,
6–7; and developing countries, 198–99,
201–2; and empirical studies, 99, 167; as
explanation for higher education changes,
3–4, 46–47, 49, 166, 167, 168; and field
theory, 11, 26, 28; as ground-breaking
contribution, 5–6; influence of, 187,
200–201; mechanism concept in, 28,
166–67, 168–69, 182; as midrange social
theory, 33, 46; on patenting, 85–86, 87–89;
and policy network approach, 11, 26;
reception of, viii–ix; studies complementary
to, 104–7; on trustees, 16, 19–21; universality
of, 49–50
academic capitalist time regime (ACTR), 56–70;
morality of, 67–68; opportunities from, 69;
paradoxes of, 59–62; postmodern capitalism
and, 66, 68; shifts in time/power relations
under, 66–67